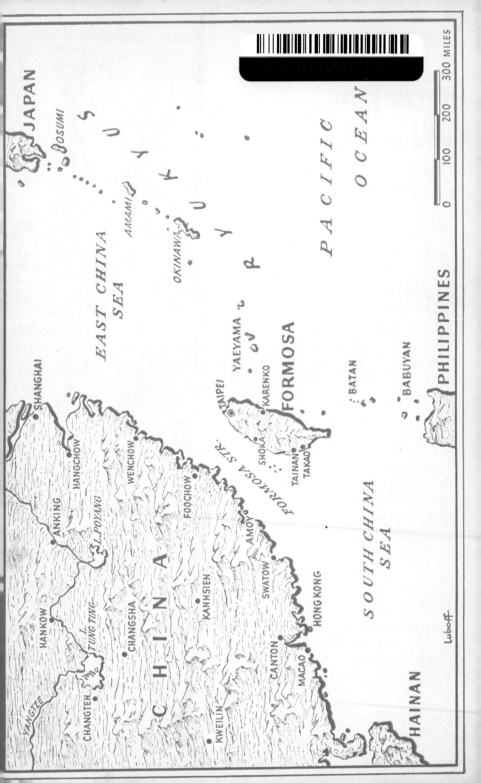

JOURNEY TO THE FAR PACIFIC

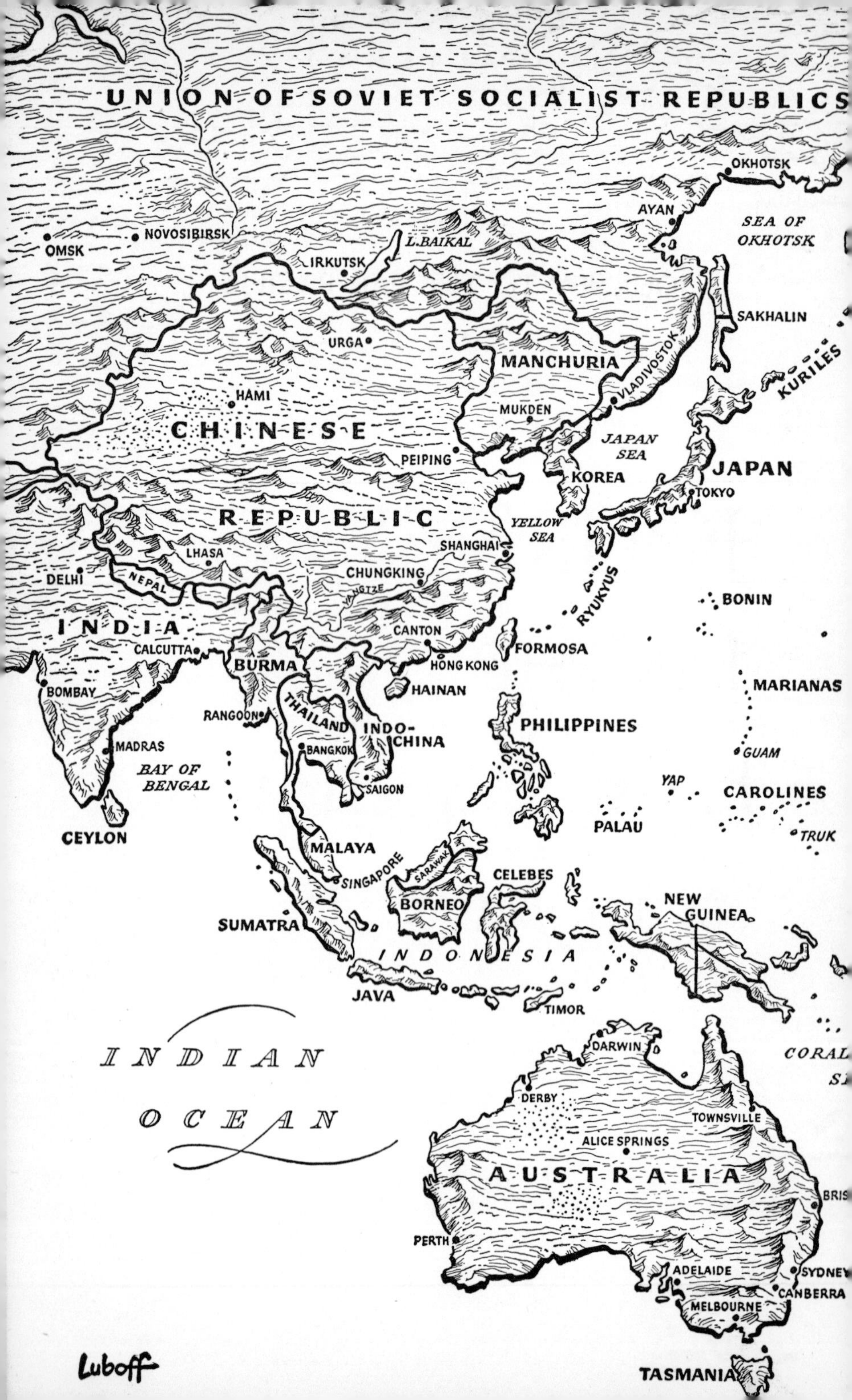
UNION OF SOVIET SOCIALIST REPUBLICS
OKHOTSK
AYAN
SEA OF OKHOTSK
OMSK
NOVOSIBIRSK
L. BAIKAL
IRKUTSK
SAKHALIN
URGA
MANCHURIA
VLADIVOSTOK
KURILES
HAMI
MUKDEN
CHINESE
JAPAN SEA
PEIPING
KOREA
JAPAN
TOKYO
REPUBLIC
YELLOW SEA
SHANGHAI
LHASA
CHUNGKING
YANGTZE
DELHI
NEPAL
RYUKYUS
BONIN
INDIA
CANTON
FORMOSA
CALCUTTA
HONG KONG
BURMA
HAINAN
MARIANAS
BOMBAY
THAILAND
RANGOON
INDO-CHINA
PHILIPPINES
MADRAS
BANGKOK
GUAM
BAY OF BENGAL
SAIGON
YAP
CAROLINES
PALAU
CEYLON
TRUK
MALAYA
SINGAPORE
SARAWAK
CELEBES
BORNEO
NEW GUINEA
SUMATRA
INDONESIA
JAVA
TIMOR
DARWIN
CORAL
INDIAN OCEAN
DERBY
TOWNSVILLE
ALICE SPRINGS
AUSTRALIA
BRIS
PERTH
ADELAIDE
SYDNEY
CANBERRA
MELBOURNE
TASMANIA
Luboff

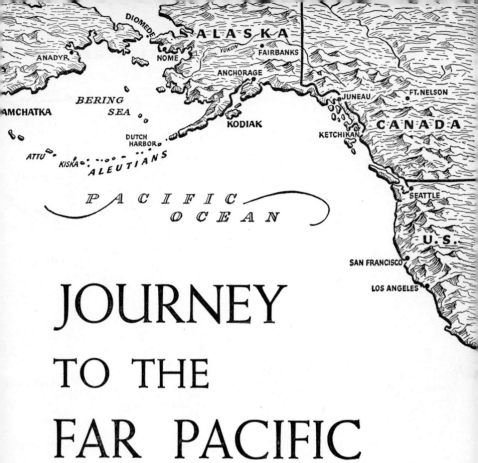

JOURNEY
TO THE
FAR PACIFIC

By THOMAS E. DEWEY

Doubleday & Company, Inc.

GARDEN CITY, NEW YORK, 1952

Library of Congress Catalog Card Number: 52-5222

Contents

6   *Contents*

Introduction

In the spring of 1951 Europe was covered with a surface calm, while five wars and revolutions raged in the Pacific. In addition to Korea, Communist attacks were being waged against Indo-China, the Philippines, Malaya, and Indonesia.

Here at home the great debate on sending troops to Europe was over. It was one of the bitterest since the Civil War, splitting both parties. For more than six months I had taken an active part in the struggle to defeat the efforts of a group in the United States Senate to throttle the program for collective defense of the North Atlantic Treaty nations. Anticipating the crisis, I had revisited the countries of Europe in 1949, to see for myself the conditions upon which so much of our future existence depended. Now I was tempted to go back again to study the progress of the intervening two years; but a newer and graver crisis was rising in the Pacific.

By a coincidence the 270,000,000 free people of western Europe are matched by the only slightly larger number of 300,000,000 in the free Pacific. Unfortunately this decisive area is largely lost from our sight in the distances of the Pacific and in the mysteries of Asian political movements and personalities. It seemed to me that I ought to go to see conditions at first hand and at least form my own impressions. The insistence of John Foster Dulles that a visit to Japan would be helpful in emphasizing the firm purpose of Americans of both parties to bring about a treaty of reconciliation contributed to my decision to go to the Pacific.

Of all the countries of the Pacific, Indo-China was the only one I was advised to avoid. It was said that relations between the French and the natives were so delicate that if I spoke to one more French than native official, feelings would be hurt and an incident created; General de Lattre was the most difficult man in the world to get along with; the Emperor Bao Dai was a French playboy puppet with no following among the people; and America was making a great blunder in supporting him against Ho Chi Minh. Moreover, it was too dangerous, I was told; people were being killed all over the place every day. None of these arguments seemed impressive to me.

So last summer I traveled forty-one thousand miles, visiting seventeen republics, kingdoms, territories, and colonies in the decisive Pacific area. I had most certainly not intended to write a book about a trip I made for my own information. During the course of the trip, however, I made extensive notes and concluded after I got home that there might be others who would like to see the Pacific countries as I saw them. Here is the result. Since I am a lawyer and not an author, this must necessarily be a simple, straightforward report.

I deeply appreciate the countless courtesies extended to me, during a purely personal trip, which made possible all of the opportunities of an official visit with few of its disadvantages. I am also grateful to Ambassador Dulles and General Lucius D. Clay for their great kindness in reading the manuscript and giving me their comments; and to many others who have read particular sections. I am equally grateful to Dr. Herman Hilleboe, Commissioner of Health of the State of New York, and to Paul E. Lockwood, Public Service Commissioner, for checking the manuscript against their own recollections and notes made during the trip. Of course I accept full responsibility for all of the facts and conclusions.

This book does not pretend to be an authoritative analysis of the social, economic, or military situation of the Pacific. Time was often all too short and even some of the things that seemed to me to be as clear as day may not be clear at all; it is certainly true that the more I knew about the Pacific the less sure I became of any dogmatic conclusions. This is just a report of what one American, who has spent twenty-one years in public life, saw and thought.

THOMAS E. DEWEY

JOURNEY TO THE FAR PACIFIC

1

Japan

The time will come, perhaps not in your day nor mine, when, unless Europe and America unite to check Muscovite ambition, it will not only grasp effete nations in its path on the Asiatic Continent, but, with the hordes thus brought under its control will overrun the civilization of Europe as did the Hun and Goth, the Visigoth and Vandal of old.

> *From* Through Manchuria with the Japanese, *by Louis Livingston Seaman, published November 1904*

WE were four hours late from San Francisco in landing at Tokyo's Haneda Airport and I had been a little anxious about the delay. On arrival I found that the legendary patience of Asia usually pays off: in this case I had missed three Fourth of July receptions. Ambassador William Sebald took me from the airport to the Imperial Hotel to freshen up for the final and most official Fourth of July reception of the day at the Embassy Residence.

The trip from Haneda to Tokyo was strange and exciting to me. Farmers and their families were working in rice paddies in water up to their knees. Every conceivable kind of cart, bus, truck, bicycle, automobile, and ricksha crowded the road. As we moved into the city, streetcars, bicycles, taxicabs, and little two-wheeled carts pulled by coolies appeared in increasing numbers. The most spectacular forms of transportation are the charcoal-burning trucks and taxicabs which carry on the rear a fearsome contraption that burns charcoal to generate a low quality of gas that runs the engine at a highly irregular rate of speed. Since Japan produces little oil, gasoline is so expensive that motor travel is a luxury enjoyed principally by foreigners. We passed some of the more prosperous Japanese coming home from work in motorcycle sidecars, with uniformed chauffeurs driving the motorcycles.

In addition to everything else, the ingenious Japanese mechanics had crossed a large number of American jeeps with some Rube Goldberg cartoons, putting the results to work on the streets of Tokyo as buses. The congestion in the streets would equal that of any American city even before adding to it jeeps, motorcycles, bicycles, rickshas, and man-drawn carts. The Japanese traffic police presented a smart appearance on their little islands at every main intersection and struggled vigorously with the vehicular nightmare, but with little success.

In the slum areas on the outskirts of the city, most of the people on the sidewalks were in native dress of the poorest quality and scarcely a woman old enough to be married was without a baby strapped to her back. The men on the sidewalks or pulling carts along the streets wore only shirts and short cotton trousers coming just below the knee. Toward the center of the city an ever increasing share of the people on the street were in Western dress and by the time we reached the heart of Tokyo more than three quarters of them appeared in clothing which would be quite at home in any American city.

There were still many marks of the war. Before the war Tokyo was a monster city of 8,000,000 people; during the war it shrank to 3,000,000; now it was back up to 5,000,000. Gaunt skeletons of bombed-out factories were to be seen everywhere and will be for many years. Long rows of brand-new houses had sprung up in many of the areas that were bombed and burned out, alternating with other rows of aged buildings which survived. One B-29 fire bombing in the war ringed a great section of the city, burning it out completely and resulting in the horrible total of 185,000 casualties.

The drive in from the airport gave me a chance to get acquainted with Ambassador Sebald and it gave him an opportunity to find out what kind of a Republican visiting fireman he had on his hands. We had a number of mutual friends and I was prepared to like him from the start. He is a quiet man, a hard worker, and has special qualifications for his difficult assignment, including, surprisingly enough, fluent knowledge of Japanese. For this there is a simple explanation: a graduate of Annapolis, William Sebald became a Japanese-language officer in the Navy, resigning his commission during the 1930s to practice law in Japan. When Pearl Harbor was attacked he immediately re-entered the Navy and served throughout the war in Admiral Ernest King's headquarters in charge of Combat Intelligence for the Pacific Theater.

After the war he joined our diplomatic mission in Tokyo, becoming in August 1947 the senior American diplomatic officer with the complicated title of Chief, Diplomatic Section, General Headquarters, Supreme Commander for the Allied Powers, United States Political Adviser for Japan and Deputy for the Supreme Commander, Chairman and Member for the United States, Allied Council for Japan. They call him Ambassador for short.

Everyone told me of the high quality of his advice during the Occupation and of his success in handling delicate problems between the Occupation and the Japanese Government. In the 1930s Mr. Sebald married a beautiful Eurasian girl who has been of invaluable help to him in the official entertaining which is one of the most onerous of the American Ambassador's many duties. Mrs. Sebald explains with a smile that her ancestry is half British and half Japanese but that the British half also includes French, Dutch, and Spanish.

We had left Albany on July 1, 1951, a party of five. Paul E. Lockwood, Public Service Commissioner of the State of New York and before that my secretary, had been on most of my travels with me, both at home and abroad, for many years. He was not only good and helpful company but expert in the handling of the infinite and complicated diplomatic, schedule, and travel problems which occur on such a trip. Dr. Herman E. Hilleboe, Commissioner of Health of the State of New York, Assistant Surgeon General of the United States Public Health Service on leave of absence, and one of the original three members of the World Health Organization Expert Committee on Tuberculosis, had planned to go to Korea anyway, and timed his trip to join our party for part of the way. "New treatments for burns have been reported from Korea which sound almost miraculous," he had said. "Many people don't believe them and I must see them. Where they may have 200 casualties in a day in Korea we may some morning have 200,000 in New York City; I have to know what's going on; it may save thousands of lives." Traditionally, a lieutenant of the State Police has always accompanied the Governor of New York and that is the assignment today of Lieutenant Edward M. Galvin. The fifth member was Raymond I. Borst of the Buffalo *Evening News*, a senior member of the Legislative Correspondents' Association at Albany, who was assigned by his paper to go along.

Our Tokyo home, the Imperial Hotel, was an intricate brick structure on many levels, designed by Frank Lloyd Wright. It has the virtue of having survived both earthquakes and bombing, though one section of it was damaged. But its appearance immediately recalled the remark attributed to Harry Thaw. Long years after he shot the great architect Stanford White, so the story goes, Thaw visited Tokyo and after one look at the Imperial Hotel exclaimed: "My God, I killed the wrong architect!"

The invitation list to the Ambassador's Independence Day reception filled three and a half single-spaced pages. It included the officials of the Japanese Government, the Imperial Household, the entire diplomatic corps, the leaders of the armed forces, American businessmen and newspaper correspondents. Since we were the occupying power, it was virtually a command performance for all except the Soviet officials.

July 4, 1951, was a big day in Tokyo. It was a big day not because of my arrival or because it was our Independence Day. It was a big day because Major General Aleksei P. Kislenko, Soviet member of the Allied Council for Japan, the highest representative of the Soviet Union, appeared at the reception; even more remarkable, he had brought his buxom wife along for her first public appearance in years; but most important of all, he was smiling.

The reception was buzzing over his presence and everybody connected it with the Russian bid for a truce in Korea which had been made only a few days before. General Kislenko was cordial even to me though on several occasions his government had branded me Public Enemy Number One.

Crosscurrents of opinion and many worries quickly emerged at the reception. Our military leaders were hopeful but wary. They were afraid the truce might be a trap. If the Communists could utilize a lull to supply and regroup their forces without bombardment from the Allies, they might launch a surprise offensive of crushing weight. The American officers were also

worried that political pressure might compel them to give up
our good positions on the ridges and withdraw to an entirely
indefensible line on the 38th Parallel.

The Japanese were worried, but for different reasons. "What
will happen if the truce succeeds?" they asked anxiously.

"Will America then withdraw all her troops from Korea?"

"Will we face another invasion of Korea and possibly
Japan?"

They saw with all the stark realism of people who sit under
Russian guns the danger of a Red-occupied Korea pointing like
a dagger at the heart of Japan. I had publicly warned four years
before that if we withdrew from Korea it would be invaded;
so I understood their fears.

The Koreans were bitterly unhappy, too, for they saw the
possibility of a settlement again dividing their country, perhaps
for many years, perhaps forever.

I never saw so many people so unhappy over the prospect
of peace—because nobody believed the Soviet would allow it
to be a real peace.

Though I had met General and Mrs. Matthew Ridgway at
the reception, I was scheduled to call on him formally at
eleven-thirty the next morning and he was to return the call on
me at noon. This seemed to both of us to be just diplomatic
nonsense so we had a long and valuable visit until we left together for lunch at his official residence. When General Ridgway was called to the command of the United Nations Forces
after the death of General Walker in December 1950, our
forces were in headlong retreat from the Yalu. All the immense
prestige we had gained in the free world by intervening to save
a helpless victim of aggression was hanging in the balance.
Erect, calm, and forceful, with his trade mark of a live grenade
on his shoulder strap, General Ridgway rallied and reorganized
our forces. Later, replacing General MacArthur, he moved

naturally into the position of Supreme Commander for the Allied Powers.

Following lunch, presided over charmingly by Mrs. Ridgway, the general and I returned to headquarters, where we were joined by Ambassador Sebald. I had accepted an invitation to address the America-Japan Society on July 6; though I had worked on my speech during the flight out, there were still some rough edges, so together the three of us went over the final draft.

Delivering the speech at the special luncheon meeting of the society the next day was another new experience for me. I had never addressed a Japanese audience. Would they understand enough to make it intelligible? And what about the extemporaneous remarks that somehow always creep in? They can fall very flat if not understood. The audience included the Prime Minister, a number of Cabinet officers, business and professional people, as well as quite a few Americans. At the opening I made it clear that I was speaking solely as a private citizen and in no way for the government of my country. Then I couldn't resist the temptation to interject an aside: "Some of you may know that I tried a couple of times to get into the national government but without success." The laugh that came from the entire audience ended my worries. I had not only a politically conscious audience but one that understood English and had a good sense of humor.

Later I was particularly interested in the mail that came in commenting on the press reports of the speech. The Japanese are one of the most literate people in the world and I am sure they are most prolific letter writers. The largest share of the letters referred especially to the section of my speech which read:

"My countrymen want no territory, no subject peoples, no domination of any other people. Our record proves it.

"What other nation in the history of the world ever fought so hard to win a war it did not start and then paid out so generously in order to lift up and restore its defeated enemies?

"Did any nation ever win a bitter war and then pay more than two billion dollars to feed and clothe and succor the fallen, as America has done in the case of Germany?

"Did any nation ever win a bitter war and then pay more than two billion dollars to feed and clothe and succor the fallen, as America has done in the case of Japan?

"Did any nation make such sacrifices and then ask not one dollar of reparations in return? I am deeply aware that a nation's purpose cannot be measured by dollars. I am equally aware that a nation's purpose must also be measured in terms of human understanding and human sympathy. I mention these facts therefore not in vainglory but in all humility to illustrate the high purpose and the sacrificial devotion of a free people to the welfare of their neighbors of the free world.

"The people of America and of the free world are building their strength for the sole and exclusive purpose of preventing war. The United States will never be the one to start a war in any conceivable set of circumstances. The United States will never attempt to use other nations for purposes of aggression. All these contemptible methods we leave to the imperialist aggressors.

"We do not believe war is inevitable.

"We are dedicated to the high purpose of making peace inevitable.

"It must be a peace of strength—not a mere peace of surrender or appeasement. It must be a peace in which free men and women can sleep calmly in their homes, serene in the knowledge of their freedom from secret police and enemy bombers."

It is easy to be misled and certainly ten days in a country

make no one an authority on anything; but I do have the firm impression that the people of Japan are grateful to the United States for our determination to create a new approach in world relations by extending a treaty of reconciliation and friendship to a vanquished enemy.

Whether the inexorable pressure of economics and world events will permit Japan to remain free is another question. In six years she has made the revolutionary change from a totalitarian, one-party nation to a genuine, constitutional monarchy with the people actually in control of their government. In almost every other country I visited, the most persistent question was: "Has Japan really become a free nation and will it last?" Americans ask as a matter of curiosity: but the people of Asia, of the Philippines, of Australia and New Zealand ask as a matter of life and death. I witnessed the depths of tragedy and bitterness with which many of them remember the Japanese conquest and occupation. They never want to live through such an experience again.

I don't know whether Japan's freedom will last. Nobody does. This is a critical time for Japan and what happens in 1952 may decide her direction for many years to come. For the Japanese the first essential is food. No one can get much interested in elections, political theories, or world affairs when he doesn't know where tomorrow's bowl of rice will come from. Today no Japanese can answer that question until he knows whether Indo-China and the Rice Bowl of Southeast Asia will remain with the free world. Every home I saw in Japan with as much as twenty square feet around it has a garden, not for pleasure but from necessity. The vegetables they grow supplement the meager amounts of rice and fish their earnings will buy.

The war was a catastrophe to Japan in which she spent her accumulated reserves of fifty years in less than four short years of disastrous struggle. Stripped of Manchuria with its rich mineral and agricultural resources, Korea, Formosa, the Kurile Island chain, and the Ryukyus, the 84,000,000 people of Japan have been crowded back into the four home islands which altogether have only 147,000 square miles, less than the State of California. While they need almost everything, the loss of rice imports from their former possessions and of some of their fishing areas has put this vigorous nation up against the haunting specter of hunger.

Nevertheless, it is generally believed that with fair business conditions the industrial workers will resist Communist propaganda and support the present liberal government. The industrial workers, however, are a minority; of all the people in Japan, fifty-five out of every hundred live on the farms and dominate the elections to a far greater extent than in this country, where the farm population is only about one sixth of the total. If the Japanese farmer is in distress as the result of further inflation, while the price of rice remains fixed, he may overturn the government. Whatever happens, right now it seems definite that he will not vote Communist.

His alternative would probably be the Socialist Party, which has two wings, one radical and one closer to the middle of the road. The Socialist Party officially opposed the peace treaty on the ground that it should be signed by Russia and Red China. This, of course, was fatuous and they privately admitted it.

The Liberal Party presently in power is made up of a solid group of able people. Under the leadership of Premier Shigeru Yoshida, they recognize that their political job is the future development of a rapidly expanding free-enterprise economy in close alliance with the United States and the rest of the free world.

One of the most encouraging aspects of the Japanese political situation is the willingness of people to vote for individuals they respect and trust. In the last vote for the Diet, more than one quarter of all the votes were cast for leading local citizens who ran without party labels. Three of the governors of prefectures, whom I visited, were also elected as independents.

After the war the Russians had a plan for a grand political coup in Japan. They held more than 1,000,000 Japanese war prisoners who were exposed to thorough Communist indoctrination; as the prisoners avowed their conversion to Communism they were sent home to take over Japan for the Kremlin. The plan misfired. Up to May 1951, the Soviet Union had returned 902,673 prisoners of war and civilians, and the more that arrived, the lower went Communist prestige until it almost reached the vanishing point in the spring elections of that year.

After one of our visits Premier Yoshida sent me an analysis of the vote in the last three elections. It showed that the Communist vote fell from nine per cent in 1949 to five per cent in 1950, to less than one per cent in 1951. The Japanese bid fair to become our most stable Pacific ally if economic conditions permit.

The brightest spot in the whole picture is the way the Occupation under General Douglas MacArthur robbed the Communists of their most effective propaganda weapon in Japan —the promise of land reform.

Before the war the Japanese system of landholding was, in the words of Minister of Agriculture Tyutaro Nemoto, "ridiculously unfair." "The Japanese farmer's life," he says frankly, "was miserable in the extreme despite his hard work and all his skill." Nearly half of all the tillable land was owned by landlords who collected as rent such an exorbitant share of the produce that it often amounted to more than half of all the crops harvested.

In America we are used to farms ranging up to thousands of acres. In Japan the average landlord who owned twelve and a half acres was rich; his tenants were extremely poor. It is almost impossible for us to realize the hunger of the Japanese tenant farmers for land.

On December 15, 1945, the Occupation issued an historic directive to the Japanese Government, calling upon it to purchase the landlords' five million acres and resell them to tenants. Absentee landlords were required to sell all their land. Landlords who were genuine farmers could retain as much as seven and a half acres; the government bought the rest of the land at about forty times the annual rent, issuing government bonds in payment. The tenants, of course, had no money, so they were allowed to buy the land on credit and pay for it over thirty years in annual installments. The amount of land available worked out to give the tenants an average of two and a half acres apiece.

Many Japanese and some Americans entertained grave doubts about the effect of such a quick and radical operation upon food production. However, all worked out well for the tenant farmers. They bought their new land in the Redistribution Program at a fair price in 1946. Then a terrible inflation swept over Japan. Rigid controls had held inflation within bounds until 1947, when the inexorable law of economics finally defeated even the best controls. The yen fell from a value of forty cents before the war to less than one third of a cent. As a result, the former tenant farmers did not need to work thirty years to pay back the government; they paid for their farms with cheap yen after two or three years. They were disturbed by the inflationary rise in the prices of the things they bought, but for the moment they were happy. At last they owned their own land and it was already paid for. Today a new song is heard on the farms:

"The same paddy field, but now my own:
The richer soil yields golden blades of rice.
Heavy is the crop and light is my heart;
Sharp is the sickle and blue is the sky.
Hail this happy harvest day!
Bright shines the sun on my own piece of land!"

The former landlords were terribly victimized by the inflation. They had sold their land at a fair price in return for government bonds. Then the government bonds suddenly lost most of their value. The government is now searching for a means to provide some fair reimbursement to the former owners.

While I am not an agricultural expert, I own and operate a 300-acre dairy farm. As a result I have found that in many nations of the world it provides me with a universal language, and whenever I am in a foreign country I try to spend at least one day visiting farms. For some reason, whatever I learn in the cities is often contradicted in the country by the thoughtful view of the man and his wife who work the soil. They live away from mass opinion and the sometimes hysterical moods of the big cities. In Tokyo I tried to follow my usual practice of arranging my farm visit so that I could go alone with an interpreter and thought I had succeeded. To my dismay, when I finally got to the country, I found myself in the company of the Minister of Agriculture, the governor of the prefecture, a dozen local officials, and twenty newspaper reporters and photographers. The chance of easy, private talks with farmers looked pretty dim.

As it worked out, the presence of others was unexpectedly helpful. Mr. Nemoto, the Minister of Agriculture, is the first in a succession of fifteen postwar ministers of agriculture to be a graduate of a school of agriculture. Governor Yuichi Oh-sawa of Saitama Prefecture was not only helpful but a fine host. Luncheon was served in his home and, following the Japanese custom, he made a brief speech of welcome in excellent English. He had worked hard on his speech and afterwards mailed me an inscribed copy of it. In part it said:

"Your visit is an unprecedented honor to the citizens of Saitama Prefecture and I am deeply grateful for this.

"These young girls are daughters of well-known families in this prefecture and they volunteered to serve this luncheon, deeming it a great honor.

"In order to show my sincere gratitude and pure heart, I had all the mats renewed and all parts of the house cleaned yesterday."

The food was delicious, the product of centuries of experience in learning how to give the commonest foods a taste and flavor which convert them into delicacies. The luncheon featured fish and shellfish, but no meat. Beef and lamb are almost unknown in Japan for the good reason that grain is too precious to be spared to feed animals. It takes about five pounds of grain to make one pound of beef; five pounds of rice can feed one Japanese for a week; there is no grain to spare for luxuries like meat.

After expressing our gratitude for the luncheon, we set off—by now a party of 40—to visit the farms in the neighborhood. The first farm we visited was owned by a fortunate young man who had been able to get three and a quarter acres—three fourths of an acre more than the national average—under the Land Reform Program. He was waiting at the house when our entourage drove up, dressed in a white, sleeveless shirt and thin, tight dungarees which came to frayed bottoms just below his knees, barefooted, alert, and anxious to be friendly. He was obviously overawed by the presence of the governor of the prefecture and the Minister of Agriculture, but after considerable effort I managed to shake myself loose from the others and talked with him alone through the interpreter. He finally relaxed and spoke freely. His house, he said, had been owned by his family for many generations but never before had they owned any farm land. The house itself was unusually large, perhaps thirty by forty feet; about half of it was entirely open at the sides, as is common in Japan, part of it having a dirt floor; the rest of the house was on a raised platform about two feet above the ground and in this part the entire family lived.

The farmer's wife came up as we talked; soon after that his father appeared, stooped and graying, with a little child strapped to his back and another tugging at his shirttail. "My father is too old to work," the young farmer explained, "so he takes care of the children." The grandfather was there, too, sitting cross-legged on the floor back in the open part of the house, bearded, frail, and dignified. Beside him was a child of about six sleeping on a mat.

The young man was definitely an upper-crust farmer. He was upper-crust because he owned a working ox. It pulled his plow and also was used for plowing by his less privileged neighbors, who paid him in hours of labor, cultivating his vegetables and his rice paddies.

Like all the farm land in Japan, his three and a quarter acres were intensively cultivated. First he would grow a crop of barley and wheat while his rice shoots were growing in a separate paddy. When they came to the transplanting stage after the barley and wheat were harvested, the paddies would be flooded and each shoot of rice carefully transplanted by hand. In addition, the farmer had an unusual amount of space devoted to the raising of vegetables of the usual American varieties— beans, eggplant, broccoli, carrots, and two rows of corn, which the Japanese eat on the cob as we do, instead of grinding it into corn meal for cooking. He even had radishes, which I learned were an important vegetable in Japan. They are pickled for use in the winter. I asked him if all the vegetables were for their own use. "No," he said, "we sell some in the village. My wife preserves some and we put others in the ground for use in the winter." What he did not say was that, in addition to cooking, bearing children, keeping the house, and putting up the vegetables, his wife spent as many hours working in the field as he did. That was taken for granted.

Since no farmer can afford to buy commercial fertilizer for all the needs of his intensely cultivated land, much of the fertilizer is night soil—human fecal matter. No Japanese, in city or country, would think of wasting precious fertilizer, and every bit is saved in earthen jars under the toilet. The farmer who owns an ox develops regular customers in the nearest village with whom he has an arrangement to collect the sewage from their homes. Neither pays the other—the farmer gets the fertilizer and the villager gets his sewage removed.

In every drive through the country I saw enterprising businessmen whose stock in trade was an ox, a long cart, and ten or twelve large wooden buckets. These merchants collect night soil from the villages and cities and take it to the country, where they sell it to the farmers who own no oxen. For every automobile I saw on the road there were as many as fifty carts bearing night-soil buckets which our American soldiers have gaily dubbed "honey buckets."

As many of the diseases endemic in the Orient are transmitted through night soil, Americans and most Europeans do not eat raw vegetables or some raw fruits. The natives develop considerable immunity but foreigners become infected with both typhoid and dysentery. Despite great medical progress in Japan, economic pressure forces her to maintain many ancient practices, including the use of night soil. There has not been enough money to develop modern sanitation, including what we regard as the barest necessities of water and sewage control. In recent years considerable progress has been made in reducing typhoid and dysentery but washing facilities are primitive in most Japanese homes, so that contamination of the hands is easy. Even worse, the wife usually washes the family clothes in the same stream which has been fed by seepage from the contaminated fields.

Despite these handicaps the Japanese live up to their reputation for cleanliness. I was much interested in a typical wooden bathtub. It was against the outside of the house under the eaves, about three feet deep, three feet wide, and four feet long, oval in shape and with a small metal stove in one end. Charcoal is put into the stove and the water is heated by the metal of the back of the stove, which forms part of the end of the tub. The barefoot family on that farm worked long hours in the rice paddies, in muddy water up to their knees or higher. Nevertheless, they were a clean family and the bathtub was the most used piece of equipment in the house.

We saw the other side of the farm picture in the course of a visit to a former landlord who had once owned 15 acres and was now reduced to three. I managed to get him away from the mob scene for a private talk and discovered that he had no sense of bitterness over the land reform.

"Even before the war," he said, "I sold portions of my land to my best tenants and they are still my good friends and neighbors today. I let them use my barn to store their crops and they still use my electric mill to grind their rice."

He had retained considerable capital equipment according to Japanese standards: a tiny electric rice mill, a storage shed about twenty by thirty feet, a horse, and a pig which was about to declare an extra dividend. Such possessions set him apart as really well-to-do even after land reform had taken four fifths of his land. He was a fine farmer and would be a success in any free country; it was natural, therefore, to find the boys of the newly created 4-H Club gathered at his farm, eager to talk of their projects, learning the best farming practices on his well-tended acres.

The Soviet plan for the conquest of Japan was checked but not defeated by the land reform. The Kremlin now expects to take over the country by gaining control of the rice and raw materials on the mainland which the Japanese need. The Communist offensives in Korea and, even more importantly, in Indo-China are seemingly aimed at distant conquests; in reality they are aimed directly at the heart of Japan by gaining control of her food supply, her raw materials, and her trading area.

While the agrarian reforms have greatly increased Japan's food production, the irresistible increase in population has also continued from 70,000,000 to 84,000,000 in the last ten years. So the Japanese people are just where they were a decade ago —still importing that twenty per cent of their rice which is the margin between life and death. Japan must trade manufactured goods and services for food and raw materials. The sources of her rice imports for 1940 show dramatically how much Japan needs her Asian neighbors if she is to survive:

	METRIC TONS
SOURCE	OF RICE
Korea	59,000
Formosa	418,000
Thailand (Siam)	284,000
Indo-China	439,000
Burma	420,000
China	54,000

Devastated Korea has little rice to spare and indeed is a food scarce nation today. Formosa is now occupied by the national government of Chiang Kai-shek and, as the result of a greatly increased refugee population, has little rice for export. Thailand, Burma, and Indo-China are the only nearby sources from which Japan can hope to buy the rice she must have: the Rice Bowl of the Orient is still Southeast Asia. That is why the Communists are concentrating there.

Japan has an equally grave shortage of coal, iron ore, and salt. Today she imports rice, grains, and minerals from eighteen nations all over the world. Half of the total comes from the United States but the costs are so great as to be impossible on a permanent basis. Just for example: salt sells for $3 a ton in San Francisco; it costs $19 a ton to ship it to Japan. Coal costs $10 a ton and another $20 a ton to ship to Japan.

So in this respect, too, Japan's survival depends upon the free nations of the Far East. Under peaceful conditions the bulk of her mineral requirements can be provided at reasonable prices from the Philippines, India, and Southeast Asia. In those areas Japan has a natural market for her textiles and other manufactured products, in exchange for the rice, coal, iron ore, and salt she so desperately needs. Free to trade with each other, these hundreds of millions of people can progress in commerce and in standards of living while becoming bulwarks of the free world.

Of course for Japan there is always the alternative of Mao Tse-tung's Communist China. Japan could get most of her needed minerals from China. But if she is forced to trade with Mao Tse-tung he will attach a political price to every cargo. That is an old Communist technique at which the Soviet Union is a past master, and Russian "advisers" are largely running Red China. Every transaction would increase Soviet influence in Japan until the Communists would have her by the throat; by turning on and off the flow of her lifeblood they would swiftly be able to weaken her to the point where she would fall into the waiting arms of Soviet slavery. If Japan is to remain free, so must Southeast Asia.

I was eager to learn the Japanese opinion about the complex problems of these countries. Surely, I thought, the Japanese must have strong views on the future of their neighboring countries, many of which they had occupied during the war. I hoped to get clear-cut opinions on the whole subject but almost always I ran into a blank wall. The reason finally dawned on me: the Japanese military and political leaders who occupied those areas have been executed or purged. The remaining people of Japan have been isolated from the world for ten long years. They have been so isolated that few are familiar with the conditions in other countries; moreover, they are so concerned today with the problems of self-preservation that they have had little time to think about anything else.

A curious psychological aspect of Japanese character also interfered with my efforts to get the opinions I sought. At first I made the mistake of talking with people in groups. Finally I realized that the average Japanese, after centuries of regimentation, still does not feel at ease expressing frank opinions in the presence of others. After almost every visit with businessmen, political leaders, judges, scholars, or other groups, one individual after another took me aside for a private conversation. Others wrote afterwards and my correspondence with people who have definite opinions but did not wish to discuss them in the presence of others is still growing.

On some subjects there was general agreement. From Japanese of every walk of life came the deep conviction that so long as Mao Tse-tung rules Red China he will remain a Communist and a Russian tool; that America must continue to maintain troops in Japan and Korea after an armistice or the Russians will move in again; that Southeast Asia, the Philippines, and Indonesia must remain free or Japan and the whole Pacific will be lost.

Definite opinions on all these subjects also came from American diplomats, businessmen, and newspaper reporters, as well as from British, Dutch, and other Europeans. I was appalled, however, at their gloomy and contradictory appraisals of the prospects for Indo-China, Malaya, the Chinese Nationalists, and the greatest new nation of all, Indonesia.

"If there is a cease fire in Korea," they said ominously, "the Chinese Communists will invade Indo-China next and drive the French out. Burma and Thailand are next on the list. Then Malaya and all Far East Asia will fall. India will be surrounded and Japan starved out: the whole Pacific will be gone.

"Indo-China is the critical spot and the Emperor Bao Dai is nothing but a puppet and a French playboy. He has no strength and is a liability. The revolutionary leader, Ho Chi Minh, is a patriot; the people love him and he will inevitably win, whether he is a Communist or not. The French won't fight for Indo-China much longer anyway."

One veteran American newspaper reporter went even further. "I did some lecturing back in the States recently," he said. "I told them that I wanted to see America get ahead of a revolution for once instead of lagging behind. I told them we should back up Ho Chi Minh and win the friendship of a new government which is bound to win out in the end."

There was equal gloom about Indonesia, the great new island republic which was formerly the Dutch East Indies. A lawyer who had spent his life in the Far East said, "Every Cabinet officer is a little king unto himself and there is no organization at all in the government. Some one of the revolutions going on down there will take over the country and set up a dictatorship. It's bound to happen before the year is out —probably before you get there."

It all seemed too pat to me, a little too ready acceptance of the Communist propaganda line; but at least these Americans and Europeans did have opinions, dubious as some of them seemed. I looked forward anxiously to finding out how all these countries looked on the spot. During the whole trip, I found that almost everything looked different at first hand from the way it appeared at a distance; it also looked much better.

One of the most interesting group meetings I had was with the members of the Lower House of the Diet, which corresponds to our House of Representatives. When the Emperor opens a session of the Diet he first receives the leaders of both houses in a small private chamber. His desk and chair are simple but the walls, covered with lacquer and gold leaf, are stunning; behind the Emperor's desk is a large fireplace flanked by beautiful posts about eight inches in diameter which run from the floor to the ceiling, each post being made of thousands upon thousands of layers of lacquer which took twenty-seven years to apply.

The Upper House of the Japanese national legislature was formerly the House of Peers, which exercised an all-powerful influence on the government. Today under the new constitution the House of Peers has become the House of Councilors, with sharply limited powers.

Following courtesy calls on the leaders of the two houses was the conference with about twenty of the leaders of the various political parties; the usual morning tea was served as we sat down around a large conference table. While most of the members spoke some English, I was delighted to find "Frank" Taziko Matsumoto serving as interpreter. He had served in a similar capacity a few months before when a group of the Diet members who visited the United States came to Albany. He is a forty-eight-year-old college professor representing the District of Hiroshima. Though nominally a member of the People's Democratic Party, he is actually a highly regarded member of the large group of non-party members of the Diet and I believe he has a fine political career ahead of him.

This was one of the few occasions when Japanese I met in groups spoke frankly in the presence of others. Highlighted by sharp controversy, we talked about the Japanese peace treaty, the danger of Communist invasion of Japan, the ubiquitous subject of food supply, the future of free government, and, of course, Japan's dire need for capital and raw materials. Every time a member of one party made a flat statement one of the others would crack back at him across the table. When a Socialist member spoke highly of the Japanese peace treaty, contrary to the public position of his party, one of the Liberals got a big laugh when he queried: "Why don't you say that in public and be honest about it?"

Premier Shigeru Yoshida has the respect of the members of all parties, even his political enemies. I had first met him at the Independence Day reception and then the next day we had a long discussion during my formal call on him at his official residence; but I first began to feel that I really knew him at the America-Japan Society luncheon. We talked easily throughout the meal, retiring afterward to a private room with two or three others to take off our coats, drink some iced tea, and cool off. We met a number of times later and each time I felt more strongly his personal warmth and his high-minded approach to staggering responsibilities.

Yoshida at seventy-three is a sensitive, quiet man of fine ability and character. In the days leading up to the war he was a steadfast opponent of the militarists who had seized control of Japan. He suffered greatly for his views both before and during the war; finally he was imprisoned a few months before the end.

He was a natural choice for Premier of Free Japan. All Americans who saw and heard on television his eloquent speech at the San Francisco signing of the peace treaty must have been impressed by the forthright honesty with which he met every issue, the sincerity of his gratitude, and his pledges of future friendship. As a statesman, I would rank him as close to Winston Churchill as any man can get; I would place him on a par with Alcide de Gasperi of Italy and Robert Schuman of France. Premier de Gasperi has singlehandedly led Italy through her postwar revolution and Schuman as Foreign Minister of France has had the great vision which may yet steer Europe into economic unity.

At one stage of his life Premier Yoshida lived in Scarsdale, New York; he speaks quite good English, has a good sense of humor, and enjoys an American cigar. At dinner at Ambassador Sebald's home one night, someone asked the Premier what he did for cigars during the war. He replied that some tobacco had come in from Formosa; then he explained: "You know, Japan and Italy have two things in common." I supposed he would refer to their common difficulties with shortage of natural resources and their excess population, but he continued: "They both produce a little tobacco and they both make very bad cigars."

At the same dinner there was some discussion of the orphanages the Japanese had established to care for the abandoned children of Japanese women and American GIs. With their varied national and racial backgrounds, our troops have left some remarkable biological mixtures behind them. Mr. Yoshida was asked if he was disturbed by this problem of racial mixture. Smiling, he replied: "Well, the Japanese haven't had any new blood in twenty-five hundred years and I don't believe it will do us any harm."

Premier Yoshida is deeply religious and his favorite spot in all Japan is the Sacred City of Kyoto. He repeatedly urged me to pay the city a visit, telling me that whenever he was in western Japan he always made it a point to spend the night at Kyoto. He, as well as many others, expressed their gratitude for the wise decisions made by our military commanders during the war not to bomb this religious and cultural center of Japan with its eighteen hundred temples and shrines.

When we traveled by train to Kyoto we rode third class; there were first- and second-class cars but I wanted to try the transportation facilities used by the mass of the people. The seats were not too comfortable but they were perfectly adequate for a trip of a few hours, and while the equipment was not new, it was spotlessly clean. Japanese railroads operate exactly on schedule; they wait for nobody and at least the train we were on started and stopped without a single jolt the entire trip. I don't remember ever having had such a smooth train ride. Japan is the only nation in the world where the railroads of the country transport more passengers than freight. The railroads are the backbone of the nation's transport, since there is only one good highway in all Japan; the rest range from poor to terrible.

For more than a thousand years Kyoto was the traditional capital of Japan. In 1869 the Emperor, after the Meiji Restoration, moved the capital from Kyoto to Tokyo; it took three months for the royal court to make that historic hegira of two hundred miles which is now covered in a few hours by rail. As we drove through the city past shrine after shrine I gained my first real understanding of the relationship between Buddhism and Shintoism. While Buddhism is the basic religion of Japan, as it is of much of the Orient, Shinto was developed in Japan during the past thousand years as a pseudo-religious cult based upon nature and ancestor worship. After the Restoration in 1868, a different aspect of the cult was added, based on the divinity of the Emperor and his ancestors, while government support of the shrines and the priests brought about a close union between Shintoism and the government. All that has been swept away in the new Japan. The constitution now prohibits government support of the shrines or the priests and forbids the government to engage in religious education or activity.

This separation of Shintoism from the government constitutes a spiritual revolution of unmeasured meaning for the future of Japan. The changed status of the Emperor alone will exert tremendous influence upon the country's political development, for better or for worse. Whether he will have greater or less influence I was not sure in the light of many conversations and I looked forward to meeting him and forming my own impressions.

When we arrived at the great Shinto shrine we were met by the colorfully dressed high priest and—despite the new decrees —a member of the Imperial Household, dressed in formal morning clothes. I was surprised that the Shinto temple was no temple at all. Instead, there were high, beautifully carved and painted torii, a few simple frame buildings of natural cyprus wood, and long covered walks through the sacred gardens. As we walked along I noticed that there were few worshipers in sight. The high priest explained that this was because it was then the hot, rainy season but that during the balance of the year there are about twenty-five weddings a day as well as a steady flow of the devout from all over Japan.

From the Shinto shrine we drove to the great Buddhist temple, a monumental stone structure built on enormous piles on the side of a mountain. Long steps lead up to the floors of the temple, whose approaches are guarded on each side by huge figures of fierce gods. At various levels in an area which is largely open there are figures of Buddha, some of great size, housed in elaborate structures with closed, grilled gates; these shrines, I found, are opened only on sacred days or on the occasions when young priests in training are allowed to see the sacred literature.

Tied to the iron gates and at other places throughout the temple were thousands of little knots of parchment upon which people who wished to be cured of illness had written their desires. Outside one gate there was an enormous pair of iron shoes, a huge walking stick and pikestaff, given many years ago by one who was cured of illness upon visiting the temple. Deep below in the ravine beside the temple a shallow pool, surrounded by stonework, is fed by a pipe through which water flows continuously from the mountain. Here the faithful make their obeisance to Buddha, then stand under the flowing water to have their sins washed away.

One of the Japanese officials at Kyoto said: "My people are more primitive in their religion than Christians. It is not a part of their daily life. It is not even a set of morals or ethics comparable to those upon which your religion is based. To the Japanese, his religion is principally a means of appealing for divine help or of seeking repose from the turmoil of the world."

Since Kyoto is also a textile center, we drove to the outskirts of the city to see the factories that produce the beautiful brocades for which Japan is famous. Many of the employees work at what appear to be ordinary hand-operated looms; but those who make the finest brocades do all their work by fingernail weaving. Their nails are allowed to grow far beyond their usual length and become so coarse and strong that they can pull the colored threads through the back of the cloth, forming the beautiful patterns of Japan's most famous products. Men and women work in accordance with their skills and all are paid by a complicated piecework system. One girl of nineteen who had been working there since she was twelve was earning 30,000 yen a month, or about eighty dollars, the highest pay I heard of for any worker in all Japan. The average earnings of the skilled workers in the factory were about forty dollars a month.

At the low extreme of wages in Japan was the seven dollars a month earned by the girls in the silk factories near Ogishima village, where the silkworm cocoons are transformed in one continuous process into bales of silk, ready for shipment.

The low wages of the girls at the factory seemed shocking at first but turned out to be not quite as bad as they seemed. The girls live in comfortable dormitories at the factory, where they are provided with all their meals and their health is cared for in a private clinic. In a revealing comment on the Japanese educational approach, the president of the company observed with pride, "We also have a private school where our girls study flower arrangement, tea ceremony, dressmaking, and other subjects useful to them when they marry and establish their own homes." By this process the girls' social standing is elevated and their chances of making a good marriage are greatly improved. Living in the factory dormitories gives the girls little opportunity to meet young men but, it was pointed out, that is of minor significance because marriages are arranged by their parents anyway. By the time they are nineteen or twenty they are out of the factory and married, adding to the burgeoning population of Japan.

The curiosity of the Japanese workers is limited by long tradition. They never looked up at the visiting party in any of the factories I visited. By the same token, every machine and loom must have been idle when we left because the windows were crowded with men and women solemnly gazing at the departing guests.

In most Japanese factories men and women work side by side, often at the same job. Elsewhere women barbers are the rule and little girls do the shoe shining in the streets; frequently the women do the harder physical work, both in Japan and throughout the whole Orient. Only in the steel mills and the shipyards were all of the factory workers men.

I had originally thought it would be inappropriate to go to Hiroshima because I felt that if I did it might look as though Americans were coming to view the misery they had created. So I had declined cabled invitations from the mayor and organizations of Hiroshima before I left Albany. In Japan, I found to my surprise that they were genuinely eager to have me come, and upon my arrival at Hiroshima I learned the reason: the people of the city have dedicated it to the "commemoration of peace."

Jouncing along narrow, rutted roads from the airport through village after village, the suburbs of Hiroshima seemed to be quite normal; but as we got into the outskirts of the city evidence of the bombing became increasingly apparent. Whole areas were still as flat and empty as a farm field, while in others a considerable amount of rebuilding had been done. Even the rebuilding, however, could not conceal the picture of utter desolation Hiroshima still presents. Near the City Hall the city has built a "Memorial to Peace" which includes in a space about fifteen feet square an exact replica in miniature of the devastation. Since that square does not represent the whole area of damage, there is painted on the sides a continuation of the scene of horror and destruction. Nothing—absolutely nothing—survived in the center of the city except eleven steel and concrete buildings and some tombstones.

On August 6, 1945, at 8:15 A.M. a pale flash startled the citizens of Hiroshima, accompanied by the sound of a slight explosion about a mile above the exact center of the city. For a few seconds a small speck was observed falling rapidly, leaving a red column of fire behind it. At a height of about six hundred yards it exploded with a terrific blast, radiating a reddish-blue glare and intense heat rays. The sudden pressure of the explosion created a violent wind which carried tons of debris high into the air only to dump it onto the northern sector of the city a few moments later. The original estimates of 80,000 killed gave no picture of the monstrous horror that followed.

Later study indicated that this estimate took no account of the armed forces or visitors in the city. The best estimate today is that more than 260,000 were killed or died of injuries. At least 250,000 more were injured.

Fifty-five thousand buildings were completely destroyed; another thirteen thousand were partially destroyed. Within a mile the destruction was total except for the eleven steel and concrete buildings. As far as three miles from the center of the blast destruction was sixty per cent complete. All this was the result of a primitive, early type of atomic bomb whose explosive power has since been far exceeded. In a little cemetery right back of the Peace Memorial, beside the Ota River at the center of the burst, even the granite tombstones showed melted surfaces. Yet despite the intense heat and the violence of the explosion, people survived in concrete buildings within less than a half mile.

The horror was compounded when a typhoon hit Japan not long after the explosion of the bomb, piling its misery and damage onto the stricken city; floods swept the area, impeding rescue work and adding heavily to the casualties; thousands more died of typhoid fever and dysentery as a result of contamination of all water supplies. Six years later Hiroshima was still struggling to its feet.

A large crowd was gathered as we arrived at City Hall and I finally believed that this visit to Hiroshima was really regarded as a good-will tour. In his little speech of welcome the mayor said: "We want the people of the world to see our Peace Memorial and be warned of the awful consequences of war. The people of Hiroshima have accepted the bombing as an incident of war but because of the terrible nature of the atom bomb we are the leading exhibit in the world for peace."

Entering the battered Hiroshima City Hall, we walked up to the roof, where the mayor had laid out on a table the plans for the new and beautiful city which is to rise from the ruins. The main street, which used to be narrow and winding, is to become 330 feet wide, a beautiful boulevard as well as a fire brake; other narrow, crooked streets are to be wide and straight; the "Peace City" which aspires to be a Mecca for lovers of peace is to be modern and beautiful too. Whatever its coming role, it is certain that the destruction of Hiroshima did save countless lives which would have been lost on both sides if the war had ground on through the invasion and conquest of Japan.

Valuable research will come from Hiroshima as the result of a project set up by Secretary of Defense James Forrestal in 1946 to study the medical condition of people exposed to atomic radiation. Dr. Hilleboe, who stayed over to examine the project, reported that research has already shown that cataracts are forming more frequently on the eyes of children who were exposed to the gamma rays; there is some evidence that leukemia is more frequent among adults who were exposed; studies in genetics and of children born to mothers who were exposed are expected to produce valuable information about the effects of atomic radiation.

Some baffling social problems have been presented to the Atomic Bomb Casualty Commission by the poverty of the Japanese and its complex relationship to their sense of personal dignity and pride. To carry out scientific studies the surviving people who were exposed to atomic radiation must have periodic checkups. The difficulty was that the patients could not accept pay for coming for the checkups or they would lose face; but by coming they would lose a day's wages and then there would be no money to buy rice for the next day. The margin of existence in Japan is as slender as that.

A young American-educated Japanese came up with the solution: they should arrange to pay a sum for "carfare" which would be equivalent to a day's wages. Then the patients could save the money by walking to the dispensary and home again; they would also save face because they had accepted no pay for coming to the clinic; still they would have the price of tomorrow's rice.

The commission faced an even more delicate task in arranging post-mortem examinations of deceased persons who had been exposed to the atom bomb. To learn the long-range effects of radiation it is imperative to examine bone marrow and also specimens of the liver, spleen, and other parts of the body. But no Japanese could possibly accept money for allowing the body of a deceased member of his family to be examined. Careful inquiry disclosed, however, that it would be entirely proper for the bereaved family to accept a gift which would help pay for the cremation, funeral, and burial feasts. By accepting the gift of the commission for these expenses, the family could avoid going into debt and at the same time suffer no loss of face. Co-operation has been quite satisfactory since this arrangement was worked out.

It rained hard the night we spent in Osaka and we came out the next morning to see dramatized almost all of Japan's critical problems other than food: the desperate shortage of capital, raw materials, and power, and the equally desperate need for flood control. By morning six inches of rain had fallen and it was still raining during the short drive from Osaka to Kobe. As we drove over a Kobe bridge an ugly brown torrent was tumbling, pouring, foaming under the bridge and down the stone-walled river. It was such a terrifying sight that I asked someone to halt the procession of cars so we could get out to see it. Both the mayor of Kobe and the governor of the province had been out on flood duty all morning. As we stood watching the wild spectacle they told us that two bridges farther down the river were in danger and might go out any moment, that immense damage had been done in the country areas and that many people had been drowned.

Mr. Nemoto, the Minister of Agriculture, is convinced that great flood-control programs are the only solution for two of Japan's top-priority problems: floods and lack of power. Of course floods are not a new problem for Japan. Nine hundred years ago the entire course of her greatest river was changed to lessen floods; today, after centuries of struggling against the annual inundations, they are still one of Japan's most acute problems. The war made them worse. The shortage of fuel was so great that freezing people chopped down every tree within walking distance, denuding many of the forests which normally retained the rainfall. Thousands of lives are lost and millions of acres of rice land are flooded out each year; the resulting loss of ten to fifteen per cent of their basic food is an annual tragedy to an underfed people.

The lack of power is equally acute. In Tokyo the streets at night give the impression of a brownout because so little power is used for lighting them; the great shipyards at Kobe are shut down at least one day a week for lack of power. The Dictaphone machine which I carried along for letters and making notes ran down several times because the current was not strong enough to operate it. In all fairness, however, I should mention that this also happened in Indonesia, Australia, New Zealand, and elsewhere.

American electrical engineers were horrified to find, when they surveyed the distribution of electric power in Tokyo, that there were no meters on houses. They were advised that the system had always been for the householders to pay a standard amount for a stipulated amount of current. Everybody knows, of course, that each householder who has a connection lets a few of his neighbors tap his power line to light their own homes, for which they pay him a small amount. The Americans naturally insisted that meters should be installed. The power company officials said that was ridiculous and impossible, arguing: "We can't possibly afford the great capital costs for hundreds of thousands of electric meters, to say nothing of the cost of installing, maintaining, and inspecting them. We certainly couldn't afford the great cost of hiring an army of meter readers. If we did, the meter readers would be underpaid so they would make private deals with the householders and put in false reports. Then we would have to hire another force to check on the men who read the meters."

As if that were not enough, they argued that the ingenious Japanese would install "jumpers" so that the meters would be by-passed and the householder would sell electricity to his neighbor just as before. "Therefore," said the company officials, "why go through all this and spend all this money when we have a perfectly satisfactory way of doing business now?"

The American engineers gave up. They had learned Lesson Number One in foreign affairs: that it is difficult and unwise to try to make the rest of the world over in our image.

At Kobe the power shortage was dramatized still further. In the midst of a driving rain we transferred to a launch and rode across the beautiful harbor to the Kobe Shipyard and Engine Works. This company has been building fine ships for fifty years; a 10,000-ton freighter was on the ways while we were there, about ready to be launched. The management is progressive and the shipyard, as well as the great steel mills we visited later, seemed to my inexpert eyes to be models of efficiency. With every passing hour I could see more forcibly than ever why Japan's productive capacity is a prime object of Stalin's desire.

During the war the Japanese suffered the loss of 6,000,000 out of their 7,000,000 tons of merchant shipping, principally as the result of our American action in one of the most brilliant naval wars in history. Of all their losses this was perhaps the heaviest blow to the Japanese economy. Before the war their merchant marine traveled the seven seas, carrying much of the goods of the world, earning dollars, pounds, lire, and francs with which to buy the rice and raw materials Japan had to have to live. Now they have not only lost all of these earnings but they must pay foreign shippers' prices, entirely beyond their purse, to get the raw materials they need for their factories.

If they could find the capital, if they could get the raw materials, and if they could get the power to operate their shipyards, the Japanese believe they could replace their lost shipping in twenty-five years. But they do not know how they will get the capital, the raw materials, or the power.

Some months after I arrived home, Mr. S. Murakami of the Kobe Shipyard called on me in Albany to deliver some photographs of my visit sent by the president of the company. He reported that conditions had worsened since I was there so that even on the four days a week the shipyards were allowed to operate they had to shut down part of every day. With daily production reduced forty or fifty per cent, he was not only worried about the effect on his company and his country; he was worried about the distress this reduction caused the men, whose earnings were sharply reduced. "They just can't earn enough to keep their families together under these conditions," he said. "Men will turn to the unknown evils of Communism to escape the known evils of hunger if we can't get more power to keep the yards going."

One of the most controversial acts of the Occupation has been the destruction of the Zaibatsu, the big business cartels. Actually the Japanese cartel was much different from the type with which we are familiar in Europe. The European cartel is horizontal, involving an agreement to control production and prices between producers of a given type of product such as steel, chemicals, agricultural machinery, or perfume. By contrast, the common form of Japanese cartel was a vertical trust integrating into one organization all phases of production of a variety of products from the raw materials at the mines to the smelters, the manufacturers, processers, retailers and marketers, including the necessary banking and financial institutions. These vertical trusts in Japan were tightly controlled within themselves but unlike the European cartels, they competed fiercely with each other in their sales both at home and abroad.

In Japan the cartel was created not to stifle competition and fix prices but for efficiency and to save raw materials. Many businessmen in Japan spoke to me in utter horror at the idea that new businesses could be started by anybody with the gumption to undertake one. As one man said: "Why, under this system anybody can go out and form a company and sell goods whether they're needed or not. He can use raw materials that are necessary for other purposes. If this went very far it could destroy the stability of the whole nation."

The basic idea of genuine, free competition in mass production of goods at the lowest possible price, which has made America tower over the rest of the world, is still little known or accepted in either Japan or Europe.

I was in the company of Mr. Hisato Ichimada, the governor of the Bank of Japan, a number of times. Both at his home and elsewhere, whenever I raised the subject of meeting the shortage of capital, all eyes turned to Mr. Ichimada. "He will have to solve that for us," they said. But he has no solution either. Even the heads of government banks cannot create capital except by printing-press money, which wipes out by inflation the same amount of capital it creates. Capital must come from the savings of the people and savings in Japan are almost impossible to achieve.

The average earnings of workers in Japan today are about 10,000 yen or $28 a month. In four different prefectures I found that also to be the average salary of all government employees, other than top executives. Married employees with children are paid slightly more and those without dependents slightly less. The engineer who drove our train to Kobe in such masterly fashion gets 7200 yen or $20 a month; he is probably single and would get a little more if he had a family. A good stenographer gets about 8000 yen, or $22, a top-flight stenographer might get as much as $28 a month. In the steel mills the skilled workers make as much as 15,000 or 16,000 yen or $44 a month. These are top earnings in Japan with a few exceptions.

According to my own inquiries, it costs about 50 yen per person or 200 yen a day to buy rice for each member of a family of four. Adding a bit of fish and one or two vegetables would bring the total cost of an average, meager diet to about 80 yen a day per person or 320 yen for the family. That is nearly $27 a month, which is just under the average pay of the employed workers of Japan. That is why gardens are found in every square foot of tillable soil around homes. It is also why more than one member of almost every family works.

Even members of the Diet and governors of prefectures are paid only $150 a month; some of the governors are provided with residences, some not. The earnings of the most successful business executives are but little more. One of the dubious blessings we have conferred upon Japan is heavy corporate taxation and heavily progressive income taxes, almost as bad as our own, and all earnings which could become capital savings are soaked up by the government. From such earnings it will be hard to find the capital Japan needs to rebuild her shipping and her bombed-out factories.

Never far from exhaustion of their food supplies, and with never quite enough of anything, the Japanese people seemed to me cheerful, hard-working, and clear-thinking on most issues. They saw their life's savings wiped out by the dreadful postwar inflation; prices are high and earnings low; they are still terribly short of housing. Despite all their difficulties, however, they have great inherent strength.

By our standards, their houses would be intolerable in winter. They are constructed of the thinnest wood, with sliding, paper windows. The average Japanese family with their thin clothes must be thoroughly miserable, with the temperature often below freezing and occasionally down to zero. They huddle around a tiny brazier fed by a bit of charcoal or whatever wood can be found. The whole family sleeps close together on the floor around the little stove with a degree of intimacy and informality which would be quite unusual in America. I repeatedly asked how they kept warm in winter. The simplest answer was from an American: "They don't."

While far superior to many Asian nations, the health standards in Japan are, also, much below our own. The greatest cause of death in Japan is tuberculosis, which in 1950 killed 145 people out of every hundred thousand. By contrast, the New York State death rate is 19 per hundred thousand or one eighth that of Japan.

Treatment of tuberculosis in Japan is particularly difficult because of the serious social implications. Japanese do not hesitate to discuss venereal diseases and report them officially; but there is a taboo on the subject of tuberculosis, principally because it affects the marriageability of young women. Marriages are usually arranged by parents and the first question asked by the parents of the young man is whether the girl has tuberculosis. She may have venereal disease or other defects and the marriage may nevertheless be consummated; but if she has tuberculosis her chances of marriage are almost nil.

Dr. Hilleboe reported one sad example: A doctor had a young sister with tuberculosis, for whom he wanted to get streptomycin. He went to the Tokyo Office of the American Medical Services and explained that he wanted the drug for his sister. The doctor in charge replied that, under the rules, he should report her as an active case of tuberculosis. The young doctor replied that his sister did not have tuberculosis, only a lung inflammation, and refused to bring in an X ray. Despite the fact that his own sister was involved and the streptomycin might have cured her, he walked out, preferring to try to get it on the black market rather than to file the report which would end her chances of marriage.

Surprisingly enough, vascular lesions of the central nervous system such as apoplexy are the second cause of death among the highly sensitive Japanese people. Down in third place are the enteric diseases, including typhoid and dysentery which are so dangerous to Westerners but to which Asians develop a degree of immunity. There is little problem of narcotic addiction, Dr. Hilleboe found, except in a Korean colony around Osaka.

In the face of their handicaps, the population of Japan is going through the roof. In 1950 there were 2,300,000 births with only 909,000 deaths. This means that there is an excess of births over deaths of 1,500,000 people a year. At this rate Japan's population will have risen from 70,000,000 in 1941 to 100,000,000 by 1963.

For years I have puzzled over the basic reason for the shift of Japan from the side of freedom in World War I to that of the Axis in World War II. The rise of Mussolini from the ruins of World War I in Italy was an obvious explanation for the Italian shift; but no such single event explained what happened in Japan. Her growing population and barren, little islands had made her hungry; her aggressive seizure of territory in Manchuria had strained relations between Japan and the United States; her attack on China in 1937 and the long history of increasing diplomatic strain were all part of the picture but did not adequately explain the successful rise of an aggressive totalitarian clique hostile to the United States but friendly to Germany. I learned one new answer in Japan. Following World War I, the Japanese, in continuing their rapid industrialization, were in great need of technical help, exchange of patents, and friendly business guidance and co-operation. They found an America completely absorbed with its own problems, busy and prosperous; they found Germany beaten, in need of friends and hungry for markets. Moreover, free-enterprise business in America between the two wars was under constant and increasing political attack in connection with any agreements made with businessmen in foreign countries, and all such agreements ran the risk of indictment for violation of the anti-trust laws; in addition the State Department maintained its historic aloofness from business and its traditional lack of interest in developing American markets abroad, a policy which has not even been changed since World War II.

On the other hand, both the government and the businessmen of Germany were searching the world for partners and markets; after the rise of Hitler this search was intensified under the direction and, indeed, the control of the Nazi government and its entire diplomatic corps. The inevitable result was that Japan found the friendly help she needed for her own development in Hitler's Germany, with all of the catastrophic results we have since seen.

One Japanese electrical manufacturer told me that he had been in America not long before, hoping to re-establish and develop an old relationship with the General Electric Company, both in his own behalf and for the benefit of his country. He came home a sadder and wiser man; General Electric had advised him that they felt compelled to avoid all such foreign contracts for the use of patents and technical developments for fear of anti-trust indictments, at least until the law had been clarified as the result of pending trials on several indictments which had already been handed up. It seemed to me that our foreign policy and our domestic policy were once again working exactly at cross-purposes. I thought how valuable it would be if we had a government in America competent to make all of our policies work together in the interest of peace and the development of our trade relations.

For centuries it has been said that "Peace follows trade"; recent history has once more demonstrated that ancient truth dramatically and tragically. We should not relax our anti-trust vigilance; we should increase it; but what we really need to do is rewrite the law so that everyone can understand it and then see that it maintains real competition in America while serving the interests of our people and our diplomacy in the free world abroad.

The cultural bars between America and Asia are as numerous as the business bars. The Soviet Union not only suffers none of the handicaps under which we struggle in a business way, they have also outstripped us overwhelmingly in their cultural penetration into the free world. Traveling Soviet ballets, orchestras, singers, and artists, as well as every form of Soviet literature, are turning up all over the world in huge quantities. Much of the music and art is entirely unaccompanied by propaganda but it is plainly the most powerful propaganda of all. For us to compete with the Soviet in cultural propaganda would probably cost billions; but as I noted the total absence of any sign of American culture in the Pacific it seemed to me that our defeat in the struggle for the minds of people in this one area alone was so decisive as to require a complete overhauling of our attitude and approach.

Of course an occasional baseball team or boxer makes a triumphant tour of Japan for profit and does some good; American movies and magazines circulate in the Pacific. But more often than not they deal with the ugliest aspect of American life, frequently exaggerating our defects for purposes of sensationalism or entertainment.

Concerning our relations with our Pacific friends, as well as with all other countries, I received from an agronomist, one of the leading educators of Japan, a bit of advice which struck me as fundamental. We were talking at the Cabinet reception about America's still budding effort to provide real technical help to the nations of Asia. In the nicest possible way he said quietly, "I do hope that in your Point Four Program when you start sending technicians you will send good ones. One good man is worth a dozen poor ones and I hope you will send only your best." Another professor joined in with a smile, saying, "There is an old Japanese proverb that one lion is worth a hundred sheep." He did not say that he had seen too many examples of America sending abroad those who were failures at home. We each understood what he meant. At the top we usually have able people; from there down, particularly in ECA and the U. S. Information Service, they are too often unfortunate fellows who couldn't hold a job at home. Probably a more generous pay scale and a more widespread understanding of the importance of their services to the welfare of America would help more than anything else in attracting and holding imaginative and able men.

In almost every country I visited except Japan I found the ugly trail of damage done to our diplomatic service by unfounded or ignorant criticism at home. A classic example was one case where the Ambassador, in the usual way, had filed a report with the State Department on the results of a visit by a traveling United States senator. As a member of a committee investigating something else, the senator later demanded of the State Department, under power of subpoena, the file concerning his visit to that country; despite their confidential nature, the State Department felt compelled to surrender the reports and waited for the explosion when the senator read a fair and dispassionate report of what he had done. The explosion never came. After holding the report two weeks, the senator quietly returned it without ever making it public; but the fact that he had demanded and read the report went all through the service.

On many other occasions, old, confidential reports have been dragged out and exposed to public inspection. The insecurity resulting from such exposure of confidential reports has swept through our whole foreign service. Men who entered the service under Wilson, Harding, Coolidge, and Hoover, as well as more recent appointees, all expressed the same opinion: "If we are going to be held up to public scorn for our judgments ten or fifteen years after they were made, in the light of changing events, we simply will not stick our necks out. We are willing to file our honest opinions and truthful reports and take our chances with changing administrations of the State Department if our opinions seem wrong in the light of later events; but if everything we say in the exercise of honest judgment is going to be held up to hostile criticism as a result of personal pique on the part of individual senators or congressmen or as a result of conditions which have long since changed, we simply won't take the chance."

One particularly able and experienced man summarized the view of many: "In the light of what has happened in the last few years, from now on I am going to report nothing but simple obvious facts and not risk losing my job or my reputation. I'll keep my judgments and opinions to myself." It will be a long time before the United States again gets the full benefit of the advice and opinion of the really able men in the career service, who will need much reassurance before they resume the filing of reports which reflect their honest opinions on political trends abroad, social and economic conditions, and the impact made by visiting firemen.

Above all the strife and confusion of the moment there remains in the background, in Japan, the still mystic figure of the Emperor. As Ambassador Sebald and I drove up to the Imperial Palace in the heart of Tokyo, I realized for the first time that the great moats and walls which surround it no longer have any significance. A wide highway runs right through the middle of the palace grounds and at lunchtime thousands of Japanese office employees stroll along the highway, sitting, lying, and sunning themselves on the spacious lawns. Turning off the highway, we soon encountered an inner wall whose gates were guarded by two policemen. Since no one was admitted to the palace except upon written authorization of the Occupation, our credentials were carefully studied by an attendant at the gate who then got up beside the chauffeur and drove in with us.

Because the main palace was destroyed by American bombing during the war we saw the Emperor in one section of the Imperial Household's office building. We were met at the entrance and taken up a flight of stairs, down many corridors, by many doors through which shirt-sleeved clerks could be seen at work. We finally entered a stately room where we were met by the two senior members of the Imperial Household. We chatted briefly in English for a few minutes and then proceeded down another long corridor to a slightly smaller room furnished in excellent taste and with fine Japanese paintings on the walls. On the way I was courteously reminded that since the Emperor could have no influence in politics our conversation would, of course, be completely confidential. "I understand entirely," I replied. "That is also the custom in our country with visits to the President or a governor. The only trouble is that some people don't respect the custom, but they usually don't get in a second time."

The Emperor entered the room almost immediately, shook hands cordially, and we sat down to talk through an interpreter. He was dressed in a dark suit with a white shirt and a casually loose tie, and peered at the world with half-closed eyes through thick-lensed glasses. Sitting straight in his chair, he spoke in a low soft voice. While discussing foreign affairs Hirohito seemed under considerable strain; but it all disap-

peared after a few minutes when he introduced the subject of
farming. He was a different man, relaxed and completely
absorbed in a conversation about comparative Japanese and
American farming methods. Obviously the Emperor knew I
was much interested in agriculture; but I wondered how he
knew in detail of my visits to Japanese farms the day before.
Later when we went from the palace to Premier Yoshida's
Cabinet reception I learned from the Minister of Agriculture
that he had provided the Emperor with a full memorandum
on our farm visits the night before. Hirohito does his home-
work.

I was also interested to discover that he understands English.
During our long farm conversation he seemed to be enjoying
it, laughing a number of times—not at the end of the interpreter's translation but while I was speaking. I gathered that
though he thoroughly understands English he speaks only in
Japanese to be sure, because of his position, that there is no
misunderstanding.

After ten days in Japan and an hour's visit with the Emperor
I do not pretend to be an authority on the Japanese monarchy.
But some things are clear: Hirohito has been through a period
of dreadful strain; he saw his country launched on a disastrous,
losing war which he had opposed; after the war both the Russians and left-wing groups all over the world demanded that
he be executed as a war criminal. The tension grew as the
War Crimes Commission wended its way through testimony
and prepared its report. When the report finally appeared, it
established that Hirohito was in no way responsible for the
war, that he had held out against war to the bitter end and to
the limit of his influence.

After the Japanese surrender the Emperor took every possible action to make it clear to the people that he fully supported the program of the Occupation, including the funda-

mental change from theoretical absolute power in the Crown
to a limited, constitutional monarchy. He publicly renounced
all divine powers and acquiesced in the abolition of government support of the Shinto religion.

The truth is that Hirohito is not by nature a politician at all;
by natural bent and choice, he is an amateur biologist. He
spends all the time he can spare in biological studies and is
the author of a respected two-volume work on the flora and
fauna of Tokyo Bay. He personally tends a small garden of his
own on the palace grounds and greatly enjoys the annual cere-
monial rice planting when tradition requires him to go into
the fields and transplant the first shoots of rice.

While the Emperor has been preserved as chief of state,
though with limited powers, other members of the imperial
family have not fared as well. For example, the stately resi-
dences of both the Foreign Minister and the governor of
Tokyo are owned by Japanese princes. The princes no longer
receive any income from the government, so they rent their
houses to the government and live themselves in the gardeners'
cottages on the edge of their own grounds.

At the end of the war the Communists came out into
the open, expecting to share Occupation powers. Their plans
were all laid to make political capital during the confusion
which followed the end of wartime controls and the disappear-
ance of a native government, before the Occupation had become fully organized. Violence reigned in many areas. On one
day alone 500,000 people gathered on the palace grounds to
listen to savage and inflammatory speeches indirectly aimed at
the Emperor. Hirohito could see from his window thousands
of red flags bearing the hammer and sickle as orators incited
the people to riot.

It appeared necessary to the Imperial Household for the
Emperor to show himself in public and it was decided to ac-

cept an invitation to visit Yokohama. Because the gravest fears were expressed for his safety, every effort was made to get adequate police protection, but in those days practically none was available. Despite the risks, the Emperor drove through the streets of Tokyo, then through the countryside to Yokohama, with little or no escort. He was met by milling thousands on the streets; but they were friendly thousands and not a single incident occurred. His personal courage left a deep impression on the whole nation.

Over the centuries the power and influence of the Emperor have waxed and waned. During some periods he has been all-powerful; during others he has been practically a captive. This was particularly true during the dominance of the Shogun warlords and more recently in the period leading up to World War II. It is a strange contradiction that today at the end of a terrible, losing war, stripped of all claims to divinity, the Emperor is in many ways more influential than before. I left Japan convinced that the Allied decision to retain the Emperor was wise. I believe, too, that the Crown will be a powerful force for a stable, free Japan.

Despite the generally promising political picture, there are small but ugly clouds on the Japanese horizon. Some of the intellectuals expressed real concern. One university professor put it this way: "I'm worried by the presence of Communists in our teachers' unions. The Communist leadership has been pretty well driven out of the trade unions but in the teachers' unions just a couple of Communists out of a hundred tend to dominate the other ninety-eight. The influence of the Communists in our educational system is already great and after the treaty is signed I am afraid they will come out in the open. To my mind, the future is very doubtful."

A leading member of the judiciary expressed another fear.

He believes that if Japan is left alone she will have few Communist troubles. What he worries about is that after the treaty she may be forced to trade with Red China. The necessities of trade will then, he fears, bring an ever increasing number of Communists into the country in one guise or another.

Later a small incident occurred to confirm those warnings. On the occasion of the Emperor's state visit to one of the great universities, 3000 students chose the occasion to demonstrate against "American imperialism," getting so thoroughly out of hand that Hirohito was unable to leave his car; afterward the students protested that they had meant no discourtesy to the Emperor. But in prewar Japan such an incident would have been unthinkable.

After nearly a century of intercourse with the Western world Japan remains today a strange mixture of influences and the Occupation's attempt to impose American ideas of democracy has produced some curious paradoxes. In the old days, for example, when rumors or charges of scandal were circulated against a government officer he was expected to resign to save face. Today, with governors and members of the Diet elected to regular terms, that would seem to be inappropriate. Not at all. If a rumor of scandal or corruption in the administration of a prefecture gains wide acceptance, tradition still requires that the governor resign. If he resigns, then he is in good standing in the community and his reputation is entirely undamaged. If he fails to resign, however, even though the rumors are entirely false, he has lost face and his honor is impugned. This practice has already lent itself to abuse by Communist and other minorities who have forced special elections to be held whenever anyone circulated a rumor, however untrue.

So far free elections have served Japan well. Emancipation and equality of women has been established by law; men and women vote freely, secretly, and to the extraordinary extent of ninety per cent of all eligible voters—far better than we do in America. The results have been good, too. I met often with the leaders of the Diet, the Cabinet, and with many of the governors of the prefectures. Most of these men appeared to me to be well educated and superior public servants; there are few signs that demagoguery has yet produced the flotsam who often turn up in elections elsewhere.

This does not mean that Japan has solved all of her governmental problems; many of them are just beginning. One real handicap is that the people of Japan, like others in the world, concentrate almost wholly on their own problems. Despite the clear and pressing danger of Soviet aggression, neither the Americans nor the Japanese have reached any clear understanding as to the immediate course for Japan in her own defense. At Yalta we unhappily conceded the Japanese Kurile Islands to Russia. The peace treaty did not confirm this concession, however, and Russia has no legal title to the islands. Regardless of legality, she has occupied them in force anyway; today Russian divisions stand just three miles away from the home island of Hokkaido. Surrounded on the northeast, the northwest, and the west, therefore, by Communist-held territory, with no army, navy, or air force of her own, Japan will depend upon America for her defense for a long time to come.

The Japanese would fiercely resist a Russian invasion to the limit of their capacity; but at the moment they have no capacity. One of the triumphs of the treaty is that it places no limitation on their armed forces and eventually they must rebuild their defenses. The difficulty is that there is little sentiment in Japan for rearmament; even Premier Yoshida, with all his wisdom, is sufficiently pacifist to be unwilling to press for a minimum of defensive forces.

Moreover, defeat has left Japan no money for rearmament. Only under the most drastic pressure from the Occupation did the government balance the present limited budget, thereby temporarily stopping the currency inflation in 1951. No one has any idea where the money for a rearmament program would come from.

The people themselves show real hostility to the military. How long this will last no one knows. One woman who lost two sons in the war summed up what will perhaps be the final Japanese decision: "I know how terrible war is. I lost both of my sons. I do believe Japan will never again start a war and I know that we will have to have a new army and navy if we are going to prevent the Russians from attacking us. I guess we will have to build strong defenses and the sooner we do it the better."

One of the most pleasant aspects of my trip has been the correspondence with Japanese friends since my return. One letter from a friend in the Cabinet summarizes what many have said:

"I do hope you will tell the people of America of the progress Japan is making in recovery and in becoming thoroughly democratic. Please tell them, too, how clear it is that she will become a member of the family of peaceful nations for all time to come. Our country will be a leader in freedom and in stopping Communism in this part of the world."

I believe those are the sentiments of the great majority of the people of Japan today. They have the will to be free; whether they will have the economic strength to survive in freedom depends in large measure upon the wisdom of American policy in Japan and to an even greater extent upon the future of Southeast Asia.

2

Korea

. . . the last act of the drama is yet to be unfolded . . . the people of America will, in some form or other, extend their dominion and their power . . . upon the eastern shores of Asia. And I think too, that eastward and southward will her great [Russian] rival . . . stretch forth her power to the coasts of China and Siam: and thus the Saxon and the Cossack will meet once more, in strife or in friendship, on another field. Will it be in friendship? I fear not! The antagonistic exponents of freedom and absolutism must thus meet at last, and then will be fought that mighty battle on which the world will look with breathless interest; for on its issue will depend the freedom or the slavery of the world. . . .

*Commodore M. C. Perry, USN,
speaking before the American
Geographical and Statistical
Society, March 6, 1856*

It is less than four hours' flying time in a C-54 from Tokyo to Pusan, temporary capital of the Republic of South Korea. We took off from the Tachikawa air base on modern, concrete runways and landed at Pusan on one of the worst air strips I had ever seen. It was just a single strip of dirt and gravel. In war, such peacetime luxuries as cross-strips and concrete runways do not exist. The Air Force has to use whatever strip is available, and the pilots can't bother about which way the wind is blowing. Our transport plane slipped into that dusty strip in the face of a nasty cross-wind which virtually skidded the plane across the dirt and gravel runway. The landing and the runway would have been unthinkable in the United States; it would have been rare in Japan; it is routine in Korea.

I had originally hoped to go on directly from Pusan to headquarters at Seoul but the American Ambassador to Korea, John J. Muccio, had insisted that I must take time out to make courtesy calls on the members of the government of the Republic who were then at Pusan. This suggestion was seconded by Ambassador Sebald, who urged that failure to make such a visit would cause hurt feelings. "There is no government so proud and sensitive," he pointed out, "as one which is in great trouble." He was right, of course, so when we landed at Pusan, Ambassador Muccio was awaiting us with a convoy of American military cars.

Each car was driven by a soldier with another sitting beside him in the front seat carrying a Garand rifle or carbine. Even in Pusan, two hundred miles from the front, no one took any chances with the constant threat of Communist guerrillas. In order to preserve good relations with the South Koreans, the Army had arranged for a convoy by Korean military police. Six jeeploads of them, all heavily armed, preceded us while others brought up the rear. As the convoy moved away from the airport it rolled up thick clouds of dust on the main highway over which our supplies are moved.

The stench that arose from the rice paddies as we drove into Pusan was almost indescribable. In the rural sections of Japan the effluvia from the night soil on the rice fields often hangs like a fog over the countryside; but it is light and almost pleasant compared with the malodorous atmosphere around Pusan. It was hard to remember that this was our main supply base. The mud huts and shacks, which grew closer together as we neared the city, swarmed with poorly clad, ill-fed people. As we came into the winding streets of the city the shacks were packed closer together amid an atmosphere of disease and the terrible pressure of too many human beings in too little space. Even the few best squares in the heart of the city were jammed with Korean refugees and their children, all bearing on their faces and in their clothing the mark of the dreadful misery brought by war.

The task of caring for the refugees is the greatest nonmilitary problem in Korea. Before the war the Republic of Korea had a population of 20,000,000 and North Korea 9,000,-000. With every shifting tide of battle, more North Koreans sought refuge from the Communists and there are today an estimated 3,000,000 of North Korea's 9,000,000 people wandering the roads and villages of South Korea, homeless, hungry, disease-ridden, and hopeless. Today it is almost impossible to believe that Korea was once a beautiful and productive land, rich in coal, iron, gold, silver, copper, and other minerals, and before the war one of the great fish-exporting nations of the world.

We found the President of the Republic, Syngman Rhee, in a modest and rather shabby brick house. President Rhee has spent half of his seventy-five years in exile, leading the movement for Korean independence, ever since his country was incorporated into the Japanese Empire in 1910. It has been a long struggle and the burden of leadership following liberation of the southern half of his country has taken a heavy toll. Having spent a lifetime to liberate the Korea of 1910, he found himself, at an advanced age, pathetically attempting to administer the Korea of 1945, divided at the 38th Parallel into hostile zones and with a people entirely inexperienced in self-government. The difficulties have been overwhelming and the war has been a crushing blow. President Rhee and his Cabinet were utterly dismayed at the prospect that the war might be settled on the 38th Parallel and their emotional revulsion was difficult to deal with. They insisted that they would accept no settlement which does not free and unite the whole country. President Rhee even said over and over again: "Give us the arms and we will drive out the invaders ourselves." It was fruitless to point out that it took several hundred thousand United Nations troops and many casualties to drive the Reds back as far as they are. Emotion completely overcomes reason.

For some reason I had thought of Korea as just one vast and desolated battlefield. I had given little thought to the actual functioning and existence of a government in Korea, during a war in which at one time the territory it controlled had been reduced to a tiny perimeter around Pusan. Yet the President and his Cabinet as well as the Korean National Assembly were here and functioning. They had even called a special session of the Assembly this Sunday afternoon, expecting me to address them. But what could I say? Clearly, they expected me to promise that their country would be united, by force of arms if necessary. That I could not do.

Nevertheless, I had to go and speak. When we arrived for the session, I found that the Assembly was meeting in the Pusan wrestling hall. At one end was a makeshift platform; in the center were a number of folding chairs, and behind a railing two thirds of the way back there must have been at least a thousand people jammed in, standing silently, looking through hungry eyes for hope, for promises, for anything I could give them. They reminded me of a crowd of campaign workers on election night, hoping against hope that the vote would produce a landslide for their candidates. It was a harrowing experience because I could give no reassurance to their obvious hopes. I did express my admiration for the Korean people for their patience and courage, for the sacrifices of their soldiers, and for their determination to resist conquest by the Communist hordes of North Korea and Red China. Even though I did not make the promises they were so eager to accept from anyone, both the legislators and the people were pitifully cordial and they swarmed all over me at the conclusion, shaking my hand and thanking me for my visit.

Through the clouds of dust and stench we went on one more sad mission—a visit to a United Nations cemetery on the outskirts of the city. As we approached it we saw in the distance the flags of all the United Nations taking part, side by side, in this effort to defend a helpless little Republic against aggression. Just as we got out of the cars it started to rain and we passed in silence through the rows upon rows of white crosses to the American flag, where I placed a wreath at the foot of the staff. It was deeply moving to walk between these rows of white crosses and Stars of David representing Americans who had died for the cause of freedom nine thousand miles from home on the soil of a country they had never seen before and of which few had even heard before the war.

One section was impressively different. A white star and crescent marked the graves of the Turkish soldiers. Here in this cemetery were the dead heroes of sixteen free nations who had fought together in battle to preserve the liberties of us all. In death, the soldiers of the United Nations were eternally united, the descendants of the Crusaders, the children of Israel, and the sons of the Prophet.

During the hour-and-a-quarter flight from Pusan to Seoul I got my first real look at the Korean countryside. Millions of words have been written about it but words cannot convey the tremendous difficulties our armed forces have faced in this battered, war-torn land. The entire country is desolate and rugged, one valley and mountainside after another. The valleys are deep and broad; the mountains tower up at angles of forty-five degrees to a razorlike edge and then fall down again into the next valley. It's the worst possible kind of military terrain and yet our foot soldiers, supported by artillery and air power, took ridge after ridge, valley after valley, as they drove the Communists north from the perimeter of Pusan to beyond the 38th Parallel.

The terrible scars of war were everywhere. Scattered peasant huts could be seen, but in valley after valley where villages had once flourished there was nothing left but semicircles of blackened earth. Surrounded by the ever present rice paddies, what used to be villages are now man-made deserts, set against the bases of the mountains.

The area we flew over was infested by at least three bands of guerrillas who constantly attacked our transport and supply lines. Lieutenant Galvin had a grand reunion with his brother at Pusan, which General Ridgway had kindly arranged. The brother was an MP riding with supply trains and he reported constant guerrilla attacks which the MPs had to repel, often without the help of the Korean soldiers who also ride the trains. In addition, the Korean train crews were so casual about schedules that it often required stern action by the American soldiers to prevent the crews from stopping the trains periodically to go off and enjoy a meal with their relatives along the way.

Seoul, the capital of the Republic of South Korea, had been captured and recaptured six times. As our plane circled the city before landing we were able to see miles and miles of what used to be a prosperous city with more than 1,000,000 inhabitants. Berlin was the most seriously wounded city I had seen until then. In comparison, Seoul was not wounded: it was dead. In many sections not a single house remained standing. Even the great modern government buildings were hopelessly gutted.

What remained of Seoul was a military encampment. Driving in jeeps into the city, it seemed impossible that any civilian could continue to live there. Nevertheless, about a hundred thousand had somehow managed to stay in the city through all the various occupations. Still another hundred thousand had slipped back in despite rigid orders from the Army against residents returning. So now two hundred thousand people were living in the cellars or in the rubble of shattered homes in a city with no electric power, no water, no sewage disposal—nothing. The American Army provides to what remains of the city government a daily supply of rice which is carefully distributed every morning among the people. This rice is virtually the sole food supply of the two hundred thousand civilian population of the city.

Driving through Seoul to the headquarters of our Eighth Army we passed over pavements cratered by artillery fire and bombing, passing a few people sitting in front of what was left of homes or stores. One bombed-out square had been cleared of rubble and two or three hundred people sat around on the ground running the city's only market. They were the one sign of commerce in the ghost city as they sat there with a few vegetables, a little rice, or their own possessions spread out in front of them for barter or sale.

The guesthouse was the former Japanese consul's home, one of the few buildings undamaged by the war. Run by the Army, it was immaculate and my room adjoined a crude but entirely workable bath which was much needed at the end of our first day in Korea. As soon as I had cleaned up we were off to dinner with General James A. Van Fleet and his staff. I had known the general when he was assigned to First Army Headquarters at Governors Island in New York after his historic contribution to the training of the army of Greece. He conceals tremendous drive and military ability under an almost boyish smile and manner. His enthusiasm is infectious and I saw evidence of his great leadership throughout my entire stay. He does not drive men. They follow him because they have faith in him. He is also a leading expert at training fighters in backward nations and his talents were never so sorely needed as in Korea.

We went directly to dinner. There were no cocktails. I saw no strong liquor of any kind during my whole stay with the Army. Maybe it was there but I saw only beer and none of that at headquarters. These men are on duty twenty-four hours of the day, asleep or awake. They may be called upon at any moment to make decisions which affect the lives of their men and they take no chances on dulling their judgment. Dinner was identical with that served to the troops: soup, steak, two vegetables, cake, and coffee. From there we went to the regular nightly General Staff briefing on every detail of the fighting front and then to the Air Force briefing. After that the sore subject of Korea's "Bed Check Charlie" came up, a nickname which was a hangover from World War II.

Bed Check Charlie was an enemy aviator. No one knew his nationality and no one cared. They just wanted to get him, for Charlie was a nuisance. Every clear night for some months, a World War I type of airplane came over our lines just as our troops were getting some much-needed sleep. Evidently Charlie knew every inch of the terrain, because he flew in so low that radar couldn't pick him up. He would fly in between the hills, reach an air strip or command post, kick or throw a small bomb out of his plane, and shoot off a pistol a few times. He never did much damage. But he did manage to ruin the sleep of a whole lot of men wherever he showed up. The Army was getting fed up with Charlie and in the manner of foot soldiers the world over, they were saying some very unkind things about the Air Force.

The Air Force was furious and exasperated. Night fighters

of every kind had gone up after Charlie and even jet planes had entered the hunt; but our night fighters and particularly the jets flew so fast that they never could find him and his eighty-mile-an-hour jenny. As we were leaving, General Van Fleet himself announced with a straight face, "If they don't get Charlie soon, I am going up on the top of this building and shoot him down with a pistol."

They finally got him. One night after I left, a bomber pilot spotted him and went after him. The fast bomber had a rated landing speed of a hundred miles an hour but the pilot dropped all his wing flaps, throttled down his motors to a minimum, and somehow kept the plane in the air at ninety miles an hour. He came in behind Charlie, gave him one burst, and that was the end of Charlie—he blew up in the air. I understand that everybody sleeps better now and even the infantry gives credit to the Air Force.

I had my first chance at these briefings to get the answer to one of the things I went to Korea to find out. Was it possible that Chinese losses were ten to one over ours? Was it a fact that our air victories over the Russian jet MIGs up to July 1951 were as overwhelming as reported? Careful study of documents after World War II showed that our successes both in the air and on the ground had been exaggerated. In the light of this evidence, many people sharply questioned the Korean figures. I thought it was important to learn the truth and, having spent some years of my life as a cross-examiner, I went to work.

The figures of ground losses of the enemy are not mere speculations, as some have suggested. They are computed by actually counting the bodies of the enemy dead and then by a careful estimate of the number the enemy may have been able to carry away of both dead and wounded. Air reconnaissance often produces pictures indicating both the number of attacking troops and their condition after battle. Commanding officers in the field are required to sign estimates and set forth the basis on which they were made. The study is amazingly well done. Nevertheless, after the figures came into Eighth Army Headquarters, they were arbitrarily reduced, sometimes by as much as half, before being released to the press. I was satisfied when I finished that the figures on enemy casualties are carefully documented and conservatively computed. But I still had difficulty imagining how the Chinese and North Koreans could take losses running into half a million men and still stay in there fighting. With that lingering doubt in mind, I planned to search for more evidence in the countries I was to visit later and from the people who had been behind the Bamboo Curtain of Communist China in recent months. I heard reports of the greatest interest in Formosa, Hong Kong, and the Philippines.

The Air Force figures surprised me even more. Fighter planes are equipped with motion picture cameras attached to every gun. When the gun starts shooting, the movie camera starts rolling automatically. No plane is reported damaged unless the movies, when developed, show a direct hit. No plane is reported shot down unless the movie camera records it or, if the guns stop firing before the plane falls, unless the report is confirmed by two independent witnesses. After a careful examination I was convinced that our Air Force reports of enemy planes shot down or damaged are honest and reliable. This does not mean that every one of our own planes shot down is reported, at least at the time. We do not always think it advisable to tell the enemy everything we know. It does not explain either the apparently superior performance of our jet fighters against the Russian MIGs. We have often gone into battle with thirty jets on our side against fifty of the enemy. It happened the very day I was in the Air Force briefing room and resulted in a clear-cut American victory. The best explanation was that, although our planes are actually inferior in some respects, our American pilots are greatly superior to the enemy aviators.

The day-to-day Air Force figures also leave out a full report of our losses from enemy anti-aircraft. The Communists have excellent radar; their ground fire is accurate and often effective, thanks to the proximity fuse the Soviet got from us in World War II.

The second day of my visit to Korea started with an early breakfast with General Van Fleet, followed by the regular morning briefing. We had dressed that morning in Army field clothes because it was suggested that the Army would "prefer" to have its civilian guests wear uniforms to avoid attracting enemy attention. One of the officers pointed out: "Korea is full of spies. You can throw a stone in any direction and hit at least one. You're going up to the front, and the presence of white men in civilian clothes makes the enemy curious. And when the enemy gets curious, he lets go with snipers and artillery fire at everybody, not just at our visitors."

Before I left home a friend had said to me: "I'm very glad you're going to Korea. You'll see the greatest Army in the world. From all the chaos and confusion of the early days when we were unprepared, this force has been welded into the greatest fighting force ever produced by the United States or any other country. You'll also see the Army, Navy, and Air Force work as a single unit." Others disputed the superlatives, saying that the armies that rolled across Germany and the Pacific were equally good. Having seen our Eighth Army at work in Korea, I am inclined to agree that it is the best and the most powerful, if for no other reason than that it is a complete and effective union of all three branches of the armed forces—air, sea, and ground—working in the closest harmony and co-operation.

Unification is still creaking at the joints in Washington and has a long way to go before it is effective. But at the Eighth Army Headquarters in Korea I found a genuinely co-operative spirit. Unlike the days past when rivalries became personal and even bitter, I found what seemed to me a genuine mutual regard and affection. If there were any serious interservice rivalries, I doubt that they could have been concealed for my benefit. I saw none. These fighting men of ours are making unification work where it counts and pays off the most—on the battlefield.

While we were in the briefing room we received a dramatic illustration. At that moment the battleship *New Jersey* was standing off the east coast of North Korea lobbing 16-inch shells into a road nineteen miles inland from the sea. Air Force photographs had shown that the road was under intensive use for bringing up supplies and reserves to the enemy lines. The *New Jersey* was busy chewing up the road to make it impassable and occasionally hitting enemy transports, all of which was shown by air pictures taken that afternoon.

Most of the officers and men with whom I talked believe they have developed fire power to the highest degree in the history of warfare. Our armed forces in Korea are passionate in their enthusiasm for concentrated use of artillery to destroy or soften up the enemy before our infantry goes in or before the enemy can reach us when he attacks. This is the secret of the enormous casualties inflicted on the enemy and the reason we have been able to resist overwhelming masses with our own comparatively limited forces.

Lieutenant General Edward M. Almond, commander of the X Corps, tells of one day in the big spring offensive of 1951 when seemingly unending masses of Chinese were finally hurled back at the end of a long and determined attack. He says he reported with some pride to General Van Fleet **the** next day that one battalion of artillery within his corps had fired 12,000 rounds of artillery shells in twelve hours—one every three and a half seconds—which he believed to be a record in the history of warfare. General Van Fleet listened quietly. Then he grinned: "That's fine, Almond, that's fine, but it's not enough."

Despite the superiority we finally achieved in fire power, the Chinese and the North Koreans have forced us to adopt their kind of warfare. They dig themselves in near the top of the ridges, put heavy logs across their trenches and foxholes, and then pile dirt on top of the logs. This makes a dugout which cannot be disturbed by any amount of shellfire except a direct hit. So our troops have been forced to climb the ridges and go along the top, taking the land yard by yard with flame throwers and hand grenades. The enemy rarely gives up. He often fights in the hole until he is dead.

When General Ridgway took over the field command after the death of General Walton H. Walker, our forces had been reeling back under the combined attacks of the Chinese and North Korean Reds. He faced a massive task and made many changes in command. One officer who witnessed the changes told me: "A new major general was put in command of our Corps and he personally inspected every section of our lines. I'll never forget his talk with one colonel. He asked the colonel what were his plans. The colonel outlined his plans to retreat first to one position, then to another. The general asked about the men. The colonel replied that their food wasn't good and it wasn't even hot; he added that their spirit was low and that morale was very bad.

"At the end of the report the new corps commander said: 'Colonel, from now on we are not retreating, we are attacking.

We are no longer thinking in terms of retreat, though of course one staff officer will have those problems worked out. You are thinking only of attacking.

" 'So far as the men are concerned, everything you report to me is your fault. The men are entitled to good food and they must have one hot meal a day except under the most impossible conditions. Their morale should be good and I will hold you personally accountable.' "

Then the officer who was telling me the story smiled and added: "A week later the general went back. There were no more retreats. The meals were good and the food was hot. The morale of the men had been revived and they were ready to fight."

Following the headquarters briefing we went to the dirt air strip and were off for a tour of the front, each of us in a little two-seater L-19 reconnaissance plane. One after the other the L-19s took their short run, bumping along the dusty air strip, and we were off up the Uijogbiu River to the I Corps command post. As the river wound back and forth beneath us we found ourselves alternately over our own lines and then over enemy territory until we arrived at another of those dirt air strips where we were met by Lieutenant General Frank W. Milburn, commander of the I Corps. New York National Guard units are in almost every corps area and I visited each outfit to talk with the men. Perhaps the most spectacular welcome was from the 955th Field Artillery of the New York National Guard, formerly the 14th Regiment of Brooklyn. After our second flight of the morning we drove directly from the air strip to this unit and just as we arrived they let loose with a dozen rounds from 155-mm. howitzers. They were shelling gun emplacements twelve thousand yards away in active support of our patrols in enemy territory.

The guardsmen are good soldiers and every time I was with a group I tried to talk to the men privately to learn how they really felt. Generally they were in good spirits, though they all asked the universal question: "Governor, when are we going to get out of this lousy place?"

The men of the 955th Artillery, the old Brooklyn outfit, were most interested in our opinions of how the Dodgers would make out in the pennant race. Of course Paul Lockwood, as a former Brooklyn *Eagle* sports writer, was most helpful in giving detailed guesses. At that time Brooklyn looked like a sure thing in the National League and I hope no one held it against us that we told them they had the pennant all wrapped up. Paul got a surprise when he asked a young Negro soldier: "What part of Brooklyn do you come from?"

"Sir," replied the soldier, "I come from Birmingham, Alabama, but since I've joined this outfit, I'm for the Dodgers too."

Later that afternoon, in visiting a signal battalion from Peekskill, New York, I found nailed on a tree a large sign which read: "The boys from New York welcome you, Tom." Again I had a chance to talk with the men and they seemed genuinely pleased to see someone from home. This group also wanted to know about the baseball race, although there were more Giant than Brooklyn rooters. One husky soldier in the back of the crowd I was talking with yelled:

"Hey, Governor, you're a lawyer, aren't you? How about some advice?"

There was a roar of laughter and I shouted back: "Sure, how can I help you?"

"I live in Peekskill and I understand I am one of the defendants in the lawsuit by Paul Robeson over that riot two years ago. Shall I stay here or would you advise me to ask the general to send me back?"

On the trip from IX to X Corps we flew through the passes

of the rugged mountains which divide East Korea from West Korea. We had to fly up to 4500 feet in the little L-19s to get through the passes, often only fifty feet above the ridges and close enough to exchange waves with the men who were manning the front-line foxholes. The terrain was awful, much worse than I had seen in the flight from Pusan to Seoul. The ridges were sharper, the valleys were deeper, but the military problem was the same—to seize and hold the ridges in order to control the valleys.

At X Corps we were met by General Almond, who drove me in his own jeep to a nearby helicopter air strip. It was a short hop over the mountains to the headquarters of the Marine Division but during it I learned of the immense affection for the helicopter that has developed among our armed forces. In the winter of 1950–51 at Chosin Reservoir and at Hagaruri, the Army and the Marines made their stand in the face of overwhelming enemy forces, suffering heavy casualties. There was no regular means of reaching either spot for evacuation of the wounded and the situation seemed desperate. The helicopters saved the day, lifting five thousand wounded men back to field hospitals. Both officers and men alike expressed their undying gratitude to the Sikorsky and Bell helicopters for the largest mass lifesaving operation ever known. Light planes picked up six hundred more from elements that were completely cut off, landing them at strips adjacent to air evacuation hospitals.

At the briefing at Marine Headquarters a colonel read a carefully prepared, scholarly analysis of the enemy. "The North Koreans are rugged," the colonel said, "used to the terrain, used to hard work, willing to fight up and down mountains all day, utterly indomitable when they are dug in, almost impossible to dig out, and fanatical in their resistance." Then he made an interesting contrast with the Chinese. "They are also well trained," he said, "but not quite as enthusiastic. They have much less determination and when they are taken prisoner, they are completely co-operative."

As to both, he had one simple conclusion: "All the forces of the enemy are well indoctrinated. But they fight for a very simple reason. If they turn around and run they know they will be shot down by their officers. So they prefer to fight, hoping to stay alive."

Late in the afternoon we started off on a flight toward the front lines of X Corps in the small L-19 planes. Almost immediately the weather started closing in and before long we couldn't see the mountains on either side of us. Soon the fog became so thick we could make out only the plane immediately behind us and General Almond decided there was no use trying to fly in that pea soup because we wouldn't see anything anyway. So he radioed to the other planes to turn back to the command headquarters. All the ships were able to keep in close radio contact and with good fortune we all landed safely at the air strip of the command post of X Corps. Only a week before the Undersecretary of the Army had crashed into the side of a mountain in one of those fogs and it was a miracle that he survived.

I have landed in many airports, good and bad, and at home on paved and unpaved air strips, in grass airports and in cow pastures. The Pusan air strip had seemed to me to be the worst in the world, but the front-line air strips are incredible. With a fluid front there can be no nonsense about wasting manpower and material on a strip which may be used for a day or a week. When a sector is taken or lost, new strips must be made available instantly. Bulldozers are brought up and the dikes around the nearest rice paddy are knocked out; even as the water flows off the field the bulldozers run the length of it and often within an hour the new air strip is complete. Only three hundred and fifty yards long and a few plane lengths wide, paved with nothing but dirt as God made it, it is sometimes as busy an airport as you will find in a big city in America. The L-17s and the L-19s take off in three hundred yards and land in two hundred yards—always in a cloud of dust in the summer. These sturdy little ships with their improvised runways are the eyes and ears of the Army.

I was amazed by the way the Army has taken to the air. Every general in command of a corps area has a standard routine. After breakfast at 7:30 A.M. comes the morning briefing, conference, and orders for the day. Then the general gets into his little two-seater L-19 and visits his command posts in the front lines. After he has conferred with the commanding officer at every front-line post, seen to the condition of the troops, their food, the hospitals, their supplies, ammunition, and military position, he returns to headquarters to begin the work of the late afternoon and evening. Sixteen hours is a short day for the command in Korea going on seven days a week without relief. I have heard a lot about armchair generals but if there are any in Korea I did not meet them. They take all the risk of flying over front lines in a tiny single-motor aircraft, making a number of flights each day. Time and time again I wished that our people at home, in politics, in business, and in industry could get some appreciation of what the officers and men of the Eighth Army were going through to keep World War III away from America.

As I went to my quarters in a "doghouse," or converted truck, I met a soldier who had just gone off guard duty. He turned out to be a farm boy from Minnesota and when I found that he came from a dairy farm, it was old home week. I asked him into my quarters and we sat down and talked dairy cows over a glass of beer. It took us both back to our farms and neither one of us realized how the time fled. Finally

General Almond came to take me to dinner. I invited him to join us and the general sat down with the private and me for the rest of our talk about dairy farming in Minnesota and Dutchess County, New York.

That night I learned some more about the ROKs, the troops of the Republic of Korea. They are ill trained and have no military tradition of their own. As a result, the United Nations has found it necessary to intersperse each narrow front held by one or more ROK divisions with strong United Nations forces. In this way the ROKs can be reinforced immediately from each side when they are attacked. All this excepts the 1st ROK Division, which guards the flank on the west coast of Korea. It has earned the respect of all of our men and it demonstrates that with proper training and equipment the South Koreans can be first-class fighters.

They are so short of trained military leadership that a former lieutenant in the Japanese Army in World War II is the Korean major general in command of one ROK division. Another ROK division is commanded by a South Korean who was a sergeant in the Japanese Army. If a recent sergeant is now a major general, it is hard to imagine the qualifications of the rest of the officers and non-coms. The ROK officers have almost no training as we understand it, in battle tactics, leadership, or care of their men. Almost immediately when the enemy attack commences communications go out, sometimes for hours. In retreat the first thing they abandon is the artillery. As a result, each ROK division has been surrounded by heavy concentrations of UN artillery which covers both the UN and the ROK front.

The 38th Parallel is a dividing line between two halves of the same nation, one of which has proven itself savage and powerful in war, while for the most part the ROKs have not.

The hard lesson is that the Soviet not only gave the North Koreans excellent training but also thorough indoctrination immediately upon occupying the country in 1945. We waited a tragic six years and only after a war and heavy casualties of our own did we start giving the ROKs the kind of training they should have had in the first place.

The South Korean laborers, on the other hand, have been of infinite value. They are patient and strong, used to taking orders after thirty-five years of Japanese occupation. With a wooden frame attached to their backs, they can carry thirty to fifty pounds of ammunition or supplies. During a major engagement in one corps area alone, 13,000 laborers serviced troops as far as fifteen miles ahead of any possible mechanized supply line. They carried the thirty to fifty pounds of supplies up the valleys and over the ridges for fifteen miles and then walked fifteen miles back—all in a day's work. Men and women alike do the work and often the women are stronger than the men. Later, at Hong Kong, the British commanding general told me of an experience of his own in Korea. A 360-pound oil drum had to be rolled onto a truck. Two of his own soldiers tried and failed. Two Korean women near by volunteered to do the job and they put the drum where it belonged.

Only the strong can survive the disease and hard climate in Korea. Another natural enemy of the Korean countryside is dust. It gets into your eyes, into your mouth, into your ears, into your food and drink. It seeps through everything you wear and gets into bed with you at night. Casualty figures include thousands of men with eye infections who had to be taken out of the lines for treatment of this quiet but very present enemy.

Early the next morning we found the fog had lifted. Following breakfast and the morning briefing, we took off again; this time General Almond and I were together in an L-17, a single-engine plane with three seats. Flying close to the ridges, we saw much of the X Corps front lines where the men had built what seemed an impregnable position. Most of them were out around the ridges doing one job or another and we waved back and forth as we flew the lines. On the way back we were caught in the middle of an artillery cross fire but landed without incident.

One military conclusion struck me hardest during these days: despite the use of airplanes for every purpose, despite our almost undisputed control of the air throughout most of the war, we have relearned the hard lesson in Korea that air power alone does not win wars. They called it "Operation Strangle" and tried to isolate the battlefield from enemy supplies. If such an operation would ever win a war it should have won in Korea, with the enemy supply lines running along narrow, well-defined routes between the mountains. At the end of a year of Operation Strangle the enemy was apparently stronger than he had been when the air campaign began.

The Air Force has done a magnificent job. It is just that the air enthusiasts claimed too much. In addition to fighting and bombing, the Air Force has carried hundreds of thousands of tons of supplies to the front lines in the midst of battles, once dropping 5000 tons of ammunition and on another occasion dropping 16,000 tons of supplies in a critical area of the front lines in a single day.

Air evacuation of the wounded has been equally spectacular. As of July 1951 the Air Transport Command had carried 152,000 casualties. The figure sounds fantastic but it's true. Sometimes a wounded or a sick man is picked up right at the scene of battle in a helicopter and taken back for emergency service. Then he may be flown to the Mobile Army Surgical Hospital, then to an evacuation hospital in Korea, and if necessary to a base hospital in Japan. In some cases the same man is evacuated more than once, either for different wounds or because of illness one time and wounds another time. Every man carried one flight counts, of course, as a flight casualty in this computation.

While I was visiting troops Dr. Hilleboe was visiting hospitals. He had come principally to see the spectacular new treatment for burns the Army medical authorities have developed and he was excited and impressed. The treatment sounded incredible when it was first reported in the medical journals; it still sounds repulsive but it is saving priceless lives.

The patient is first carefully checked for the extent of his burns and other wounds and for shock. Then he is put on a schedule of 300,000 units of penicillin twice a day, which is usually continued for the first week. Within twenty-four hours he is taken to the operating room where, after he is put under anesthetic, the burned areas are scrubbed with sterile gauze soaked in a mild detergent. This gets rid of the blisters and the loose skin and dirt that may be imbedded in and around the burned area. Amazingly enough, after the burns are scrubbed no medication or dressings are put on them and the patient is returned to his bed. Serum then starts oozing out and, within twenty-four to forty-eight hours, it hardens to form a crust which protects the burned area and also keeps out infection. For some reason the crust seems also to allay pain, for after the first night no sedatives are administered and the men sleep well. At the end of twenty-one days, if the burn is first or second degree, the area under the crust is usually fully healed. If it is a third-degree burn the tissue usually remains soggy, and the surgeon will then proceed with skin grafting.

While this new treatment of burns is not always useful, particularly where the burn has gone through all the surfaces of the skin, it is one of the most spectacular medical advances made in Korea. Moreover, Dr. Hilleboe reported many cases which he saw, three or four weeks old, where the skin was already beginning to look normal, entirely free of the scars which follow the traditional treatment of burns. If we ever suffer atomic bombing at home these techniques will save hundreds of thousands of lives which would otherwise be lost for lack of the thousands of doctors and the enormous volume of medical supplies necessary for the old-fashioned treatment.

Air evacuation of the wounded has been equally effective in saving lives; handling of casualties in the Chosin Reservoir action was typical of the procedure. Litter-bearers took the severely wounded back to the battle aid station for emergency attention. Then they were taken to the Mobile Army Surgical Hospital or MASH units, which are housed in separate tents connected together with tent canvas to make surgical and medical wards, cook tents and mess tents for patients and staff. Each has complete, self-sufficient water, electricity, sewage disposal, laundry, pharmacy supply, and record units. Each of these 200-bed field hospitals can run on a twenty-four-hour schedule with 60 cots for surgical cases and 140 cots for medical patients. Most of the cities in the world would give anything to have a hospital as good as just one of these MASH units.

Ninety-eight per cent of our wounded evacuated to Japan have gone by air. The evacuating planes do double duty, carrying combat supplies and medical equipment from Japan to the war areas; returning, they are flying ambulances carrying their cargoes of wounded American soldiers.

This whole air evacuation program is a modern miracle. On the 152,000 casualty flights made only twelve men have died in transit, and those were during the early stages of the war. That is a record of achievement in handling wounded that has never been even remotely matched in any war in history.

Soon after I returned home I saw in a New York newspaper

a bitter attack on the medical services, reprinted from a Midwestern newspaper. My boiling point is not usually low but this made me furious clear through. On the basis of both my own observation and Herman Hilleboe's thorough professional examination, I am convinced that the medical branches of the armed forces are doing the most magnificent job in the history of warfare. The figures prove it. In World War II, deaths from disease were fewer than deaths from wounds for the first time in history and deaths from wounds were decreased to 4.5 per cent of all wounded men. In Korea that 4.5 per cent of deaths has been cut in half under the most difficult conditions ever seen in modern medicine.

Stalin has had his day with Korea. It is my own opinion that the invasion of Korea was just another step in his scheme of world conquest. In fact I warned against it specifically back in November 1947, saying:

"At this moment, Soviet occupation forces hold the northern half of Korea and American occupation forces hold the southern half. The Communists have completely regimented the northern half, installed a totalitarian government and built up a well-trained, well-armed fighting army of 250,000 men under puppet leadership. In the American half there is no civilian government, no native military force—nothing but a political void.

"We have now, with great pains, prepared for a plebiscite in Korea which the Soviets are cynically boycotting. They are boycotting it because they anticipate that immediately upon the withdrawal of American and Soviet occupation troops, the armed forces of the North will engulf all of Korea."

Our government ignored the warning and withdrew our troops. Then it committed the incredible folly of announcing that Korea was outside our defense perimeter. That was an open invitation to the Communists to move in. They accepted the invitation with all the horror which has since followed. The tragedy could have been averted and should have been. Failing in that, we had no choice.

I regard our intervention in Korea as the single action which saved American influence from disappearing in the Pacific and stopped further Communist expansion, at least for the time being. The day the President announced American defense of Korea I publicly supported his action. I was sure it was right and necessary; I still am; but no one can witness the terrible sacrifice of our youth without having many pangs of doubt.

There is even doubt as to just why Stalin pressed the button for the Korean invasion. Was it just for another easy conquest? Or did he have other more significant motives? A remarkable letter I received from a Japanese political leader asserts:

"The USSR had four objectives in the Korean conflict:

"a. Testing of the kinds of new arms of the United States and the power thereof.

"b. Testing the attitude of the United Nations and its capacity to react.

"c. Studying the effect of military cooperation of the People's Republic of China and North Korea.

"d. Examination thereby of the strength of the defense of Manchuria.

"Each one of these objectives reflects the Russian mentality and the whole war is reminiscent of the utterly unprovoked invasion of Finland before World War II. The only difference is that the Russians were then testing their own arms."

The Japanese continues his letter by saying that he believes all four objectives have now been achieved and he adds:

"The students' view is that Soviet Russia will now proceed to accumulate military power and further study the tactics and power of the United States until 1955. Then she will move out resolutely and fearlessly upon aggression, when there appears to be a relaxation upon the part of the United States as the result of a Soviet 'peace offensive.' "

Perhaps it is true that this was just a probe, a testing exercise for Stalin, and that he had a far more sinister motive than merely the acquisition of new territory.

Whatever the reason, four blazing truths have emerged:

The United States did react in defense of the integrity of a helpless allied nation.

Our arms are generally good. At first they were not in sufficient number but we are proceeding to cure that defect.

The United Nations did react by swift and affirmative action.

The Chinese and North Korean Reds have suffered terrible casualties and Stalin knows that the free world can fight.

I am deeply convinced that, if we had not sent troops to defend Korea, American and United Nations prestige in the whole Pacific would have collapsed. All Southeast Asia would probably have gone Communist by now. The danger is still great and growing but at least our act of springing to the defense of Korea has given hope to the people of Japan, the Philippines, Free China, Southeast Asia, and Indonesia. It has also given hope in the great cause of collective security through the United Nations.

3

Okinawa

Japan grants, and the United States of America accepts, the right, upon the coming into effect of the Treaty of Peace and of this Treaty, to dispose United States land, air and sea forces in and about Japan. Such forces may be utilized to contribute to the maintenance of international peace and security in the Far East and to the security of Japan. . . .

Article I of the Security Treaty between the United States of America and Japan, signed at San Francisco, September 8, 1951

O<small>KINAWA</small>, half the size of the State of Rhode Island, and scene of the last great battle of the Pacific, was our midway stop on the way from Japan to Formosa. It is said that the Japanese were jealous of the Okinawan civilization, which had flourished on the island for hundreds of years. Whatever the reason, they invaded and conquered Okinawa in 1609 and the island was seldom heard of in the Western world until the final stages of the Pacific war.

At dawn on Easter morning April 1, 1945, the armed forces of the United States launched their attack on Okinawa. After eighty-three days of savage fighting the end came when the two Japanese commanding generals committed suicide and this key base for the projected attack on Japan's home islands was surrendered. More than 175,000 American fighting men had taken part in the struggle, suffering 49,000 casualties, of which 12,500 were killed. One hundred and nineteen thousand Japanese troops were killed and 7400 were taken prisoner. The Japanese also lost 7800 aircraft to our 760. Of our 1300 naval vessels participating in the invasion, 36 were sunk and 370 were damaged, mainly because of the incredible fanaticism of the Kamikaze suicide pilots. The signs of that desperate struggle are still to be seen from one end of Okinawa to another.

With military hindsight it is now argued that much of this bitter fighting could have been avoided. When we conquered the airfields and beaches, the Japanese holed up in caves and trenches on one end of the island. Many now believe we could have contained them at their end of the island and left them there instead of digging them out in hand-to-hand combat with flame throwers, hand grenades, machine guns, and bayonets. Could we have made effective use of the island as a base while a good part of it was held by a large, well-fortified, dug-in enemy force? I don't know the answer. I am not a military expert. But the debate is hot.

Okinawa is the largest of the Ryukyu group of islands which were taken away from Japan in the postwar settlements. India's Prime Minister Jawaharlal Nehru thinks we should give them all back to Japan. By contrast, he thinks the Soviet should keep the Kurile chain of islands, north of the four Japanese home islands. It is not quite clear who legally owns the Ryukyus now but possession is nine points of the law. We possess them and I hope we never leave them. It is hard to imagine a more powerful strategic air base. More than $100,000,000 has been spent in developing Okinawa and a second $100,000,000 is now going into the island. If we want to keep future wars away from our shores, this is some of the best money we have spent in the postwar period.

Okinawa, far to the south of Japan, is the base from which our B-29s are bombing North Korea. Tokyo and Okinawa are almost exactly the same distance from North Korea—a thousand miles. Okinawa also commands much of the coast of China, the Formosa Strait, Formosa, and the Philippines. With radar, even small patrols can keep a close watch on that vast expanse of Chinese coast line, ocean, and strategic islands. For these operations we have based large units of the Air Force, a substantial naval force, and, of course, a large Army contingent, on the island. Here again the success of unification seemed to me very real and the relationship between the officers and troops of all services to be genuinely cordial.

While I was at Okinawa I heard a story of the growing pains of unification. I cannot vouch for it but it came from a man who should know. During the early days of the war in Korea a high-ranking officer in the Army asked his opposite number in the Air Force for close air support for the ground troops. "You know we're not equipped for that kind of work," said the Air Force officer. "It's never been part of our mission and we're not trained to do it."

"Well, that's too bad," replied the Army officer. "We sure do need the air support, so I guess I'll have to ask the Navy. Maybe they'll give it a try."

"There's nothing the Navy can do that the Air Force can't do better," bristled the air officer. "I'll see what I can do."

The Air Force undertook the mission of close ground support. But the issue as to whether it is an Army or Air Force job and whether or not the Air Force is primarily designed for long-range bombing and interceptor fighting is not yet settled.

Before I went on the trip my friend Henry J. Taylor had urged me to stop at Okinawa to see how the housing problem was coming along. He had been there a year before and was shocked at the housing provided for American troops. He said: "It's bad enough out there eight thousand miles from home with the heat and the duties and few friends. But it's inexcusable to have nothing but a miserable shack which is boiling in the summer, cold in the winter, and leaks all the time."

It was good to learn that part of the second $100,000,000 is going to build decent housing for these thousands of Americans who are manning our front lines in the Pacific. Recreation halls and movie theaters are also approaching completion to provide some community life for both the married couples and the single men.

The armed forces on Okinawa are a long way ahead of many of our people at home in shedding race prejudices. The officers have a choice of homes in order of their rank, if their families are there; then the enlisted men in order of their rank and length of service. There are no color lines and there have been no reports of racial friction in this great new American outpost. A Negro private lived with his family next door to the brigadier general who was then in command of the Army post.

The armed forces also get along well with the native Okinawans. Out of a population of a half million, 55,000 Okinawans are working for Uncle Sam. The military has not moved in and recklessly thrown American dollars around, wrecking the economy of the island. We are paying the native people at the going rate of wages. The labor relations are good and so are the human relations. Too many times, in Asia, all over South America, and in Europe, other agencies of our government have walked in and, either out of a starry-eyed idealism or a desire to show off, have paid two or three times the prevailing rate of wages. The results have always been the same: envy and hatred of us at the time and nothing but enemies and a disrupted economy when we withdrew. The armed forces are making friends in Okinawa.

Sometimes things do get a little complicated. One major effort has been to persuade the Okinawan farmer not to use night soil. The purpose, of course, is to achieve a state of sanitation for the whole island so the many thousands of Americans can live there in good health, free to eat whatever is produced locally. The natives were quite agreeable about abandoning the use of night soil—so long as the Army provided them fertilizer at half price. When we settled down on the island as a permanent operation the Army tried to stop the subsidy and proposed to sell the fertilizer at full cost price. At this point the natives became less co-operative. They indicated that they could not afford to pay the full price for fertilizer and, of course, they could always go back to using night soil which didn't cost them anything. The Army was still selling them fertilizer at half price when I last heard.

Sometimes the Okinawans admit we know what we are doing. They learned one lesson the hard way last May. The island is in the center of the typhoon belt where the storms hit in September, October, and November. Last May, however, the Armed Forces Weather Bureau picked up an off-season typhoon roaring along the coast of China, predicting it would reach Okinawa the following afternoon. The Okinawan fishing fleet was promptly notified, but the native fishermen shrugged off the report. "It's impossible for a typhoon to come in May," they said as they took off to sea. They ran right into the storm. When the fleet managed to limp back into port as the typhoon blew itself out of the area, sixty-five fishermen were missing. An immediate search by the Air-Sea Rescue Command saved thirty, but thirty-five were never found. To-day, the Okinawa fishermen listen respectfully to the weather reports.

When we returned to the airport we were again reminded sharply that there was a war going on. Every air base is rigorously guarded and protected by radar. Jet fighters are on the line twenty-four hours a day. If the Russians should decide to launch their adventure in world conquest they will find no Pearl Harbor at Okinawa today.

4

Formosa

In dealing with people of Asia, we submit the question of face is very important. For instance, extensive American aid is given to an Asian country like Korea, but President Rhee and his government were criticized by American officials for one reason or another with the result that President Rhee and his government lost prestige in the eyes of their fellow-countrymen and the world. Under such circumstances, a government cannot wield influence and receive wide public support. It would be better for such an administration to get less aid and more lip service.

That is exactly what the U.S.S.R. is doing vis-à-vis Peiping and other satellite countries. Mao Tse-tung is puffed to high esteem by Moscow, which tells the Chinese and the world that this puppet is a saint and savior.

Excerpt from letter received in Albany from a group of Chinese scholars in exile, November 19, 1951

Two hours after we took off from Okinawa the rugged pattern of Formosa rose out of the Pacific. As I went forward to talk with the pilots I could see the peaks of the mountain range that runs the length of the island. "Formosa's shaped like a long slender leaf," the pilot remarked. A few minutes later as we headed in between two mountain peaks he said:

"That's where we go in. It gives you an idea why we don't like to make Taipei after dark or in soupy weather." We passed between the peaks and headed up a deep valley with a silver river winding below. It is lush and lovely country, divided into countless tiny squares of rice paddies between the mountains and the sea.

The Portuguese mariner who first sighted the island in the fourteenth century shouted "*Ihla Formosa* [Beautiful Island]." Formosa is about two hundred miles long and a hundred miles wide, one and a half times the area of Vermont, and has almost as many people on it as all of New England. This is the seat of the government of Free China—on Chinese territory but in exile from the mainland. Here is the flower of Chinese culture: the Chinese men and women who were educated in American universities and who understand freedom, respected elder statesmen, young political leaders, soldiers, scientists, scholars, and poets. All are scarred with the bruises of military and political defeats; all have suffered a fearful spiritual buffeting and have a sense of abandonment and frustration; but they share a common determination to return to the mainland and liberate it from the Communist conqueror.

I was met at Taipei, the capital of Formosa, by Karl Rankin, American Minister, and K. C. Wu, Governor of Formosa, whom my friends at home described as one of the ablest administrators of the Chinese Government: we greeted each other, shook hands, and then were engulfed. For half an hour in a broiling sun I felt the glowing, somewhat desperate warmth of the welcome of a people sadly in need of friends. Thirty or forty reporters were mixed in with the crowd but their attempt at a press conference evaporated in the pressure and nobody seemed to mind. Photographers were in the melee, too, climbing on top of chairs, boxes, and automobiles; one even clambered up on the wing of our plane and fell off while trying to take a picture. Fortunately neither he nor anybody else was hurt.

In the crowd were members of the Legislative Yuan, the first elected legislative body in the history of the Chinese Republic; later the government sent me a book of press clippings that included a delightful comment on two of the feminine members who were present, in language alternately libelous and flattering: "Both of them, clad in white, looked much younger than their age, just resembling a pair of flowers from the same branch."

When we finally edged our way through the crowd, Karl Rankin accompanied me to the Taipei guesthouse, our home on Formosa. They call it a guesthouse; in fact it is a palace built by the Japanese as an official residence for the Governor during the fifty years the Japanese held the island, from 1895 to 1945. Formosa is known in both Japanese and Chinese as "Taiwan." Just as Britain has its Prince of Wales, so the heir apparent of imperial Japan was the Prince of Taiwan and Emperor Hirohito stayed in this palace as a youth; the Chinese still point out the tree in the palace gardens which was planted by the young prince.

We were greeted at the guesthouse by a jovial mountain of a man, Lieutenant General J. L. Huang, Deputy Commanding General, Combined Service Forces, who has charge of the house and was our host. General Huang stands six feet four inches and weighs two hundred and forty pounds. Educated at Vanderbilt and Columbia universities, he declared with a rolling laugh that General George Marshall called him the Grover Whalen of China.

Madame Chiang Kai-shek had sent me at Tokyo an invitation to stay at their guesthouse in the hills where it would be considerably cooler; but I had decided that we would see more of the life of the people on Formosa if I stayed down in the city. After the broiling reception at the airport I had some doubts about the wisdom of my decision, but as soon as I entered the guesthouse all my doubts vanished. We were the only guests and I was assigned to the suite the Prince of Taiwan had used. The stone walls made it seem cooler, while spacious rooms with high ceilings and great open doors and windows gave a sense of easy comfort. Ed Galvin put it well when he came in to set up my dictating machine: "This makes me feel right at home: it's as big as the Executive Chamber in Albany." Walking out on the wide balcony that runs the length of the building, I was enchanted by the beauty of the gardens which was not even spoiled by the presence of the soldiers of the Guard—some pacing up and down on duty with fixed bayonets, some in shorts sun bathing, some doing their laundry and drying their clothes on the shrubbery, some just sleeping.

A shower, a change to fresh clothing, and a chance to relax over a cup of tea had never been so welcome. After two hours of sleep the night before, we had already been up fourteen hours, toured Okinawa, traveled more than a thousand miles by air, and still had a heavy evening ahead. First, however, came the inevitable problem of schedule. In nearly every country I visited, the government and our own American mission had worked out a "tentative schedule," always devised upon the theory that a guest should be continuously entertained; but I had not come to the Pacific for entertainment: I had come to learn. Cutting down the schedule this time was particularly difficult because the Legislative Yuan had set up a luncheon on one day and the Control Yuan—the council of elder statesmen—on another day. If I accepted both engagements it would ruin at least one of the days when I wanted to get out into the country to see the farms and military installations.

Working out the schedule with General Huang and Mr. Rankin, I suggested that the two luncheons be merged. This was a revolutionary idea: "The two Yuans are not always on the best of terms," it was explained. "The Legislative Yuan is the elected legislative branch; the Control Yuan, with about a hundred elder statesmen as present members, exercises supervisory and disciplinary authority. They never meet together."

"Nevertheless, I should like to meet both," I said, "and I'd prefer to do it on the same day. I wonder if they wouldn't like to meet jointly for a novelty." The proposal struck both of my hosts as a diplomatic miracle if it could be achieved; to the great surprise of all, the two Yuans agreed to meet and lunch together for the first time in history. Paul Lockwood arranged the rest of the schedule with his usual skill.

My introduction to Formosa was at a dinner given that night by Prime Minister Chen Cheng. We drove unescorted through the streets of this fortress capital to the simple frame house of the Premier of the Republic of China where only two soldiers were on guard. We stepped directly from the front porch into a comfortable, combination living room-dining room, where we were welcomed by the Premier. He is a tiny, thin man, so short that he barely comes up to my ear; dressed in gray trousers and peasant's tunic buttoned up to the neck, he would pass unnoticed in a group if it were not for his piercing eyes, erect posture, and quiet dignity. As we sat down to tea—not cocktails—Shen Chang-huan, the official government spokesman, sat next to me to act as interpreter.

Unlike most of the leaders of Free China, the Premier speaks no English despite the fact that thirty years ago he was an English teacher in a Chinese university. I gathered that his English was a good deal like my French—too rusty for use.

Chen Cheng gave up teaching in the 1920s to join the revolutionary movement, working his way up to become one of Chiang Kai-shek's ablest and most respected generals. Despite his success as a military leader, however, his basic interests are philosophic and political; as Premier he is acutely concerned with the problem of restoring order and personal liberty on the mainland and with the urgent administrative tasks that would fall upon him "when the day comes." He is already at work on a complete program of land reform for the mainland, based upon the promise of much lower taxes and land ownership for all with special assurances to those who support the Nationalist Government.

The dinner party included twenty-four, which I learned was something of a magic number. The Chinese prefer a round dinner table of twelve. If there are going to be more than twelve, they like to make it twenty-four so there will be two full tables which are small enough for lively, across-the-table conversation. However dark the world may seem, eating should be a cheerful, social occasion and should be spread through as many courses as possible. For centuries, tomorrow's food has been the greatest worry of the Chinese. As a result, it is an ingrained tradition that eating is important for all, rich and poor. Drinking at meals is never for the sake of drinking—it is to give or respond to a toast or pleasantry. Even more civilized is the custom that permits—or rather expects—the guest to rise at the end of dinner and, after ten minutes or so, go home to bed. The evening has been spent at the table in good company; the night is for sleep as the table is for dinner.

The first course was piping hot, served in a large hollowed-out melon, and included a wide variety of components. I recognized a few: pieces of chicken, shrimp, mushrooms, crab, ham and beef all cooked together. It sounds confusing; it was delicious. Like each succeeding course, it was placed in the center of the table and the Premier served me and Mr. Shen, the other guests helping themselves in turn.

Someone recalled a current Formosa joke which asserted that Confucius had said, "There should be no talking during eating." Then Confucius had gone to America and upon his return he talked gaily through each meal. Asked why, he replied that he had become used to the American custom. "You see, in America each guest is served individually so they are free to talk. But in China the food is in the middle of the table. We can't afford to talk because we must watch each other to be sure we get our share of the food."

The Chinese differ from the Japanese in their use of English. Almost all well-educated Japanese I met spoke English, many of them very well. A number, however, had so much difficulty with their English that it would have been much easier to speak through an interpreter; but it is almost an affront to any Japanese to suggest it. Many of the Chinese leaders are American-educated and speak flawless English; others who have never been to the United States, such as Madame Wu, the wife of Governor K. C. Wu, also speak beautiful English. The important difference between the Chinese and the Japanese is that if the Chinese can't speak good English they don't try. The Chinese have the better system.

The meal was by way of a state banquet, the best the island afforded, but everything served was comparatively inexpensive food. What made it so good were the centuries of culinary skill behind its preparation.

The second course tasted like chicken soup but I never did learn what was in it. The third was a type of crawfish with a delicate flavor, called Lung-hsia, which in Chinese means "Dragon Shrimp." It was a sort of giant crawfish much like those found in Florida and other southern parts of the United States. With it came forks, the first we had used at the table.

The first course we had eaten with chopsticks, to which I had become relatively accustomed in Japan. I was getting to use them fairly well, although I still missed about one stroke in three.

About this time the Premier suggested that perhaps I might like to take off my coat. As it was hot and a little damp, I thought it was a splendid idea. I asked whether this was desired by the others and he said he thought they might like it. When I stood up to take my coat off, everybody at both tables stood up and cheered, taking their coats off with enthusiasm. The party began to feel like a family dinner.

About this time I got into a discussion with Governor Wu about Chinese table manners. Short, plump, and with an engaging smile, he is not only an excellent administrator but a merry soul. He announced in no uncertain terms that there are no Chinese table manners. Others vigorously disagreed with him, saying that there certainly are Chinese table manners. After a spirited debate everybody agreed that there are Chinese table manners and they are simply: "Whatever the guest does is right. The only condition is that he enjoy himself."

By now, the rice wine had been poured in the tiny thimble cups and the ever present beer had made its appearance. The wine is much like French sauternes, with a low alcoholic content. From one side of the table to the other there were constant cries of "*Kan-pei!*" which means "Bottoms up!" always accompanied by a toast involving one or more of the dinner guests. That must be why the wine is served in glasses no bigger than half an eggshell.

Succeeding courses included soybean sprouts, soybean curds with mushrooms, a pickled Chinese cabbage served with wild mustard and pickled eggs. The eggs had a most curious appearance, almost black in color. As I looked at mine with considerable suspicion, George Yeh, the Foreign Minister, noticed my doubt and, with a grin, warned me: "You know, these eggs might be one or two years old or perhaps a thousand years old —you never know." To my amazement the eggs were excellent, tasting much like the yolk of a freshly laid egg on my own farm.

Fried chicken seems to be a universal dish and, sure enough, it turned up late in the meal, broken into small pieces so it was easily picked up with chopsticks. I have never had finer chicken, and as a seasoned political campaigner, I am an authority on chicken dinners.

Then came a platter of something that was off-white, looked like a jellyfish, and was shaped like an oyster. To my dismay the Premier put two of them on my plate. "Here," I thought, "is where I quit." But it turned out to be nothing more complicated than my old friend ravioli—Chinese ravioli. It immediately provoked a dispute over whether Marco Polo had brought ravioli from Italy to China seven hundred years before or whether Marco Polo had taken ravioli back with him to Italy. My hosts insisted that the dish had been served in China for thousands of years before Marco Polo was born.

The next course featured slivers of baked ham and then followed a broth with noodles. The noodles were eaten with chopsticks and the broth was drunk from the bowl. The last course was a platterful of twelve slices of what they called a Taiwan melon; it looked like good old-fashioned American watermelon and turned out to be just that; the only difference is that because of the tropical climate they enjoy it the year around. In all there were a dozen courses and the meal stretched out over nearly three hours. Each course was small so no food was wasted and no one left the table feeling over-fed.

During the course of this happy dinner a few things on this incredibly complex island came into focus. There has been a

real house cleaning at the top in the Nationalist Government.
The men in authority today are young: Shen, the government
spokesman, a graduate of the University of Michigan, is thirty-
eight; Governor Wu, of Grinnell and Princeton, is forty-eight;
Sun Li-jen, Commander in Chief of the ground forces, graduate of Purdue and Virginia Military Institute, is fifty-one;
Foreign Minister George Yeh, graduate of Amherst, is forty-
seven; the Premier himself is fifty-four. All these ages are in
Chinese, which is one year more than ours, because a Chinese
child is considered two years old on his first New Year's Day—
a system which is biologically reasonable if rather confusing
to us.

These men are spirited, bitterly experienced, and aggressive.
They admit responsibility for many factors which led to their
defeat on the mainland. One, for example, was the attempt to
hold Manchuria. Precious military supplies were flown into
Manchuria by their limited air force to pockets of Nationalist
resistance at a time when it was perfectly clear that Manchuria
could not be held. The practical reason for this action was not
merely to try to save the priceless resources and industry of the
area, but that many members of the Legislative Yuan represented districts in Manchuria and North China. They clam-
ored for more aid to Nationalist troops in those areas. These
demands mounted in intensity until it became apparent that
the government and Generalissimo Chiang would lose their
support if some action was not taken. So a political and economic decision was made to send aid to Manchuria even after
it became useless from a military point of view. Politics sometimes gets in the way of defense, even in China.

They also admitted that Communist propaganda had been
exceedingly successful on the mainland. "The Communists
preach hatred and incite class struggle," one said. "They
promise each peasant his own land. They don't tell him that

they will take his crop away from him after he has grown it, so the promise is very attractive and they win his support. He is happy for a while even though he only gets an acre; but soon the taxes become so heavy that he finds he is paying more in taxes than he used to pay in taxes and rent combined."

"Most important of all," said another, "the Communists are leading the fight for Asia for the Asians. It can't be denied that the people of the Orient feel that the white man has oppressed them for centuries; they want to throw off the domination of the West. So the Communists have the popular side even though it is hard to teach Chinese to hate Americans because they have always thought of your country as a great and friendly power which never exploited them. The people have seen the American missionaries who came to teach, to heal the sick and take care of the orphans and the aged; but the Communists are even succeeding in teaching our people to hate Americans today."

All these Communist tactics were abhorrent to this decidedly pro-American group, but they admitted their effectiveness. The people of Asia want no more domination from the Western world and they do not intend to have it. By posing as the enemy of foreign imperialism and promising the unattainable to all, the Communists have reaped rich rewards from the surging nationalism released by World War II.

One of the wisest men at the Premier's dinner told me with deep earnestness: "The reason American propaganda has failed in the Orient is that you have not been able to convince the Asians that you believe in their freedom. The people see America allied in mutual defense with the British and the French and the Dutch in Europe. The Communists harp on this as proof that you are not friendly to the freedom of India, Burma, Malaya, and North Borneo from British rule. The people of Indonesia are just free after centuries of Dutch rule and the Communists are pounding away at your alliance with the Dutch in Europe. In Indo-China your alliance with France is again a favorite subject of Communist propaganda.

"You should drive home the truth that America liberated the Philippines and gave them their freedom. You should tell the Asians that America is defending Korea from its enemies today. You should tell the Asians again and again that America is for China for the Chinese, not for the Russians; for Indo-China for the Indo-Chinese, not for the Russians; for Japan for the Japanese, not for the Russians. The Russians are the real imperialists who are trying to conquer the world. Why should America allow them to get away with claiming they are liberators? They accuse you of imperialism and of exploitation while they actually practice both. You must get that story over to the people of Asia."

Our propaganda, or lack of it, was sharply criticized by another: "You have played right into the Communist hands. You have been telling the people of Asia all about your automobiles and shoes and homes and clothes, your super-modern kitchens, radios and television sets in every home, your telephones in every home, and even your green-tiled bathrooms. Asians can't even understand such riches and luxury. Their worry is tomorrow's bowl of rice.

"Worst of all, the Communists simply take the American propaganda and spread it. They say: 'See, this is just what we told you. All Americans are rich. How did they get that way? They got it by stealing and by exploiting the peoples of Asia.' 'Throw off the yoke of imperialist Americans,' the Communists are shouting. 'Follow the Communists and you will have Asia for the Asians.'"

It seemed to me that another secret of Communist success is that to most of the people of Asia all government is a symbol of abuse. For centuries they have accepted government authority imposed from the top. They expect nothing from government and they have received little. Public health service has been scanty and poor. Practically none of the other facilities ordinarily provided by American state governments is available, such as tuberculosis hospitals, conservation programs, public housing, good highways, regulation of public utilities, adequate schools and universities.

One of the most damaging mistakes in the East has been our seeming insistence on making Asia over into our own image. "This is absolutely impossible," said one of my hosts. "The East is old. Its cultures are deeply rooted. We love our cultures and our traditions and our people do not feel inferior to anyone.

"Our people want social reform and the ownership of their own land, but 'the American way of life' has no helpful meaning. 'Freedom and democracy' do not mean anything either. To our people, 'freedom' is a strange word; they don't know what it means. According to the philosophy of Lao-tze, all government is a nuisance. The people know there must be government and if there is government 'how can there be freedom?' You understand what you mean by 'freedom' but the Asian doesn't understand your ideas. All he wants is more personal liberty and a little better life. Free elections are a strange idea to him; but foreign domination is all too familiar. He will take a native government, good or bad, in preference to one run by foreigners."

I had originally thought that the mass executions by the Communists in China would boomerang. From our American point of view, it would seem natural that such a reign of terror would cause the people to be first sullen, then fiercely resentful, and finally to rise in armed revolt against their oppressors; but the recent history of Russia and its satellite nations shows that the Communist practice of killing or arresting their political opponents has been successful. Finally, there are few people left who dare disagree with the government. The Chinese on Formosa agree that the mass terrorism by the Communists is effective and powerful. One said: "If the Communists keep China for ten years, they will have an unbreakable hold." Another said that they could achieve it in two years. Some of the details of cruelty seemed almost too terrible to believe. Before long, I was to be in Hong Kong with a chance to check with people who had recent personal knowledge of the Communist atrocities in Red China.

It was conceded on Formosa that the Communists had succeeded in slowing down inflation though they have not stopped it; steady depreciation of the currency fits nicely into their plans for depriving the people of the impulse to save, so they will be wholly dependent on government. Just as inflation is a valuable Communist tool, it had been for years the curse of the Nationalist Government and was a major factor in its downfall. The reasons for inflation, which finally became violent, are obvious. Most of the world has forgotten how long China suffered from wars and destruction. The Japanese attacked China in 1937, four years before they attacked us at Pearl Harbor, and the war ravaged the nation for eight years; then, when peace came to the rest of the world, it did not come to China. Mao Tse-tung's Chinese Communist armies received from the Russians a fresh supply of captured Japanese arms, so the war-weary and exhausted Chiang government faced a new attack from a fresh, well-supplied enemy. Betrayed by Russia in 1945 almost as soon as the ink was dry on Stalin's thirty-year treaty of friendship and alliance, Chiang also found himself deserted by his other wartime ally, the United States. Instead of support he got abuse and public repudiation.

The Chinese are a very polite people: they are also bright. Never did both characteristics show up more than in their answers to my delicate questions about our failure to supply arms when they needed them most. No one raised the question; I had to raise it. Even the answer from one of the most important members of the government was mild: "We did receive some guns, ammunition, and aircraft. But for some reason we never got the right ammunition for the guns or the right guns for the ammunition. Whatever was sent was always too late. We could never get parts for the aircraft we had and the planes that were sent to us were always short of tails or some other essential part.

"I don't believe this was government policy. I don't even believe it was the fault of any individual man. I can't believe it. It must have been just the result of your letdown after the war and the complication of bureaucracy, with which we, too, are familiar."

Throughout my trip, I got frank answers on almost every subject. Perhaps because of my own natural bluntness, perhaps because they regarded me as a friend and knew I would not reveal who made a particular statement, I was usually able to break through their natural reserve. This time I did not try. What my friend really thought, I will never know. All I can report is what he said.

Luncheon with the Legislative and Control Yuans was almost like a college reunion. As we gathered before lunch, I met one after another of my fellow alumni from the University of Michigan, where I received my B.A., and from Columbia University, where I got my law degree. We talked about our college days and about the members of the faculty we remembered. They proudly explained that there were sixty Columbia and eighty Michigan graduates on the island, many of them in the Legislative Yuan. More than five hundred members of the two Yuans were present, some dressed in native clothes, more in Western garb. They included merchants, scholars, herb doctors, soldiers, and farmers. A number of the members were women. Together they represented a large majority of the first elected legislative body in five thousand years of Chinese history.

During the luncheon I was seated beside Yu Yu-jen, President of the Control Yuan. He is a lifelong revolutionary and today, at seventy-three, bearded, ascetic, dressed in flowing Chinese robes, he is a striking and powerful figure in the government. At the end of the luncheon Yu Yu-jen welcomed me with a gracious speech followed by a brief and delightfully humorous speech by the President of the Legislative Yuan.

As I was introduced my mind flashed back to the time I had addressed the members of the legislative body of the Republic of Korea in Pusan. Then, as now, I was embarrassed because I knew I could not possibly give them the words of encouragement and all-out support I knew they hoped to hear. At least I could give them words of personal friendship and cheer. Every two or three sentences I would stop for the translator and I found that everything I said was greeted with applause, either courteous or enthusiastic: I never figured out which. I was able to give them reassurance that the people of America had an ancient and abiding friendship with the people of China; that we have proved our friendship many times in the past and that I personally believed we would prove it again as America and Free China worked out our difficulties as free men and as equals. I reiterated my own conviction that our relationship was that of equal partners, and I was impressed, as I was throughout the trip, by the warmth with which this assertion of mutual interest and equality as human beings was received.

Formosa was settled by Chinese who migrated to the island from Fukien Province during a period of strife and great distress in the seventeenth century. Nearly 2,000,000 came during that period, bringing with them the culture and skills of China to what was then a sparsely settled island. In later periods of distress on the mainland, an additional 1,000,000 Chinese came to the island and migration continued even after Formosa had been ceded by China to Japan at the end of the Sino-Japanese War in 1895. After fifty years of occupation and of the teaching of Japanese in the schools, the basic dialect is still that of Fukien Province during the first half of the seventeenth century.

The name Taiwan comes from the aborigines who inhabited the island before the Chinese settled there. They were known as the Dai-Wan. Sometime during the centuries the D was changed to a T and the official name in both Japanese and Chinese has long been Taiwan.

The aborigines still live on the island. They are a fierce, head-hunting tribe of primitives who make their homes in the high mountain fastnesses running up and down the center of the island. Five costly military expeditions were sent into the interior by the Japanese over the years; two of them never came back. Nevertheless, while the Japanese reduced the aborigines by economic and military measures from an estimated 350,000 to 150,000, they never succeeded in conquering or civilizing them. The Chinese have no trouble with the head-hunters: they do not molest them and in turn they are not molested.

Formosa was efficiently if sternly administered during the Japanese occupation, producing a substantial surplus of sugar, rice, and other exports. At the end of World War II in 1945, when the island was transferred back to China, the Chinese Governor was welcomed by the populace as an emancipator.

At last they were rid of their oppressors. They could be Chinese again. But unfortunately the Governor was a bad one. An incident involving the cruel and senseless beating of a native by Chinese soldiers inflamed the people of the island. Soon the young native men all over Formosa were approaching any stranger and asking for his name and identification. If he did not speak the local dialect he was given a severe beating.

Violence raged through the island. Pretending to seek peace, the Governor sent for native leaders to ask for the names of all whom he might appoint as a committee to restore good relations. As soon as he had his list of names the Governor deployed troops all over the island and practically all of the leaders whose names were on the list were seized and killed. The best estimates are that between three and five thousand of the ablest people on the island were dead when the massacre ended. The bitterest hatred of the Nationalist Government resulted. It was not until 1949 when the whole Nationalist Government moved to Formosa that the Governor was called to account and executed. This retribution and the appointment of K. C. Wu as Governor brought about much better feeling and the relationship between the government and the people greatly improved.

With inflation eating away at its vitals, Formosa is in trouble. The island took a bad beating from American bombs during the war. A large share of the factories and power plants built by the Japanese were bombed out; airfields were knocked to pieces and transport was almost paralyzed; food supplies and production of both food and industrial goods fell disastrously. This island, which had previously been quite capable of supporting 5,000,000 people, suddenly found itself carrying the whole government of China, 600,000 troops and more than 2,000,000 new civilians—merchants, farmers, teachers, government employees, and refugees who had come with the Nationalist Government to Formosa. By 1951 the population had increased to more than 9,000,000 and the problems of food supply, housing, and sanitation were crushing.

It is agreed by disinterested witnesses that the members of the government are not making money today, whatever others may have done formerly on the mainland. The gold reserves that were brought to Formosa have been reduced to a dangerous level to carry the terrible deficit. Government officials are paid little enough; the members of the Legislative Yuan, for example, draw the equivalent of about fifty dollars a month. Madame Wu is a distinguished artist, and to make ends meet for Governor Wu and herself they held a public auction of all her paintings at Manila, bringing in $20,000 American money. The Wus have been supporting themselves on the proceeds ever since. Other leaders of the government are living in actual want. Even the Generalissimo and Madame Chiang live in a modest home in the hills. The average civil servant gets about ten dollars a month in American money, which is not enough to live on. Many hold other jobs at night; usually more than one member of the family works. An army private gets two dollars a month, plus his food, clothing, and medical care, or about twelve dollars. An army major gets fifteen dollars plus fuel and rations for himself and his family. He is actually not much better off than the private.

The basic staple, rice, is artificially held down to a low price; tea and vegetables are grown on the island in large quantities and are reasonable in price; but other food is high. Beef and fresh eggs are almost prohibitive; milk is scarce and butter must be imported from Australia; coffee costs two dollars a pound. American advisers have stimulated the rapid growth of the fishing industry to provide a better diet for an underfed people and altogether conditions are improving but there is much still to be done.

Under the leadership of Governor Wu and with the important help of American engineers, factories, bombed-out electric power plants, airports, highways, and transport facilities have been rebuilt, and production increased above prewar levels. A new system of irrigation has been devised to increase production of sugar cane. The schools established by the Japanese have been continued and greatly enlarged, with Mandarin becoming the official language. Medical health centers have been expanded and new ones created.

The tax structure has been reorganized with interesting results. The sales tax had been three per cent. It was cut to six tenths of one per cent with the amazing result that collections actually increased. That experience underlines my own observation that in many nations of the world nobody pays any taxes except those who get caught. Certainly that is true in Asia and in many countries of Europe and South America.

Land reform was the next great task. While plans were being discussed and are still under way to buy up the land held by large holders and sell it to the tenants, one broad step was taken immediately. Rents had run to half and more of all crops. By law rents were reduced to 37.5 per cent. This created great good will among the tenant farmers, and with new incentives before them rice production increased to a record, leaving a surplus for export after feeding the whole population of the island.

I heard about all these improvements from one after another on Formosa and the story was the same from both Americans and Chinese. As usual, I was looking forward to my day in the country when I could see these agricultural changes at first hand; as always, they looked different face to face.

In the company of Dr. Raymond T. Moyer I set off to see

some Formosa farms. Dr. Moyer made a fine impression on me and I was delighted to find that he was a graduate of our State College of Agriculture at Cornell. Despite his own immense personal contribution, it was not long before I found that he was discouraged by a number of factors and he has since resigned and returned home, to the great loss of our Chinese friends.

The first farm we visited was about twenty miles out of Taipei and here it seemed to me that I found all the problems of the island rolled up into one. As we stopped by the roadside, a half dozen naked youngsters were swimming in the brown water of an irrigation ditch. Overcome with embarrassment by this visitation, they scrambled out and ran for the house to get their shorts. The farmer, middle-aged, stooped, bearded, and wearing just a gray shirt and tattered shorts, seemed to epitomize the Asian peasant. This time there was no large group of government officials, only Dr. Moyer, Paul Lockwood, Ed Galvin, and an interpreter. We had even persuaded our Chinese hosts that we did not need a military guard. I had insisted upon a native interpreter because a government employee who spoke with a strange dialect would not as easily gain the confidence of the natives. So our interpreter was a native Taiwanese who spoke their seventeenth-century Fukien dialect and pretty good English.

The farmer ushered us into the living room of his long, one-story, ancient brick farmhouse. The room was ten feet square, dominated by a painting of Buddha over the mantel; one rough, strong table and three narrow benches were all the furniture in the room, the benches being standard farmhouse equipment—three to four feet long, six inches wide, and worn smooth by many decades of use.

Once again I had difficulty in getting the farmer's family straight. There was a young woman carrying a baby; he explained that she was his daughter, but later it developed that she was really his adopted daughter. If a farmer's family has no daughters or sons, it is the custom to adopt a daughter. When she marries, her young husband moves into the family and carries on the father's work. More women and children kept coming in until I was thoroughly confused. It finally evolved that the farmer was a widower, operating the farm with his brother-in-law, his son, his son-in-law, and their wives and children.

The whole farm was an acre and a half and supported seventeen people. The farmer was happy that the government had cut his rent but added: "My rice brings little more in Taiwan dollars than it did before, but everything I buy has gone up two or three times in price. Things are very hard."

This was a new side of the picture. At a stop at a co-operative, I learned more about it. The co-operative was a substantial brick building, old but serviceable, set back from the road. There were about fifteen poorly dressed men and women working at desks. Before long I was off in the corner with the manager, the assistant manager, and a clerk, drinking a cup of tea. Each was an old-timer with fifteen to twenty years' service in the co-operative. It was curious to see Chinese whose manners were more Japanese than Chinese; they even looked a little Japanese because they had typical Japanese dentistry with the gold around and between the biting edges of their teeth. Like all country people, they were remarkably open and frank, often interrupting each other to pour out their opinions. It soon became clear that the co-operative was not a co-operative at all, but a government-operated agency which collected taxes paid in rice by the farmers. It also sold the farmers seed, corn-meal cake, and other supplies, sometimes on credit.

The credit function of the co-operative is very important because the usury on Formosa is the worst I have ever seen.

To borrow money for business or farm use, the ordinary rate of interest is a hundred per cent a year; as further evidence of this inflation, the Bank of Taiwan pays its depositors an interest of four and a half per cent per month—or nearly sixty per cent a year. All of this shocked me, but like everything else in Asia that seemed so strange, there was an explanation. The co-operative manager explained: "Inflation has been raging in Formosa. If a moneylender has a hundred dollars to lend, he must bear in mind that at the end of the year it may be worth only fifty dollars in purchasing power. If he is going to lend his money he must get at least a hundred per cent interest if he is to have the same amount of purchasing power at the end of the year, without any profit. If a lender can't get his hundred per cent interest, he'd be better off buying a pig or a few bags of rice. At least they will still be worth the same in purchasing power when he wants to sell them.

"The farmers have been hit hard by the inflation too," he continued. "In many ways they are worse off than before the land reform. For one thing, the landlords used to repair the drainage ditches and keep them in shape to flood the rice paddies. Now, after the owners pay their taxes, they don't have enough money left to maintain the ditches.

"The price of rice is worse too. Rice used to bring the world price. Today, with price control, the farmer gets less than the world price and part of the time as little as half. We understand the government's problem. They can't let the price of rice go up to the city people, but when the price of land, machinery, and fertilizer all go up, the farmer suffers badly."

Fertilizer is still high on Formosa and the average farmer meets about half his needs with night soil. As in Japan, farmers collect night soil in the villages and cart it out in "honey buckets" for use on their own farms and to sell to their neigh-

bors. In Formosa carts as well as plows are usually pulled by
water buffalo. I had never been close to one before and I was
first impressed by his huge size, smooth skin, and ferocious
appearance. Actually he is a patient, hard worker in the fields
and on the roads; he can be handled by the smallest child in
the family and is dangerous only to strangers and, particularly,
foreigners, they say.

Driving down the road, I noticed a colony of half a dozen
houses which Dr. Moyer said were on the poorest farms in the
neighborhood. I said I wanted to see them so we got out of
the cars and walked up the narrow, dusty road between the
rice paddies. On one side a farmer was plowing a paddy in
water up to his knees, while a farmer on the other side was
harvesting his rice. This was a family job. Two small boys
were cutting the yellow rice with long curved knives and tying
the stalks into bundles. Another small boy took the bundles
to a little box about three by four feet. It turned out to be a
Formosa threshing machine, with a treadle which turned a
drum whose spikes knocked off the heads of the rice. Another
boy would carry the rice to a flat sun-baked space where it was
raked out on the ground to dry. This is woman's work and
either the mother or one of the daughters rakes the rice back
and forth for one or two days until the heat of the sun has
dried it. The process of raising and harvesting rice by hand
is infinite labor; it is terribly hard to see how one family can
raise enough to feed itself and pay the taxes.

At the end of the road we stopped at the first house. In the
small front yard was a pen holding four half-grown pigs while
a half dozen chickens scratched in the dirt. A big, cheerful
woman appeared at the door; taller than the average Formosan,
at least five foot seven, she said with a glowing smile: "You
are welcome." The interpreter introduced us and asked if we
might come in to see her home. "Of course, it is a great

pleasure to have you visit me." In the little living room she showed us her pride and joy, a worn-out Singer sewing machine. Beside it there was a pile of clean cotton cloth. "I do some sewing for our neighbors," she said. "It helps with our income."

Her husband was off working, not on his own land or even as a tenant—he was working as a farm hand for whoever had a job to be done—the very bottom of the economic scale. When I asked how he made out, she said: "He gets work about half the days of the year, wherever he can find it in the neighborhood. The farmers always pay him in rice." I did a little mathematics which showed that his pay amounted to about fifty cents American money a day when he could get work.

She showed us through their tiny, immaculate house and as we came back out into the front yard I pointed to the pigs.

"How do you feed them?" I asked. "Where is your garden?"

"We have no garden. We can't buy any land and there isn't any for rent. We buy the grain we feed to the pigs."

This stopped me completely. "If I raised pigs on my farm," I said, "and bought the feed for them, I would lose money. How can you afford to buy feed to raise them and make any profit?"

She laughed heartily: "We don't expect to make anything. That's just the way we save money. Whatever happens, when the pigs are fat, they will bring a good price. Then we can buy more pigs and more grain to feed them."

This buxom, happy, thirty-year-old woman with no education had mastered the secret of inflation. These pigs were her hedge against the decline in the value of the Taiwan dollar. She knew that if she and her husband saved their money and put it in a bank it would go down steadily in value. She also knew that if she put her tiny savings in pigs they would go up in value.

On the way back to town I mentally rearranged some more of my ideas about the people of Asia. Perhaps the greatest mistake of all is to assume that intelligence and education mean the same thing. They don't. In country after country, talking with farm people, I found that though they could not read or write they had a fine understanding of agriculture, of the good and bad points of their government, and of human relations. They have something else, too. However unskilled and backward they may seem, there is a tenderness of family devotion and a strength of family ties from which most of us could learn a lot. It is true that life is held cheap in Asia; but it is also true that family ties there seemed to me to be closer than in most other parts of the world I have visited.

Formosa today presents an interesting picture of the new China that had grown up before the Reds took over. For centuries China was a man's world. Under the new constitution, women have been elected to the Legislative Yuan and hold appointive offices. Their position and influence have increased enormously.

The emancipation of women has had some interesting by-products. A recent Chinese visitor from Formosa relates the sad tale of Miss Chu Chen-yun who committed suicide by jumping into Sun-Moon Lake, one of the most beautiful in all Formosa. The case was widely reported in the local press and attracted much attention because the young lady was a well-known teacher at the engineering college. Before long it got around that for some time prior to her death she had been having an affair with Wang Shi-an, dean of the college, which was broken up when Wang's wife arrived from the mainland. Everyone believed that Miss Chu committed suicide because she was despondent over her broken romance and a wave of indignation swept through all the women's organizations; meetings were held and resolutions were adopted demanding that Wang be arrested. Of course there was no particular statute that he had violated but the criminal law in Asia is not so much a matter of what is written in books as what a judge thinks the law should be.

The pressure from the women's organizations finally caused the police to arrest Wang and place him on trial, charged with inciting Miss Chu's suicide and with "using the influence of his position to seduce." After a widely publicized trial the judge dismissed the first charge for lack of evidence but found Wang guilty of seduction and sentenced him to a three year term in prison.

The sentence divided the island into two warring camps. The men were outraged, believing Wang had committed no crime; the women were outraged, believing that he was not only guilty of a crime but that the punishment was much too light. The latest report was that the prosecuting attorney, a man, had finally filed an appeal to a higher court on the ground that the sentence was not heavy enough.

The level of health on Formosa is surprisingly good despite the presence of all of the usual endemic diseases of the Orient. There are three kinds of doctors on Formosa: the few Anglo-American-trained doctors who use modern scientific techniques; the Japanese-German school of doctors who practice the old arts of medicine with few modern techniques and little scientific laboratory work; and the ancient Chinese herb doctors, who horrified Dr. Hilleboe. The herb doctors still practice the ancient basic Chinese medicine. They teach that the Wu-hsiu or five factors in the body are: metal, wood, water, fire, and earth. According to their theory, illness is a maladjustment of one of those elements. By taking the pulse, they determine which one of the elements is out of order and prescribe ancient herb medicines. Many of them have an intuitive sense of the psychology of the patient and are able to do some good, but their medicines are regarded by modern doctors as virtually useless. If the herb doctor decides you have too much iron in your system, he takes a batch of powders, including ground "unicorn" horn, and mixes them together. He tells the patient to swallow the concoction three times a day for about two weeks. "If they don't kill the patient by that time," said Dr. Hilleboe, "he is usually over what he had anyway and the herb doctor gets the credit."

Every effort to regulate the herb doctors in the past has been fruitless, partly because in many areas of China they are the only doctors available. Now a new factor has arisen: several of them are members of the Legislative Yuan. Whenever any attempt at regulation is introduced they see to it that there is "a grandfather clause" attached to the proposal—one which protects all who are already practicing or studying the profession.

There are some fairly modern hospitals in Taipei available to a limited number of people. Dr. Hilleboe inspected a rural general hospital, which is available to the masses of the people: "The halls were dirty and there were two or three stray dogs in the lobby," he reported. "There were no screens on the windows. As we walked through the wards and rooms, the smell was almost overwhelming. When a patient is sick, he rents a room or a bed in the ward and gets some service from his visiting doctor. The hospital provides no food or nursing services; so the family moves in. They stay in the ward and build a little charcoal fire on the dirt floor to cook food for the patient. If he becomes seriously ill, all of his relatives come and they sleep around him. Toilet care and personal hygiene of the patient has to be done by the relatives; waste is simply thrown out the window. While the doctors do their best, I'm afraid that this hospital is more of a place for dying than for getting well." It was reminiscent of his reports on rural hospitals in Japan.

By contrast, his report of other efforts in the rural areas of Formosa was more encouraging. There were some comparatively good hospitals; in Taiwan Province there are 22 health centers and 240 health stations, each station having a physician, a nurse, a midwife, an inspector, and a laboratory technician. The Chinese physician in charge of a health station often gets more salary than his superior, who is in charge of the whole province. The nurses take their work to the whole countryside, one nurse handling calls on a hundred families, giving them bedside care, obstetrical care, and all other nursing in the home. "I smiled to myself," said Dr. Hilleboe, "when I thought what one of our public health nurses in New York State would say if we asked her to travel over dirty, bumpy roads on a bicycle with two medical bags on the handlebars, to take care of a hundred families.

"The head nurses in two of the centers are American-trained and speak good English. They really know their jobs. With all they have to do, I don't see how they can face it; but I guess they don't have time to stop and think, or they would have given up long ago and gone someplace else."

The American-trained local doctor in charge of one province told Dr. Hilleboe that there is one trained doctor for every 2400 people, which is high by all Asian standards, and that, despite all of the handicaps, the facilities for medical care are better than ever before: "We can make Formosa a model of health for all Asia if we're given time, more trained people, and more of the medical supplies that can only come from America."

The Nationalist Army on Formosa is a military question mark. It was a broiling hot day when I went for a military inspection in the company of Major General William C. Chase, chief of our MAAG for Formosa, and General Sun Li-jen, commander of the ground forces.

The members of our MAAG group on Formosa have the refreshing point of view that they are guests. They do not think of themselves as bosses sent out to give orders to inferior people. They have set up no fancy headquarters; they have not commandeered the best buildings in town; they work well and effectively with the Chinese; there has been no brawling or rowdiness, no effort to take advantage of their position or to impress the natives. All 300 of our officers and enlisted men are making friends for us every day. I wished our civilian missions in other lands were all as competent, as quiet, friendly, and effective.

The day before our inspection trip one of the American officers told me something of General Sun: "He is a graduate of Purdue and of V.M.I., you know. He is a real fighting man and a great leader. In 1942 a British division was surrounded by the Japanese on a mountain in Burma and the commanding general advised Sun Li-jen by radio that he would have to surrender. Back came a message from General Sun: 'Hold out two days and I will fight my way through to your rescue or die in the attempt.' With 8000 men, Sun attacked the Japanese, turned their flanks, and cleared an escape route for the British; out of his 8000 men, Sun suffered 2000 casualties. In gratitude for his exploit the British Government conferred upon him the Order of the British Empire.

As we arrived for the inspection, a regiment of 1100 men broken up into squads were scattered all over the field. Stripped to the waist, wearing only shorts, they were engaged in the most vigorous training exercises: throwing dummy hand grenades, engaged in bayonet practice, in machine-gun assembly, assembling Signal Corps radios, and in dry-run training in how to shoot American Springfield rifles.

When we came to the group who were doing straight athletic work from parallel bars, I noticed that quite a few lacked the strength to pull themselves up and over. General Sun quietly remarked: "They are not getting enough food." Later General Chase, Madame Chiang, and the American reporters all confirmed that the army was not getting enough to eat. In addition to rice they get some fish but altogether their diet has little more than half the calories served the average American soldier.

We did not witness the more rugged training. In this a number of soldiers are divided into two groups. One man of the first group throws a live grenade at the second group, one of whom must throw it back before it explodes, while the first group takes cover. General Sun admitted that it was tough but added, "We have had very few casualties, less than one in a thousand. This kind of training will save thousands of lives in combat." Final stages of training also include taking "enemy-occupied" hills under both live machine-gun and rifle fire.

I could understand why our MAAG group were impressed. Their general opinion was that about 200,000 are well trained and another 100,000 fairly well trained; the remaining 300,000 are yet to be trained or have special assignments.

Our military men like and admire the Chinese soldiers. By the end of the day I understood why: they are playing for keeps. When they were on the mainland they had been promised that if they surrendered they would be given honorable discharges by the Communists and railroad tickets home. They now know that hundreds of thousands who did surrender were immediately impressed into the Communist army and many were sent to be slaughtered in Korea. In the face of the doubts that many others have expressed, I personally believe

that few of them would desert to the Reds if Nationalist landings were made on the mainland. They tell me that you can
double-cross a Chinese once but not twice.

Colonel Leroy G. Heston of our Air Force spoke in the
highest terms of the Chinese as combat pilots, having trained
them in the Philippines and later on the mainland during
World War II. He says: "They make as fine pilots as there are
in the world. All they need is airplanes to fly."

Of course Free China's army needs much more than planes.
They have little artillery, only small arms which will be useful
in guerrilla warfare. Their leadership needs better training and
better pay. They have never had a retirement system and few
if any resign. In the three branches of the armed services of
the United States there are 1100 general officers; on Formosa
there are 1700 generals.

Chiang Kai-shek is the prisoner of his own successes. When
he started his long effort to unite China it was ruled by many
local governors, generals, and warlords. Instead of eliminating
them all by conquest, he won many to the Nationalist Government by persuasion and of course gave them positions in the
government. As a result, his very successes in bringing about
the unity of China overloaded the Ship of State so heavily
that they were among the reasons for the downfall of the
government. Here on Formosa were 1700 generals still dream-
ing of leading armies back to the mainland, but meanwhile
contributing to the factionalism of the island and undermining
the authority of Sun Li-jen over the ground forces. This is
another reason why the strongest advice must accompany our
aid to Formosa if it is to be effective.

Whatever its defects, the army on Formosa is the largest
army in the Pacific on the side of freedom in the event of
World War III; it is a stabilizing factor which many believe
has thus far helped prevent the Red Chinese from launching

an attack on Indo-China. It would be unwise to think of this army as a means of invading the mainland to hold territory today; but its potential is important for the future and for possible guerrilla action sooner; meanwhile it holds this invaluable island fortress in our defense structure.

The most furious man I met in the Orient was Generalissimo Chiang Kai-shek; the most furious woman was Madame Chiang. I had met Madame Chiang during her wartime visits to this country where her eloquent speeches did much for the cause of Free China; and I had deplored the growing chilliness of the White House towards her after the war.

Chiang Kai-shek I had never met. He has never been to the United States; as a matter of fact, the farthest west he has ever traveled was to Moscow in 1923 and to Cairo, during the war. Except for brief journeys, he has spent his active life on Chinese soil and, having made himself the symbol of a united China, he is one of the most controversial figures of our times.

I had a rather confusing picture of the Generalissimo as a great patriot, as a stubborn and unyielding man, and as the only leader for many centuries who had ever reached the dizzy height of rule over a united China, however briefly. His extraordinary career shows why he has earned all of these reputations. He was educated in Japan; he was under Soviet influence for several years; and he led the cause of a free and united China for a quarter of a century. He was kidnapped by two generals under Communist influence in 1936 but his moral leadership was so strong that they did not dare kill him. He fought the Japanese for eight years, the Chinese Communists for twenty-five. He became the wartime partner of the "Big Four" in world affairs and won through to triumph as the ruler of 450,000,000 people. Then exhaustion, followed by catastrophe, drove his government from the mainland and here he was with his army and his government in exile on the little island of Formosa.

I was curious to learn whether the Generalissimo's dramatic changes in fortune had affected his acknowledged power of leadership. He still seemed to command a mystic loyalty from unnumbered followers. Corruption in his far-flung government of the mainland? Yes. Failure? Yes. Yet millions of Chinese idolize him as a personally incorruptible, matchless spiritual leader. Both Chinese and Americans agree that his leadership is largely spiritual. One outstanding figure on Formosa told me: "Chiang is the only man who can hold this government together and he is the only man under whom it cannot succeed." While this bitter aphorism is partly false in both its aspects, it represents the viewpoint of one faction.

Another story I had never heard before partly explains his tremendous moral influence. When the Chinese were hard pressed by the Japanese during World War II the German Ambassador in Japan was working to get China out of the war. A great many of Chiang Kai-shek's closest advisers were convinced that China should make a separate peace with Japan. They knew the strength of the Communist armies in the north and from long experience they mistrusted all assurances of coöperation from Stalin. They felt that the ultimate danger would come from the Communists, arguing powerfully that they should settle with Japan and get busy eliminating the Communist armies.

"The Generalissimo would have none of it," one Cabinet officer told me. "In the face of increasing pressure he stubbornly resisted every proposal for a negotiated peace. 'If I have to lead the fight against the Japanese alone I will do it!' he exclaimed. 'I will never betray my American allies.'

"The report of his attitude went all through China. Even though many disagreed with it, they were forced to admire his courage and his loyalty to his allies. He may be a terrible administrator and he certainly has been betrayed by many of his associates. But his personal courage and adherence to principle have cemented our loyalty to him."

I had to travel to Formosa to learn another pointed lesson in modern history, one which I believe should be taught in every American school. In 1919 Sun Yat-sen, father of the Chinese Republic, asked the United States to provide military, technical, and economic advisers for the new Chinese Government on a ten-year basis. The American Government turned down the request. So did Great Britain and France when Sun approached them. Only Soviet Russia remained and Russia quickly accepted the invitation. As a result, all of the Chinese leaders in the early days of the Republic came under Communist influence and it was on the orders of Dr. Sun Yat-sen that Chiang visited Moscow in 1923 for four months, having interviews with Trotsky and the then Foreign Commissar, Chicherin, among others.

Perhaps as a result of this visit, Chiang Kai-shek was one of the first to recognize the evil threat of Communism and to break away from Russian advisers, sensing that Russian friendship for China was the kind of friendship a wolf has for a lamb; and so began his ceaseless twenty-five-year struggle for a free and united China. In the course of this struggle he married American-educated Mei-ling Soong; together they are the "first couple" of Free China, working for liberation. Paradoxically, Madame Chiang's elder sister, the widow of Sun Yat-sen, is a Vice-President of the Communist People's Republic of Red China.

My first visit with the Chiangs was at tea and there was no indication that it would lead to one of the most violent political discussions I have ever had. Madame Chiang welcomed Karl Rankin and me to the simple combination living room-dining room as the Generalissimo joined us. It was a charming party—at first. Madame Chiang and I recalled our meetings in America; the Generalissimo asked me many questions about Japan and I asked him his estimates of the military and economic conditions on the mainland.

At sixty-five years of age, as the Chinese compute it, he is still vigorous, both physically and intellectually. At times he paces up and down the room and speaks with great force. At other times he sits quietly and speaks with the calm of a Chinese philosopher, wiggling his foot in the traditional gesture of an Asian scholar. At the end of a pleasant hour I was sitting on the edge of my chair, ready to leave, since this was merely a formal preliminary call. Then somebody mentioned the Japanese peace treaty and there was nothing formal or pleasant about the hour-and-a-half that followed. For all his charm, Chiang Kai-shek can convey more sense of fury, frustration, anger, and bitterness through an interpreter than any man I ever met. When he paused for breath, Madame Chiang went into action in her beautiful English. It just happened that I was the first American the Generalissimo had seen since the published draft of the Japanese peace treaty had announced that neither Free China nor Red China would be allowed to sign it. The strength of his feeling was so powerful that it swept away the ordinary social amenities in a blast of searing emotional bitterness:

"I will accept full blame for losing the mainland in the struggle against the Communists. But must we become the victims of total abandonment by all those on whose side we fought so long and so hard when freedom hung in the balance?"

Fortunately I knew rather intimately the whole story of the Japanese peace treaty from the day John Foster Dulles undertook to negotiate it. I explained that his difficulties had been almost insuperable: the Russians were sabotaging all treaty discussion and were successfully sowing seeds of suspicion not only in Asian countries but among our European allies; all Southeast Asia, including Indonesia and the Philippines, had been occupied by the Japanese and many were insisting on enormous reparations, which Japan obviously could not pay. I pointed out that the world's last great treaty of vengeance—Versailles—had led straight to Hitler and the explosion of World War II. This time we hoped to sow the seeds of friendship and freedom, without the night soil of dictatorship and war. America proposed to negotiate a treaty of reconciliation that would restore Japan as a free and democratic partner in the defense of the free world. This was vital not only to China but to the whole world.

The Philippines, Southeast Asia, Australia, and New Zealand, fearing a resurgent militarist Japan, wanted to prevent Japanese rearmament. To meet their fears Ambassador Dulles had proposed treaties of mutual defense between the United States, Australia, New Zealand, and the Philippines as guarantees against future Japanese aggression. The British insisted on many provisions, including one for the benefit of their shipping industry which would prevent Japan from rebuilding her own merchant marine; they also insisted that Red China be a party to the treaty. Ambassador Dulles had flatly refused to negotiate such a treaty with Red China, whose armies at that moment were killing both British and American soldiers in Korea; as a matter of principle, he refused to accept Red China while Free China was excluded. This raised such a crisis that, after completing his preliminary negotiations with the Pacific nations, he went to London to thrash it out. The Labour Cabinet twice rejected the American concept of the treaty and were brought around to our point of view only after superhuman efforts.

I patiently explained all this amid many interruptions and in the face of great emotion. I described the urgency of the treaty: if the British Government did not sign, then the British Dominions would probably stand aside and with them most of Europe. The British Foreign Office could not be persuaded to sign the treaty with the Nationalist Government of China since they had recognized Red China, even though Red China had not recognized Britain; to persuade them to omit Red China from the signatories was a great triumph of American diplomacy.

I might as well have whistled in the face of a China Sea typhoon. After years of insults by our government and what he believes to be our abandonment of China after the war, the Generalissimo's feeling swept aside all argument: China had fought the Japanese for eight years, suffered 3,000,000 casualties in the armed forces and uncounted millions of casualties among their own people; China had been our staunchest ally, engaging millions of Japanese troops on the mainland when those troops might otherwise have been fighting Americans all over the Pacific. On top of that his government had fought a bitter and bloody battle against Communist aggression, before, during, and after the war. While the Communist troops gave the Japanese little or no trouble, they harried the Nationalist forces even after the Axis attacked Russia. Then in flagrant violation of the treaty of friendship and support which Moscow signed with Chiang on August 14, 1945, the Chinese Communist troops had fought their former allies for four years while the United States looked away. The final exclusion of Free China from the Japanese treaty had again humiliated the government of China before the world; defeated Japan was to be allowed the power of the victor, to choose whether she would sign a peace treaty with her old enemy, the Nationalist Government of China, which won the war, or with the Communist usurper, Mao Tse-tung; betrayal was bad enough but humiliation was a blow from which recovery would be difficult in a land where face means so much.

I couldn't refute the Generalissimo's argument because so much of it was true. What I could do was point out the reasons for what had been done and the advantages which would flow from it. With the Japanese peace treaty completed, both America and Free China would be in a far better position in the Pacific. Without a treaty, we would corroborate the Communist propaganda charge that America intended to stay in Japan forever and ultimately to conquer Asia. With the treaty accomplished, the Communist propaganda line would be weakened. Then we could concentrate on a general treaty of mutual defense in the Pacific area.

The discussion was by no means fruitless. It served to bring up many factors which had not been well known on Formosa and, naturally, it was all on the most friendly personal basis. But I felt I had not succeeded until, as we stood up to leave, Karl Rankin spoke for the first time. In five minutes he summarized the situation better than I had done in an hour and a half. It was perfect; I was proud to have him representing our country.

Twice in the course of his service in Europe he was in the midst of war as invading troops shelled and occupied Brussels in 1940 and Belgrade in 1941. On his tour of duty in Manila the Japanese invaders caught him and his wife, interning them for two years. The Rankins were exchanged late in 1943 and next assigned to Cairo at the height of the war in Africa; then to Greece in time for the Communist revolt of December 1944.

Karl Rankin is a dedicated man in the leadership of our mission to Formosa and the more I saw of him, the more I respected him. The members of our mission got on well together and there was no backbiting either at the general conference we had or when I talked with them alone. They work well together as a team; the only thing they lack is any encouragement from their own government.

Of course, no single factor dominates this complex situation, just as no single factor was responsible for the defeat on the mainland. Perhaps one of America's greatest diplomatic blunders was the language of President Truman's order in December 1945, when he sent General Marshall to China. This order made it clear to the world that Chiang Kai-shek had been directed by the American Government to settle with the Communists under pain of withdrawal of all American aid. To the Communists the President's order meant that all they had to do was stall for time and demand a larger and larger share in the Chinese Government. They had the written assurance of the President of the United States that he would give no more aid to the Nationalist cause unless the Communists got everything they asked for.

Four years later came the famous White Paper, issued in 1949 by our State Department, attacking the Nationalist Government on many counts and explaining why we could not extend more aid. It hit Formosa like an atom bomb. There it was regarded as the most bitterly unfair attack ever launched by one so-called friendly nation against another. As one Chinese put it to me: "The White Paper did us more harm than all the years of Communist propaganda because it came from those who were supposed to be our friends." The Legislative Yuan was outraged by this attack on their government and acted as any legislative body would, demanding a strong, detailed answer. George Yeh, the Foreign Minister, steadfastly advised against any official answer. During a long and turbulent debate he explained his position to the Legislative Yuan; twice he resigned his office and twice he was restored to it. His views finally won out. It was better to take the insult in silence than to issue a detailed documentary reply which, however sound it might be, would further increase the animosity of those in control of the American Government. For Free China must die without American support.

Just a month before I left on my trip, President Truman had made a political speech in Tennessee in which he had again referred to the Nationalist Government in scathing terms. This speech repeatedly came up during my visit to Formosa; again and again I was reminded how important it is for our American officials to learn that their words echo and re-echo around the world. The slightest comment by the President, the Secretary of State, or lesser officials echoes like thunder throughout sixty nations. The most irresponsible statement by a congressman or senator, speaking for nobody but himself, is headlined around the world and is often mistaken to represent American policy.

Material help is essential to the survival of Formosa; with a defense cost taking sixty per cent of the island's small revenue, financial help is imperative; but what her leaders want most of all is the simple gesture of faith and friendship—which costs nothing. Premier Chen Cheng, one of the wisest leaders of the country, said:

"What we need most of all is moral support, so that we are not continuously shamed before the world by our greatest traditional friend. Next we need technical support so that we can do our jobs better. After that, we need political support in our relationships with other countries. Lastly we need material aid."

He was deeply grateful for the technical assistance, the material aid, and occasional political support we have given his country; but like everyone else on Formosa, he utterly failed to understand why America, which is leading the world's fight against Communism, should continuously give aid and comfort as well as material to Soviet propaganda by making political attacks on our wartime ally, the Nationalist Government.

They certainly have no illusions on Formosa about the nature of Communism. Major General Chiang Ching-kuo, the eldest son of the Generalissimo, is in command of the island police. In fact, it is said he operates eight different groups of police, including counter-intelligence, army education, and anti-Communist indoctrination, each spying on the other and on everybody else. Moscow-trained and married to a Russian woman, he is nevertheless thoroughly anti-Communist, though he uses some Soviet methods. Chiang Ching-kuo has also established a system of political commissars in the army over whom General Sun Li-jen has no control. The political work in the army was explained as necessary for the indoctrination and education of the troops. Whatever the explanation, our MAAG group takes a dim view of it.

However repulsive this intensive police work, I found that it was set up to deal with something even more repulsive—sudden death. The government of Free China was in deadly peril from the moment it moved from the mainland to Formosa. It was sad to hear how some of the high-ranking officials had been entrapped by the Communists. Many of their sons or daughters had been in schools on the mainland; those whom the Communists converted were sent personally to Formosa to urge their fathers to collaborate with the Reds under promise of protection when Mao took over the island; others were forced to send messages to their fathers, warning that failure to collaborate with the Communists would result in the execution of their sons and daughters by the Chinese Reds. Faced with this terrible choice, some Chinese Nationalists betrayed their trust and went over to Communism.

"We now know," said one of my American friends, "that Chiang's government was threatened by attack not only from the mainland but from within. Many Communist spies and traitors came to the island along with the government, the troops, and the millions of refugees.

"Investigations disclosed that treason ran almost to the highest levels. The Deputy Minister of Defense was caught with a two-way radio right in his own office, communicating every day with the Red Government on the mainland. He was quietly arrested and the radio taken over by the secret police. For three months messages continued to be exchanged with the mainland and a list of traitors and collaborators was gradually compiled. It included many in powerful positions such as the head of all the electric power and other utilities on the island, as well as many minor figures.

"The scheme for seizing the island from within had been worked out in every detail. The head of the public utilities, for example, was carefully instructed during this period how and when to cut off all electric power on the island; but he was also carefully instructed not to allow the destruction of any plants."

When the Communists on the mainland finally discovered they were being duped and the arrests came out in the open, the spies and traitors on Formosa were tried and shot. No one thinks that all of them were caught, and on Formosa the price of continued existence is eternal vigilance. Two Red spies were caught and executed while I was there. These stern security measures have paid off in law and order, however, for Formosa was the last country I visited until I reached Australia where Communist assassins and guerrillas were not a constant menace. Members of the Cabinet told me that two years earlier they could not possibly appear on the street without a heavy bodyguard and could never travel at night. Today both Chinese and Americans agree that order has been so effectively restored that they can walk the streets alone in perfect safety by day or night.

One of the things I sought on Formosa, as usual, was the opinion of the newspapermen stationed at Taipei. I have found that the press and radio representatives have at least a refreshing judgment on matters where statesmen walk delicately and with reserve. So I arranged a completely off-the-record social meeting with the American and European correspondents on Formosa. In that small group from all over the world I found every kind of opinion and background because no two of them agreed on anything. We had a lively two-hour argument: some felt that all of the over-age generals should be retired and removed from power so they could not undercut those who carried on active responsibility; others argued that many of the generals on the island had the genuine admiration and loyalty of 50,000,000 to 100,000,000 Chinese on the mainland. Many Chinese "generals" are politicians, they argued, not soldiers; some were originally teachers and scholars and they see nothing inconsistent in the idea of seeking to promote their country's welfare in politics as in war. No one had any illusions that the Formosa army could immediately land on the mainland and hold large areas. Its chief immediate use is to restrain the aggressive ambitions of both Russia and Peking. There was a strong feeling that this army and guerrillas in South China should be given every possible support. The whole Chinese Army of 600,000 men costs less than $100,000,-000 a year; it would cost thirty to fifty times as much to support an American army of similar size.

One American remarked: "It would cost comparatively little to put this island on a sound financial basis. With its forty air fields and two naval bases, Formosa is essential to our own defense perimeter. A bankrupt Formosa would be a liability and not an asset, just as a bankrupt Japan would be. A little more technical aid, coupled with a little more money, could turn this island into a tremendous fortress. Nowhere can so little aid gain so much strength for our side."

The Nationalist Government still controls many islands in addition to Formosa. One group, the Pescadores, lying between Formosa and the mainland, is of great strategic importance for reconnaissance of the China coast and in intercepting ships with contraband for the Reds on the mainland. Other Nationalist islands are even closer to the mainland and I asked why the Reds had not seized them. One explanation was that the Communists had launched an assault on one island and had been driven off with great losses after a two-day battle; another explanation was that a certain amount of trading useful to both sides goes back and forth from those islands. I was inclined to believe both.

Formosa has another strategic importance: the immense spiritual influence it exerts upon the overseas Chinese in Southeast Asia and throughout the Pacific. In Indo-China, 1,000,000 Chinese do much of the region's business; almost half the population of Malaya is Chinese, as are 800,000 out of Singapore's 1,000,000 people; in the Philippines 400,000 Chinese dominate the business community, as do the 2,000,000 Chinese in Indonesia. So long as Formosa remains free, these overseas Chinese will not be forced to look for leadership to Red China.

Unlike Japan, Formosa was keenly aware of the problems of the rest of the world and particularly of Asia. The Free Chinese know that Southeast Asia is a magnet to the Chinese Reds, for the mainland of China has just too many people and too little land, while Burma, Thailand, and Indo-China have a land surplus. So do the Philippines. So does Indonesia. These areas have a fatal attraction for the Chinese just as they had for the Japanese so long as they were a militarist, aggressive power. Now Mao Tse-tung, with unlimited manpower and Russian support, has taken their place.

One experienced Chinese leader summed up the general Formosa attitude: "Your action in moving into Korea saved the position of America and the free world in the Orient. Now we are worried over what will happen with a cease-fire. If the Red Chinese troops are released for other adventures, I very much fear they will join in an attack to run the French out of Indo-China and take over all Southeast Asia.

"There are 200,000 to 250,000 Red Chinese troops stationed along the north border of Indo-China. At present, these Red Chinese troops are leaving the job of fighting the French to their puppet Ho Chi Minh and confine themselves to training officers, indoctrinating troops, and providing supplies.

"But this is just a stalemate, it is no solution. I believe that the only solution is for Britain, France, and the native governments to enter into a firm partnership within the structure of the United Nations. They can agree among themselves to provide total defense for Southeast Asia. If they do, it will never be attacked."

"What about the raw materials?" I asked.

"It is equally important that you set up among you total control of resources. Rubber, tin, copra, and everything else is now leaking out of those countries to the Communists. If the great powers will work out a partnership with these Asian governments, providing a genuine system of control of all exports, you can prevent this diversion of critical materials to the Communist countries. You should move boldly to see that it flows only into the free world."

"Assuming that were done," I inquired, "what is your approach to the guerrilla problem in all these countries?"

"You should learn, if I may suggest it, that Communism in Asia is not the same as Communism in Europe or America. The Asian peoples do not understand that Communism is a new and worse form of absolute tyranny. Most of them just think of it as another economic theory. In Asia, the only possible solution for Communists is their total obliteration. One Communist is a cell and he divides and subdivides like an amoeba. Among uneducated people this spreading poison can destroy a country.

"I don't believe that any American aid should be extended to any country in Asia which tolerates Communists. You never know when they are going to conquer a government from within or by their guerrillas and everything you have given them may turn out to be money wasted."

Chiang Kai-shek and his Nationalist Government are controversial subjects. Despite all the arguments, one thing is clear: Free China and its Formosa stronghold are essential to Pacific defense. The solid line of our Pacific defense structure runs from Alaska down through Japan, Okinawa, Formosa, and the Philippines. Without Formosa, the whole chain of defense would be cracked wide open; with it, the free world holds a mighty position which both serves the free peoples of the Pacific and also helps keep the threat of war thousands of miles from American shores.

Even if Nationalist China were as bad as its enemies paint it, I would favor supporting it as one of the forces necessary to keep the Communists from overrunning the whole Pacific. If Chiang Kai-shek were as bad as his enemies claim he is, he would still be a thousand times better than Mao Tse-tung, who has been killing American boys in Korea.

There is no choice. In a fiercely troubled and dangerous world, we need all the friends we can muster for our own survival. Nationalist China is on our side; Communist China is our self-elected enemy.

"Nothing—absolutely nothing—survived in the center of Hiroshima except eleven steel and concrete buildings and some tombstones."

After luncheon at Governor Yuichi Ohsawa's home.

Premier Shigeru Yoshida of Japan.

A briefing in a front-line command head-quarters in Korea.

(Collier)

(Collier)

"We flew over the worst possible fighting terrain in the little L-19s."

"General James A. Van Fleet [*left*] does not drive men—they follow him."

"General Matthew Ridgway moved naturally into the position of Supreme Commander for the Allied Powers."

Yu Yu-jen, President of the
Control Yuan on Formosa.

Generalissimo and Madame Chiang Kai-shek.

"The Old City of Manila, once wholly contained within medieval walls, was used as a last-ditch defense by the Japanese."

"Manila Bay is full of sunken ships whose rusting hulls jut out at crazy angles."

"In Hong Kong 1,000,000 refugees live for the most part in tiny shacks thrown together with waste pieces of galvanized iron and driftwood."

"Others live on sampans, acres of sampans, miles of sampans, stretching from one end of the harbor to the other."

(Collier)

"From a police observation post in the New Territories of Hong Kong we had a glimpse of Communist China."

"The finest rice of all China grows in the New Territories."

Bao Dai, Emperor of Indo-China's Viet Nam.

(*International News Photo*)

Ho Chi Minh, Communist leader in Indo-China.

The late General de Lattre, Marshal of France.

(*Collier*)

"I had always wanted to see the remains of the capital city of the once great Khmer kingdom, which had been lost to civilization since the fifteenth century and reclaimed from the jungle only in the last hundred years."

"The incredible towers of Angkor Vat appeared above the jungle."

"We also passed a gilded Buddha seated on a raised platform under a high thatched roof."

"The Borneo head-hunters can track an enemy through any jungle in Malaya."

Commissioner General Malcolm MacDonald looks at a captured Communist flag.

"Traveling along a winding, deeply rutted road" on a farm visit in Indonesia.

Ambassador Merle Cochran and Foreign Minister Achmad Subardjo, Indonesia.

(Collier)

An Indonesian rice paddy.

(Collier)

"Young girls dressed in
sarongs were pounding rice
in a small open shed."

President Sukarno of Indonesia explaining a painting behind his desk of "tattered Republican soldiers carefully cleaning weapons, putting fuses in dynamite, and bandaging . . . wounds, while a man off in a corner is sadly counting his last three bullets."

5

The Philippines

... From the status of a dependency enjoying for four decades the protection of the sovereign power, the Philippines rose ten years ago to take its place beside the United States in the war to repel imperialistic aggression in the Pacific. The Filipino people, by bearing loyally their share in the great struggle, conclusively proved not only their right to freedom but also their willingness and capacity to defend it.

> Carlos P. Romulo, Foreign Secretary of the Philippines, at the signing of the United States-Philippines Mutual Defense Pact, August 30, 1951

THE SOUTHERN TIP of Formosa dropped behind us and we were out over the South China Sea, heading for the Philippines, where the United States had conducted its greatest experiment in colonialism. Settling back in my seat, as the plane droned over the empty sea, I recalled some of the stories I had heard about the Philippines. They were discouraging to say the least, stories of the Communist Huk guerrillas who, it was reported, were terrorizing the countryside, even venturing at times into Manila itself. "It is absolutely impossible to go out into the country because no roads are safe from Huk ambush," I had been warned.

On the flight out from Honolulu to Japan, I had met a

young couple who lived at Clark Field, about sixty miles north of Manila, where the young man had been stationed since the end of the war. His report on conditions was decidedly unfavorable. After the Philippines had been granted their independence, the American armed forces hired Chinese guards for the air field. They were excellent, the young man said; the guards had few friends in the area and nothing to do but their duty; but local political pressure finally forced the Americans to dispense with the services of the Chinese and substitute Filipino guards who had altogether too many friends. It was good patronage but bad security. Discipline became lax and the Huk guerrillas infiltrated the whole district. "Today," he said, "the area is so bad that the automobile trip from the field into Manila has to be made in a military convoy."

Economic conditions in the islands were so serious that President Truman had appointed a mission directed by Daniel W. Bell, president of a Washington bank, to make a study which had been published the preceding October. I had the report with me and it made gloomy reading. With unconscious irony, this mission from Washington sharply criticized the Philippine Government for deficit spending, graft, favoritism, and reluctance to face the problems of the country. "The economic problem in the Philippines is over-population and very low incomes," it went on. "In the past 10 years the population has increased by 25% . . . wages are wholly inadequate, in some instances less than one peso (50 cents) a day.

"The Treasury has a large and mounting deficit with taxes covering only 60% of the expenditures. . . . School teachers have not been paid. . . . New taxes, voted by the special session in Congress, cannot meet the budget needs and the cash position of the Treasury is becoming steadily worse. . . ."

The report forecast a "new outburst of inflation, the burden of which will fall on those struggling for a living in a land of very high prices and very low incomes. . . . Prices on the average are three and one-half times as high as prewar. Most agricultural and industrial workers have no faith that their economic position can or will be improved. Businessmen fear a collapse of the peso. . . . Inefficiency and even corruption in the government services are widespread. . . . The situation is being exploited by the Communist-led Hukbalahap movement to incite lawlessness and disorder."

It was a dismal outlook. In fact, I do not recall ever having read a more discouraging document.

I was just finishing the report when Paul Lockwood tapped me on the shoulder and pointed out the window. In the distant haze we could make out the mountains at the north end of the main island of Luzon. As we approached Manila, we flew over Lingayen Gulf, scene of one of the great naval engagements of the war. Crossing Subic Bay and immortal Bataan Peninsula, we could see no scars of war since the lush tropical growth came down to the water's edge. We circled the island of Corregidor, heading across the immense reaches of Manila Bay for Nichols Field, the Manila International Airport.

From the cool altitude of ten thousand feet we came down to the sticky, tropical, midsummer heat of Manila. We were met by Ambassador Myron M. Cowen and went off to the Embassy Residence. While Bataan and Corregidor looked untouched from the air, we now saw that the marks of war are still heavy on Manila. The savage fighting that took place in the liberation of Manila left a city in which scarcely a building is unscarred. The Old City of Manila, once wholly contained within medieval walls, was totally destroyed. Every government building, the great university, and every church was used for last-ditch defense by the Japanese and it took artillery, flame-throwers, napalm, grenades, and machine guns to dig them out. When the Old City was finally leveled, the New City also took a bad beating before the last resistance was stamped out.

Manila Bay is full of sunken ships whose rusting hulls jut out at crazy angles above the surface of the water near the shore. The damage in Manila is not as bad as in Seoul or Berlin and since 1945 the United States has spent $500,000,000 in reconstruction, rebuilding much of the city; but the devastation of war is still to be seen everywhere.

The city, like Tokyo, presented a curious mixture of the Occident and the Orient. Aside from a few who were smartly dressed in Western clothes, most of the men wore thin cotton pants and thin shirts, sometimes brightly colored; the women wore the simplest cotton dresses. The ever present American jeep was there, usually made over into a small bus called a "Jeep-ney." By the time Filipino mechanics got through tinkering with the jeep-buses they looked thoroughly uncomfortable, but it was amazing how many adults and children, live chickens, baskets, and bundles one of them could carry.

It was a new experience to come to a city where Dewey Boulevard is the best street in town. My name struck the Filipinos as a particularly useful subject of conversation and also tickled their sense of humor. Even at the luncheon in the palace, President Elpidio Quirino opened his speech by saying, "Dewey has taken Manila again." All were interested in my relationship to the admiral and I had the feeling that they didn't quite believe me when I told them I was only his fifth cousin.

Driving up Dewey Boulevard, Ambassador Cowen explained that the Embassy Residence had been taken over for offices and that he lives in a rented house formerly owned by a leading businessman who was caught aiding the guerrillas and executed by the Japanese.

I had thought that the explosion over the Japanese peace treaty on Formosa would be my last experience of that nature, but my illusions were quickly shattered. Formosa was furious because it was not to be allowed to sign the treaty; by contrast, the Philippines were furious because they were asked to sign a treaty without cash reparations. The treaty was the principal subject of bitter conversation all the time I was in Manila.

The Filipino people suffered greatly during the war; their land had been overrun, devastated, and ravaged by the Japanese. President Quirino lost his wife and two daughters from wanton Japanese machine gunning just two days before Manila was liberated; the Solicitor General lost his father, two brothers, and a sister in the same way. There is scarcely a family in the Philippines that does not carry the scar of personal loss and hatred for the Japanese. Their intense and universal hatred will last a long time.

One distinguished Philippine citizen summarized the situation when he said: "I simply have no solution for the terrible emotional upheaval which has affected the opinion of our people concerning the Japanese peace treaty. They will never understand it if our government signs a treaty without war reparations. In their own minds they have built up an impossible and fantastic figure of $8,000,000,000 they insist must be paid in reparations by Japan."

As I met more of the working people and farmers my concern increased. The bitterness was greater, more intense, and more personal than I had ever seen before, even on Formosa. One American summed it up: "The average Filipino thinks of war reparations as a large sum of cash to be paid to the victor by the vanquished and then distributed to the people. They expect the government to receive a huge amount of money from the Japanese Government and divide it equally among all Philippine citizens. When the text of the treaty made it clear that there were to be no reparations, everyone felt he was being cheated out of money he had coming to him.

"If anyone could explain to these people," he concluded, "that even if they did get reparations there would be no personal distribution of wealth, they would quickly lose interest in the subject."

While my visit was wholly unofficial, Ambassador Cowen put me to work "selling" the Japanese peace treaty at every meeting and at every meal. The Filipinos were not easily sold. They had their own point of view; they knew that Ambassador John Foster Dulles, the architect of the treaty, was my close friend: so couldn't I explain to him the shameful way the Philippines were being treated? They admitted that the American Government had paid for reconstruction of destroyed buildings and homes, of roads, bridges, ports, harbors, fisheries, and power plants; it was true that the American Government had given back pay to all the Philippine armed forces and compensation to their families; that Philippine veterans were receiving the same benefits as American veterans. It was true that the Reconstruction Finance Corporation had given them a large loan. All these benefits had run to nearly $2,000,000,000 and they were grateful. But the point was simply that the Japanese had done them terrible damage and the Japanese must pay $8,000,000,000 in reparations.

At meeting after meeting I found myself explaining the simple facts the Japanese people were facing: how they had lost 6,000,000 out of their 7,000,000 tons of shipping and all their overseas possessions, their sources of raw materials and of rice imports. I described the destruction of the factories and the total absence of capital for the reconstruction of the country. Japan simply had nothing with which to pay reparations.

I explained the theory of the treaty. We did not intend to repeat the mistakes of the Treaty of Versailles, which led to the rise of Hitler and another war. History shows that there are only two alternatives: a defeated enemy should be wiped out and his people enslaved in the brutal fashion of the ancients; or he should be restored to good physical and moral health so he can become a useful, free member of the family of nations for the future.

The first, savage alternative is entirely foreign to our civilization. The only course open to us was to restore Japan fully as a friend and ally so she could survive economically and be strong enough to resist Communist aggression. We were attempting the greatest treaty of reconciliation in history; it would fail if we imposed harsh conditions on an already impoverished and desolated country.

It was an uphill job. I will never forget the morning after a long evening on the subject when a top member of the government called the Ambassador on the telephone at seven-thirty to say that he had stayed awake all night worrying about our discussion: "It's very simple. I have it all figured out. Last night Governor Dewey was simply helping his friend Dulles out of a tough spot. Things in Japan can't possibly be as bad as he describes."

Underlying every other objection was, of course, the deep fear that Japan might rise again and launch another campaign of conquest. I urged that a treaty of mutual defense between the United States and the Philippines, which had already been proposed in general terms, should allay their fears. The suggestion seemed to be quite helpful and was eagerly followed up. In all of these matters Ambassador Cowen was an effective influence toward the end we both felt so essential for the peace of the Pacific and of the world. Realizing that trade between Japan and the Philippines was necessary to both, we also knew that unless both signed the treaty it might irreparably damage their recovery.

I never worked so hard in my life on a job that wasn't mine; nor did I ever have a sterner taskmaster than Ambassador Cowen. Despite everything, public sentiment against a treaty without reparations was so inflamed that when I left it still appeared unlikely that the Philippines would sign. Some time after I got home a modification was arranged which recognized more clearly the moral right of the Philippines to reparations in cash and also their right to receive certain services from Japan. The treaty of mutual defense between the United States and the Philippines was also negotiated. When I next saw President Quirino it was in Washington after the San Francisco Conference, where the Philippines had signed the Japanese peace treaty.

Soon after, there were elections to fill a third of the seats in the Philippine Senate. President Quirino's party lost every seat. Statesmanship is not always good politics.

Twenty million human beings in the Philippines live in 115,000 square miles, an area slightly larger than the State of Arizona, but the main island of Luzon is by far the most densely populated. When the treaty of peace between the United States and Spain was signed in 1898, land title was confirmed and ownership continued and much of the farm land on Luzon is still owned by old Spanish families. Under the Spanish system which still prevails, a tenant's debts carry over from year to year and are inherited by his children and his children's children. Entirely by accident, the Japanese occupation came to the rescue of the heavily indebted tenant farmers. It was the one bright, amusing episode of a terrible war.

When the Japanese moved in they issued their own currency, the prewar American-sponsored peso declining in value until it was practically worthless. When the American troops returned three years later the Japanese currency took a nose dive but was still legal tender during the liberation period. Many enterprising tenant farmers dug out their savings, bought cheap Japanese pesos, and quickly paid off their debts to the landlords in the almost worthless paper. They not only paid off their own debts, but they were able to wipe out the debts of their fathers and their fathers' fathers. Today the Japanese peso is a curio universally called "Mickey Mouse money."

With the coming of peace industrial and agricultural production soared to near prewar levels but the farmers and the city workers were still having a miserable time meeting the high cost of living brought about by postwar inflation. Embassy employees with their extra allowances are suffering.

Housing is desperately short. The guerrilla warfare of the Huks has driven an estimated 150,000 refugees from the outlying regions into already overcrowded Manila, adding grave burdens to the city's food supply, its electric power, and its water supply, which, under American guidance, was once the finest in the world. Wages are miserable and a desperate situation has been saved only by adoption of a minimum wage of a dollar a day, as recommended by the Bell Report. In a few highly skilled trades the minimum is as high as a dollar and a half a day. In America those same skilled trades would earn twenty dollars a day; in Alaska, thirty-five dollars a day.

Many other recommendations in the Bell Report have also been adopted, at least in part. Income taxes have been raised to the point where they are almost as confiscatory as those in America but they remain largely nominal since less than 12,000 people bother to file returns. A heavy seventeen per cent tax on foreign exchange has been imposed. Exports are up and imports down to the point where there is actually a surplus of exports. This is an unsound tax, damaging to any island economy; like Japan, the Philippines must trade or die. But the budget is balanced. The government has increased salaries and the graft denounced in the Bell Report was believed to be decreasing. Greater confidence in the government and its currency has halted the flight of capital, and employment opportunities in factories and plantations have increased. Instead of the gloomy picture I expected to find, the economic life of the Philippines is improving in every direction.

During the war thousands of young men went into the jungles to fight against the Japanese as guerrillas. At the end of the war they just continued to be guerrillas. Some had grievances against the United States; some grievances against the native Philippine Government; some came from tenant families who believed the Communist promise of land reform; others just couldn't settle down to work. Ever since the liberation they have robbed, killed, and sabotaged. The great majority are not Communists but they were easy prey to the Communist leadership of the Huk movement.

Hidden in the mountains and in the jungle is a Communist national congress which elects a central committee that in turn selects the ruling Politburo. The Philippines are divided into ten regional commands, each led by trained Communist guerrilla leaders. Two "Stalin Universities" have been established to give mass indoctrination on Communist theories and practices. Not much has been established about the actual relationship between the Huk Communist leadership and the Kremlin, though there have been many rumors of foreign submarine landings and the sighting of two strange submarines off the coast has been confirmed.

The guerrillas still have a large supply of weapons and ammunition provided by our forces during the war. They extort money from the people in outlying villages and they also receive financial support from Chinese in Manila who contribute either willingly or under threats against their families on the mainland. Food comes from friendly villagers with whom the Huks often live during the daytime. Operating as guerrillas, the Huks have excellent intelligence and can choose their own points of attack; they can concentrate forces of 300 to 400 men for a hit-and-run raid or ambush and it is impossible to have government troops at every threatened point in the island.

Under heavy pressure the government finally appointed Ramon Magsaysay as Defense Minister in 1951. Incorruptible, brilliant, and indomitable, he has reorganized the army, increasing it to 40,000 men. At the same time, he is steadily cutting down the constabulary, which was often corrupt and preyed upon the people under the pretext of attacking the Huks. Magsaysay is in the field much of the time directing actual operations and has made magnificent progress in the months he has been in office. His motto—"Better to die on your feet than to live on your knees"—has been adopted by his troops in their bitter struggle to put down the Huks.

Under the stimulus of Magsaysay's leadership the government finally broadened its approach to the whole problem of internal order. In addition to military action against the Huks, the government announced a reward to any person giving information leading to the capture of a guerrilla, dead or alive; it also promised twenty acres of free land on Mindanao, the large undeveloped southern island, to any Huk who surrendered and who was not found guilty of any crime after a fair examination. Those taking advantage of this offer were offered three months of agricultural training as well as the materials to build a home for himself and his family.

Within a few months prior to my arrival, Magsaysay and his army had killed or captured 4000 guerrillas and many of the members of the Huk Politburo were captured, tried, and convicted. An additional 1000 Huk guerrillas had surrendered to take advantage of the offer of land. From an estimated 15,000, the Huk forces had been cut down to 10,000. Travel on the highways and life in the country was becoming safer throughout the islands.

The Huks are being driven and harassed by the government. They are still there in force and it may take a long time to eliminate them; but as of today they are fighting a losing battle.

Other equally important progress is being made. Public education now receives seven dollars per capita, which is a tiny fraction of what we spend in this country, but a great advance in the islands. School population has doubled in the last ten years and almost half the people can now read and write.

As a result of more than forty years of American administration, the Philippines became one of the healthiest places in the world to live, far healthier than any other nation in the Orient. World War II interrupted all the progress we had made: laboratories were destroyed and hospitals bombed out; epidemics broke out and 5000 lepers were turned loose; tuberculosis ran high, as did beriberi, malaria, and venereal diseases. Immediately after the end of the war the United States Public Health Service started a rehabilitation program and the Philippine Government is now carrying it on, though without adequate financing. In addition to efforts to improve nutrition and the known methods of meeting the problems of tuberculosis, a novel attack has been made on beriberi.

Throughout the Pacific, I was shocked to discover that the people who live on rice throw away the part most important to their health. We do the same thing but rice is not a main staple of our diet. In the Far East they grind away the brown husks before they eat the rice and if a housewife sees any brown grains she picks them out of the rice and throws them away before she cooks it; but it is the brown husks that contain the indispensable vitamin B complex. The people will not eat brown rice even when they are told that it will save their lives. They are almost as stubborn in their insistence upon eating divitaminized rice as we are about eating divitaminized wheat. They know that beriberi produces enlarged spleens, swollen legs, heart trouble, miscarriages in women, and often death. Even when they know that the brown husk carries a vitamin that will prevent it, they simply say: "I don't like brown rice."

Two young American scientists recently went to work on a new approach to the problem; they saved the husks from the rice mill and reduced them to a colorless liquid which was sprayed on the polished grains of white rice, at a cost of one cent a pound. Then they launched an experiment in two control areas on Bataan, with spectacular results: exhaustive tests revealed that beriberi disappeared in the group eating the sprayed rice while it increased in the group eating the standard white rice. Among those who ate the sprayed rice, the death rate dropped by two thirds in a single year, from 246 to 80 per 100,000. It is ironic and exasperating that more than 1,000,-000,000 people, nearly half the population of the world, most of whom are underfed, polish the vitamins and iron out of their rice before eating it. Efforts are now being made in a number of countries to encourage the people to use the rice spray or to eat the rice as God made it.

As usual I spent a day visiting farms and if I were a Philippine tenant farmer I would feel pretty unhappy over my lot. Land reform has progressed with leaden feet. Minimum wages do not help tenant farmers. While many were able to pay their debts with depreciated Japanese currency, rents are still high and plots of ground small. Living conditions are miserable in the little shacks built on stilts to keep them above the level of the flooded rice paddies around them. These tenant farmers are free to go to the great island of Mindanao with its rich, free land for all; but it is hard to leave home and loved ones to strike out in a wild, strange territory even though it is in your own country.

In contrast to the average farmers' plight were the excellent conditions of the farm employees on the 18,000-acre sugar-cane and coconut plantation of Jose Yulo, thirty-five miles outside of Manila, one of the largest single plantations under cultivation in the world. Though born and raised on his family plantation on the island of Negros, Mr. Yulo is not a farmer but a distinguished lawyer. When the Japanese came they demanded that Mr. Yulo co-operate with them. Under great pressure to become a collaborationist, he finally accepted the post of Chief Justice so he could use it as a cover for sabotage, espionage, and guerrilla activities. He actually received in his home in Manila during the war an agent of Manuel Quezon, President of the Philippines in exile, who was in Washington. It is said that of the twenty-two Filipinos and Americans who entered Manila during the Japanese occupation on espionage missions, twenty-one were caught and executed; the only one who escaped was the messenger from President Quezon whom Mr. Yulo smuggled out of Manila to a waiting submarine.

During the occupation Mr. Yulo, under the pseudonym "Mickey Rooney," was in constant touch with General MacArthur's headquarters, transmitting information his employees gave him about conditions throughout the islands and the deployment of Japanese troops. Mr. Yulo had two brothers in Luzon, both of whom were active in the guerrilla movement against the Japanese. One is still living but the other was caught, tortured, and killed and his body left on Mr. Yulo's doorstep.

In addition to the plantation we visited, he has a farm in

the mountains north of Manila where the Japanese tried to make him grow sugar cane. Mr. Yulo shrugged them off, saying that his employees were completely out of his control and the Japanese would have to take charge. They did but, by some strange coincidence, every time a crop of sugar cane was about to be harvested it was burned. When the Japanese came to Mr. Yulo, he explained that he was in Manila and had no control. When they investigated at the farm the employees shrugged their shoulders and said, "The guerrillas." It was from this farm that his faithful employees were able to smuggle small supplies of food to him in Manila, which made life tolerable during the occupation. In the same way loyal and friendly Filipinos found secret passageways to smuggle in vegetables, rice, and clothing for the 6300 Americans who were interned at the university through the whole war.

The great Yulo plantation we visited is mostly devoted to growing successive crops of sugar cane throughout the year. There are also some 220,000 coconut trees and a large number of acres are given over to the employees for growing their own food. It is a vast enterprise run by some 2000 field workers in addition to supervisors, foremen, and factory workers. In all, 11,000 men, women, and children live on the plantation. Every home was destroyed during the war, and they have all been rebuilt in good sturdy fashion. Mr. Yulo has built and staffed a forty-bed hospital and maintains free medical care, grade schools, and a high school. He also built a church and brought out a priest who has since been busily engaged in marrying several hundred couples, some of them grandparents who had never got around to getting married before.

One hundred miles of roads give access to all parts of the plantation and as we drove through I saw armed men quietly patrolling the fields. They are part of the private police to which I became so accustomed in all the harried and troubled

Asian countries, at mines, factories, and plantations. There were 82 on the Yulo plantation, headed by a hero of the resistance during the war.

We came to a herd of 130 dairy cattle which Mr. Yulo had unhappily acquired only a few months before. In the preceding March the owner had been killed by the Huks and the family offered the herd for sale; just as it was about to be disposed of as beef, Ambassador Cowen persuaded Mr. Yulo to buy it and save the largest single source of Manila's milk supply.

In charge of the herd was an Igorot tribesman from the mountains. The least-educated and the wildest inhabitants of the Philippines, the Igorots are among the best workers. The herdsman spoke to me in good English and discussed the problems of hoof rot, mastitis, Bang's disease, and fast milking as though he were a graduate of a first-class American dairy farm.

I was interested to learn that the Igorots still maintain many of their early tribal customs. When young people get married it is not considered permanent until a child is born. By ancient custom they smoke their dead as we would smoke hams: then when the bodies are properly mummified they are ceremoniously placed on leaves in a cave where they remain in perfect condition so their families can visit them from time to time. Early in the year, before they start planting crops, the men in the tribe divide up into two groups and throw rocks at each other. It is a good omen for the crops if several heads are cracked open. Whatever their tribal practices, I know a good many New York farmers who would be glad to have a herdsman as good as the Igorot on the Yulo plantation.

In Manila, I became acutely aware of the importance of Formosa as a key to the attitude of the overseas Chinese throughout Southeast Asia. A deluge of telegrams upon my arrival came from Zamboanga, Bulan Sagon, Catanduanes, Nagu City, and countless other places, greeting me as a friend of Free China and urging my continued support of Chiang Kai-shek. They were signed by individuals, by Chinese Chambers of Commerce, by the Philippine Chinese United Organization in support of Anti-Communist Movements, by Chinese Youth Movements, and by local branches of the Chinese Nationalist Party. Of course, I do not know that these messages were spontaneous and I suspect from similar experience elsewhere that they had been stimulated. Whatever the reason, they dramatized the basic fact of the enormous Chinese influence in the area. Four hundred thousand Chinese do much of the business of the Philippines and their attitude toward their home government is important both to the Philippine Government and to the free world. While I did not see enough Chinese to be sure, our own people in Manila believe that a majority of the Philippine Chinese have at last taken sides. So long as Formosa stands, the great majority will be loyal to Chiang Kai-shek and anti-Communist. If Formosa should fall and there should be then only the Red government of Mao Tse-tung, it would be a different—and a more dangerous picture.

Most Oriental countries do not enjoy the guarantees of habeas corpus and a trial by jury. Justice, according to the views of the government or the judge, is swift and final. The 20,-000,000 people of the Philippines are in the curious position of being Asian but with a Constitution modeled after our own. Only Japan and the Philippines present this paradox. So the Philippines, while observing their American-style Constitution, have solved many of their problems like Asians.

A rich Chinese in Manila was caught contributing large amounts of money to the Communists, thereby presenting a delicate problem to the Philippine Government. It was finally solved by inviting him to visit President Quirino, who was then in the mountains. The Chinese boarded a plane at Manila and off it went; but not to the mountains; it came down on Formosa. The Chinese Communist contributor was escorted off the plane into the arms of Formosa police. He has not been heard from since.

There was no lack of opinion among the Filipinos on the subject of Chiang Kai-shek. Many believed that the most important thing was to send an increased number of high-class American advisers to Formosa; others proposed that Chiang should publicly announce that the defeat on the mainland was his fault, that he was clearing out his bad advisers and taking personal command. They believed this would thrill the world and particularly the Chinese everywhere, providing the spark that could set off a counter-revolution within China. Others insisted that there are at least 500,000 guerrillas still resisting in South China; that all they need is gold and ammunition to prevent the Communist government from launching any new ventures of conquest. Well founded or not, there was among American, Filipino, and Chinese groups a real conviction that China is not lost and that the Red government has been greatly weakened by the Korean adventure.

As to Indo-China, two different, well-informed people explained: "The reason the Communists failed in their big drive in the winter of 1950–51 was that they made their attacks as a guerrilla operation. They were not sufficiently trained for guerrilla work and that was not the way to handle it," they said. "Since then the Chinese Communists have given the Indo-Chinese Reds rigid training in guerrilla warfare, in service of supply, and in command operations. The next offensive will be much more effective." This sounded fishy to me and how accurate it was I learned quite soon in Saigon.

One firsthand story was reported by one of our own American officials. He was attached to our United States mission in an important Chinese city at the time the Communists occupied it. As soon as the Reds marched in, he was greatly surprised to find that four of his twenty Chinese employees admitted that they were members of the Communist Party.

The Communists are not only smart in getting their people into high places; they are so much smarter than we are in propaganda that it is tragic. For example, when the Indonesian Government cut the value of its currency by one half in order to stabilize it, it was merely recognition that the currency was depreciated and it was a sound move. If a man had five dollars before the decree, he had two and one half dollars the day after it and the two and one half dollars commanded full value on the world exchange. Since inflation and the misery that accompanies it are great allies of the Communists, the Indonesian Reds promptly set to work undaunted. Through every village and every city they spread the whisper: "When will the next cut occur? I hear it is going to be in less than two months." With an illiterate people rumors gain great force and travel even faster than they do in America. Those tactics work.

I was deeply impressed with the need for a genuine American message. The Communists have such a simple story to tell: "You have been oppressed all your lives by foreigners," they say. "Rise up, throw them out, and you will be as rich as they are." They play on the swiftly moving tides of nationalism. To the Chinese and the Malays, they preach hatred of the British. To the Indonesians, they preach hatred of the Dutch. To the Indo-Chinese, they preach hatred of the French. To every Asian nation, hatred of the Americans.

Communist propaganda against America has had hard sledding in the Philippines and the Japanese peace treaty was their first break. They could now shout, "America betrayed you. See

how she sold out your claim to reparations. She's building up
Japan at your expense. Then she'll withdraw her troops from
Japan, leaving the Japanese free to invade the Philippines
again." Consistency is no problem to the Communists. In
Japan they were claiming, "America is your enemy. She has
robbed you of all your possessions and even plans to quarter
her troops on Japan so she can drag you into another war."

The people of the Philippines are still not buying the anti-
American propaganda. After we defeated the Spanish we were
absolute masters of the islands and could have exploited them
for our own use. Instead we poured hundreds of millions of
dollars into the islands, educating the people, checking malaria,
stamping out disease, building highways, and preparing the
country for free government. After forty-eight years of defending them, educating them, improving their health, their defenses, and their capacity for self-government, we voluntarily
gave them absolute freedom. There is great basic friendship
among the people of the Philippines for America.

The Philippine Republic is our great example of colonialism
in reverse. We can tell what we did there in every country in
the world. We can prove our good will. We can prove that
we want nothing except to live at peace in a peaceful world
of free men and women. In every country I visited I ached
to see a genuinely effective anti-Red propaganda program
reaching the people under native sponsorship, telling them
the true story. We should be saying: "You are now free. You
have thought the French or the British or the Dutch, as the
case may be, were tyrants. But now you know they developed
your country and you have your freedom. Don't exchange
your independence for a Russian tyrant. Don't fall for a native
leader who takes orders from Moscow. It is the route to
slavery."

The truth can be told if it is done with sufficient vigor.

Surely America, which has more great salesmen than all the rest of the world, can again convince people that we represent their own hopes and aspirations. We should tell them and tell them and tell them: "We were for the Philippines for the Filipinos and we proved it. We are for Korea for the Koreans, not for the Russians. We are for Japan for the Japanese, not for the Russians; we are for China for the Chinese, not for the Russians. We are for Indonesia for the Indonesians, not for the Russians." On our record, we can prove it. It struck me very hard that for our own self-preservation we should set about doing a much better job of selling ourselves and our cause.

No one knows this better than President Quirino; he also knows that American friendship and a treaty of mutual defense will not save his country once the solid free Pacific is cracked. At luncheon at the Presidential Palace, he said to me: "Before his death our great President Manuel Quezon, looking into the future, prophesied that our next menace was from the Chinese. Of course, he was thinking of our under-developed islands and the Chinese hunger for land. He didn't foresee the tragedy of a Communist China, but his prophecy has been borne out all too soon. Our country is on the perimeter of the Pacific and we see the danger face to face. That's why when I saw you in New York two years ago I was even then calling for a treaty for the united defense of the whole Pacific. It's of supreme importance and I feel even more strongly today than before."

"I have always thought," I said, "that the constant menace of a Communist invasion from the outside was a greater danger to a nation than internal revolution if the government was at all sound. Do you share my view that you, Indo-China, Malaya, and Indonesia can all put down your own Communist rebellions if you are free from the menace of invasion from the outside?"

"Of course I do. We are making steady progress in putting down the Huks and I believe the other nations can put down their guerrillas, given time and freedom from invasion by Communist China. Some of our Chinese are under pressure from the mainland, but otherwise today there would be no flight of capital and very little help given to the Huks if people were not afraid—trying to keep a foot in both camps just as a sort of insurance policy. A treaty of mutual defense with the United States will help us a great deal; treaties between your country, Japan, Australia, and New Zealand will also help; but the only treaty that will work in the final analysis is the one I have been calling for, to include the whole free Pacific. If we get such a treaty the Chinese Communists will never invade Indo-China or Burma and the whole Pacific will remain free."

"We have some timid souls at home," I observed, "who are afraid to go ahead because one or two nations such as Indonesia or Burma might not sign. Would that be a reason for failing to go ahead—would it make the treaty too weak in Asian eyes?"

"I think every other nation in the Pacific would sign that treaty promptly. Of course, Burma and Indonesia have difficult political problems, but I think we ought to go ahead and make the treaty; you watch, you'll find Burma and Indonesia coming along and we will have a safe, free Pacific. It will have great repercussions in the rest of Asia, too. India and Pakistan would at least have a chance; but if Southeast Asia goes they will be surrounded on the land and isolated by Russian submarines in the Indian Ocean."

In my own mind I am sure President Quirino is right. Perhaps Indonesia and Burma might drag their heels for a while but I am confident they would join in the end. Then, though

India and Pakistan, not being Pacific nations, were not members of the alliance, they would have time to work out their complicated problems without being surrounded and choked to death before they get on their feet. The chance to build a firm peace in the Pacific for our own defense and that of the free world is still available. It is not easy, but human freedom has never been cheaply gained or easily held; it will require hard work and great leadership. It can be done if we start now. I hope it will not be neglected until it is too late.

6

Hong Kong

"But must we be your enemies? Will you not receive us as
friends if we are neutral and remain at peace with you?"
"No, your enmity is not half so mischievous to us as your
friendship; for the one is in the eyes of our subjects an argument of our power, the other of our weakness."

> Dialogue at Melos reported
> by Thucydides

THE KOREAN WAR has given Hong Kong a new character.
Its fame as a free port has long been legendary. Today it is the
spy capital of the Far East—the peephole in the Bamboo Curtain. In and out of this magnificent British-held rock which
rises out of the sea a half mile from the Chinese mainland
pours a stream of information as well as a steady flow of spies
and counterspies, Reds and anti-Reds: Chinese businessmen
who deal with both Mao Tse-tung and the free world; here
are hundreds of thousands of refugees from Communist terror;
here was the place where at last I could check the varying
reports I had received about Red China.

The flight from Manila to Hong Kong was made by Philippine Airlines. In Tokyo and Manila we had heard gossip that
the airline was having labor trouble with its pilots, and we
were warned that the service might be disorganized and dangerous. This gossip turned out to be typical of the exaggeration

that flows from one end of Asia to the other. Two years ago the company had had a wage difference with the pilots but it was settled without interruption of even a single flight. The weather was fine and our flight was perfect. In just a little over two hours the mainland of China appeared on the horizon, then the mouth of the great Pearl River and the island of Hong Kong itself. We were glad it was a pleasant day, for everyone agrees that the Kai Tak airport at Hong Kong is the worst major airport in the Pacific. For lack of any flat space on which to build a long landing strip, the British had filled in part of the harbor, with the result that the air strip has a steep mountain at one end and deep water at the other. Our pilot flew around the mountain, banked sharply down the side, and came in for a perfect landing. We were lucky. During the rainy season planes from the Philippines often have to circle the airport for as long as two hours before visibility is good enough for a landing. Sometimes they cannot land at all and have to go all the way back to Manila. Earlier in the year a friend of mine had left Manila for Hong Kong, circled the airport for two hours, and returned to Manila for the night. The same process was repeated the next day. Only on the third day were they able to land.

From the airport we were taken across the bay in the Governor's launch to Government House, where I had a happy reunion with Sir Alexander Grantham, the British Governor of Hong Kong. As holiday visitors to Bermuda in the 1930s, Mrs. Dewey and I had come to know Alex and his lovely San Francisco-born wife, Maurine, and we had all been good friends ever since his days as Colonial Secretary of Bermuda. Promoted and knighted, he was now Governor of explosive Hong Kong, and their letters to us had revealed the terrible strain of the post, living as they did under the guns of Communist China. We sat down almost immediately for a briefing

on conditions in his colony and in Red China; he quite naturally reflected the views of his government, on which we had
disagreed vigorously in our correspondence; we now found
we still disagreed on many topics, but that made our long and
thorough discussion of the Far East sharper and more interesting.

Government House, the residence of the Governor of the
colony, was a Japanese palace. With serene confidence in their
conquests, the Japanese had commenced during World War
II to build a new palace for their Governor of Hong Kong.
They had just completed it when the war ended; its first occu-
pant was the British Governor.

The spacious halls and lofty ceilings of the stone palace gave
it a feeling of cool comfort, though we were there in the hottest
time of year. Unfortunately, the Japanese had chosen a poor
spot for the palace, since it was only halfway up the side of the
mountain and missed most of the cooling breezes in summer,
while their architects had also forgotten to put flues in the
chimneys for wood fires in winter.

The magnificent panorama of Hong Kong Harbor spread out
beneath us. The stunning blue of the harbor, the beauty of the
mountainside, and the fascinating mixture of every type of
Eastern and Western architecture in the city below conceals
as much human misery as I ever saw in one place. At night the
lights of Hong Kong and of Kowloon across the bay on the
tip of the mainland presented an enchanting spectacle.

Situated in the mouth of the Pearl River, which leads to
Canton, Hong Kong is a tiny island barely more than ten
miles long, which the British have occupied since it was ceded
to them by China one hundred and ten years ago, after the
Opium War; in 1860 the tip of the Kowloon peninsula, including the city of Kowloon, opposite on the mainland, was also
ceded and in 1898 some additional Chinese territory on the

peninsula was leased to the British by the Chinese Government for ninety-nine years. This is called the New Territories. The area of Hong Kong is thirty square miles; the whole colony, including the New Territories, is three hundred and ninety-one square miles, about one third the size of Rhode Island—a pinpoint almost lost in the vast map of China.

Another political pinpoint on that map is the island of Macao, a Portuguese colony of only six square miles just across the bay. Macao is a busy trading port and there were many dark rumors of smuggling, of running contraband up the river from this busy little spot where it is not considered wise today for Europeans to be on the streets after dark.

From the air Hong Kong appears to be a beautiful green mountain rising from the sea. All over the mountain are scattered foreign consulates and attractive homes of Chinese, American, and European residents. On the ocean side of the mountain are wide beaches, many of them with resort hotels, while on the northern side the city proper is perched on a narrow ledge of land between the harbor and the mountain with office buildings, closely packed on the streets winding up its side.

Before the Red conquest of China 900,000 people lived in Hong Kong, and an additional 300,000 resided in the New Territories. Today 1,000,000 Chinese refugees have crowded into the Crown Colony, bringing its total population to 2,200,-000. Nobody knows where the refugees sleep or how they eat and live. It is one of the most concentrated and tragic human problems I have ever seen.

"We assume you are making arrangements to feed the refugees," London had written the government of the colony when they started flooding in.

"If we make arrangements to feed all refugees, we will have 300,000,000 before the year is out," was the reply: a harsh but true answer.

I asked about hospitals. "We have three fine hospitals," I was told. "But if we provide hospitals for the million refugees, we shall have all the sick of China pouring in and starvation, disease, and chaos will result." Again a harsh but true answer.

So there they were, more than 2,000,000 people crammed into no space at all, the refugees living for the most part in tiny shacks thrown together with waste pieces of galvanized iron and driftwood; other Chinese live on sampans, acres of sampans, miles of sampans, stretching from one end of the harbor to the other, extended in three, four, five, even six layers out from shore. Every sampan, eighteen to twenty feet in length, houses a family, sometimes just four or five people, more often ten or fifteen, comprising two or three generations. Their children are born without the aid of doctor, nurse, or even midwife. Children play on the decks, jumping back and forth between sampans. Often I saw a Chinese father tenderly bathing a baby over the side of his sampan home in the waters of Hong Kong Harbor, which served all the purposes of a bathroom for this huge floating population. The mixed odors of swarming, insanitary human life hang like a miasma over the whole waterfront and extend deep into the city itself.

The more fortunate Chinese live in tenement houses which stand eight to ten stories high away from the waterfront, in slums, many of which would have been condemned twenty-five years ago in any American city. The usual rule in these apartments is one Chinese family for each room. The people in the back and front rooms are particularly fortunate because they can see out the windows and use the railings for hanging out their washing. Those in the rooms between are less fortunate. If the family does not use the whole floor for sleeping they will rent a few square feet to a wayfarer or another resident. There are no toilets. There is no running water, no electricity, no heat. Even at the common tap on the ground floor, water is strictly rationed, because most of the supply in Hong Kong comes from the mainland and there is just not enough for the swollen population.

"Why do most of the Chinese women and men of the mainland wear black?" I asked.

"Because both here and on the mainland there is so little water available for washing," was the reply. "Black shows the dirt least."

In spite of these crowded conditions there is no malaria in the city. Tuberculosis, the white scourge of Asia, rules as the chief killer, followed by diphtheria, dysentery, and some smallpox. Despite everything, there are about 60,000 births compared with 18,000 deaths each year in Hong Kong—the same old problem of the Far East: increase and multiply and starve.

There is the same congestion on the two main streets, which are wide enough to carry trolley cars and two lines of traffic, and on all of the rest of the narrow, crowded, winding city streets: buses, trolley cars, automobiles, rickshas, carts, and people; men and women pulling carts, people selling trinkets, youngsters selling newspapers; men and women carrying heavy loads hanging from each end of long poles balanced across their shoulders; people just sitting on the steps of shops; people sleeping on the sidewalks, in the alleys, everywhere,

Business space is at the same premium as housing. T. Y. King, regarded by many as the leading authority on Chinese antiques, has a tiny room on the second floor of the Hong Kong Bank Building. The merchandise he has jammed into those quarters would require a large store for proper display in an American city. In many stores with ten-foot fronts there are so many varieties of goods that an American would use ten times as much space to display them. In the back of the stores there is often a little workshop with a dozen workmen carving ivory or wood. Many of the shops show evidence that the treasured heirlooms of generations of Chinese families are being sold for tomorrow's bowl of rice.

No report of conditions in the colony could ignore the fact that, bad as conditions appeared by American standards, it was generally conceded that Hong Kong is a paradise of cleanliness and plenty compared with the cities of Red China. The British authorities have made impressive progress in dealing with the disaster conditions to which they returned after the Japanese surrender.

Not long after my visit, Winston Churchill's Colonial Secretary, Mr. Oliver Lyttleton, paid sober tribute to the achievements of the colony in the course of a visit to Hong Kong. He pointed out that the population of the colony is "over double that for which houses, schools, and hospitals could be provided before the war. It would be interesting to see what the administrators of any of the major cities of the world would have done if within two or three years the population of their cities had been doubled. . . . In 1940 there were 110,000 children in schools in the colony; today there are just under 180,000 and almost the whole of this increase has had to be dealt with since 1947."

He also commended the local measures to increase the number of doctors, build new clinics, and expand hospital services in dealing with the colony's health problems. He had a word of warm praise, too, for the characteristically efficient Hong Kong police force, pointing out that it has proved competent to handle its tremendous problems, even though it had been literally built up from scratch since the war.

After two days in Hong Kong we had to say good-by to Dr. Hilleboe, whose schedule required him to return to his post in Albany. He had worked so hard that he had to take a long enforced rest when he got home. Every place we went he had disappeared soon after our arrival to have a reunion with some old friend of the United States Public Health Service, or the friend of a friend who was in charge of hospitals or American medical services. He visited hospitals, clinics, and public health offices for sixteen or eighteen hours every day. He returned from these forays laden with reports on medical care and health conditions, alternately appalled and enthusiastic. He took home with him a sense of the tremendous challenge to the West implicit in the suffering, overcrowding, and want of which he had seen so much in Japan, Korea, Formosa, the Philippines, and Hong Kong.

Despite its apparent sunny British calm, Hong Kong seethes underneath with Asian intrigue. Everybody is living under some kind of a gun: the whole colony under Communist guns, the mainland under British guns, with the refugees afraid for their own survival and in terror of being sent back home. But there are few privately owned guns in Hong Kong. The law forbids carrying an unlicensed gun under pain of five to ten years in prison and the law is rigidly enforced. A recent case involved a man whose wife committed suicide with his unregistered gun. When the police found it, the bereaved husband was promptly sentenced to five years in prison.

British policy is a mixture of Asia's traditionally closed eye and firm, honest British justice. The tiny thatch-roofed shacks which the refugees have built all over the island are an acute fire hazard; but the closed eye lets them stand rather than throw the people into the streets.

Communist infiltration has been serious in Hong Kong and, again, the British have followed a cautious course. In 1949 the Communists were holding mass meetings, inflaming the Chinese population against all foreigners. Sentiment became increasingly tense and dangerous until early in 1950, when there was a showdown. The Communists led a strike of all trolley facilities. The British let the strike wear its way along until finally the Communist leadership committed the strikers to violence. Then the government cracked down hard; the violence was crushed, the Communist leaders were arrested and promptly deported.

Under the law anyone who is not a British subject may be sent from the colony without cause. It is a felony for him to return, and if he does he can be imprisoned for many years. As a result of this device the British got rid of many of the most virulent Communist leaders.

Aside from the official closed eye and temporizing with local conditions, the British have played it strictly according to their book of rules. They recognize Red China, even though Chinese Reds are killing British troops in Korea. Meanwhile they are spending millions to strengthen their defenses against possible Chinese aggression. There are only 9000 Europeans and Americans among the 2,200,000 Chinese. The government has to walk on eggs in this hate-filled atmosphere and the book of rules comes in handy.

The book of rules is no help to the cause of freedom, however, particularly when it is enforced in favor of the Communists. For example, the British are a serious handicap to our Intelligence. Since they recognize Red China they must, as they see it, thwart efforts hostile to Red China, which include American efforts at espionage and activity by the agents of Chiang Kai-shek. Shortly before I arrived a secret Free China headquarters had been raided. All the code books had been seized and the eight Chinese in charge of the office locked up.

The heavy hand also sharply restricts the movement of the refugees. They are by no means all peasants; despite the poverty in which most of them now live, many were business leaders, newspaper publishers, professors, and other intellectuals in Free China. One rule provides that no resident of Hong Kong may be given a visa permitting him to leave the colony and return unless he lived in Hong Kong at least three years prior to July 1951. This effectively stops most of the Chinese intellectuals from paying visits to Formosa, though several thousand refugees emigrate from Hong Kong every month to stay on Formosa, adding to the population burden of the Nationalist island. A similar restriction operates against the Communists. No visa to leave Hong Kong and return is granted to any Chinese unless he speaks the Cantonese dialect. Since the Communist hold on Canton Province in the south of China is weak, this has stopped some of the movement in and out of the colony by trained Red spies.

Another new regulation requires a deposit with the government of $10,000 Hong Kong (about $1600 American) by every newspaper. The Chinese loyal to Chiang Kai-shek say: "That was aimed directly at us because none of us has that much money. The Communists have unlimited money and soon they will be printing all of the newspapers." The other side retorted: "This will operate against the Reds. None of the big newspapers in Hong Kong is Communist. The big ones can make the deposit and the fly-by-nights cannot." Actually the truth lay in between. The good non-Communist Chinese- and English-language newspapers could, of course, put up the deposit; but many of the small papers were put out of business and a majority of those happened to be for Free China.

Few bookstores in all of Hong Kong sell anything except Communist literature. Prominently displayed in nearly every bookshop are books giving the fullest details of Communist doctrine and tactics, all proclaiming the right of Communism to rule Southeast Asia. They savagely assail Great Britain, France, and always, of course, America. Much of the literature concentrates on Indo-China, the crisis spot of the Pacific, if not of the world; significantly, this Communist propaganda lays great stress on the Tonkin Delta. I could not help but wonder whether the British, in their strict adherence to the rules, were playing cricket or Russian roulette.

Again Paul Lockwood solved the schedule problems with the help of United States Consul General Walter P. McConaughy: we were to meet with the American community at a reception; with Mr. McConaughy and his first deputy at lunch; with the ranking British diplomats and military leaders at a small dinner at Government House; and with American, British, and French business leaders at the home of Mr. and Mrs. John Keswick at Shek-O. Private meetings with Chinese leaders of a variety of shades of opinion preceded dinner with the whole group at the Consulate Residence. In between times I saw members of our consular staff, individual reporters, and many other Chinese and Americans. I had long since stopped trying to learn real opinions from Asians in groups, particularly in these tense and troubled areas where spies lurked always in the shadows.

Shek-O, the home of the Keswicks, is situated well up the mountain on the ocean side. As we sat on the lawn gazing down on the Pacific, somebody casually mentioned that one of the neighbors had caught a cobra in her bathroom the other day. They were all amused at how frightened she had been until her Number One boy came and killed it. Another neighbor had killed a cobra in her garden a few weeks before. The bamboo snake is an even more unfriendly visitor. Only about a foot long, he sometimes leaves the mountains where he belongs and wanders into people's front yards; his bite is fatal in twenty minutes. The mountain was about thirty yards from where we were sitting but none of my hosts took the snake problem seriously. "Why, I don't ever remember when anybody I know has died of a bamboo-snake bite," said Mrs. Keswick. "If they bite you, you can usually get help in time to have it treated."

Political opinion was divided even among this small group of good friends; but they are used to amicable disagreement, and conversation wandered off into anecdotes. One was about a former American marine aviator who later became one of Chennault's Flying Tigers and then a civilian pilot for CAT, the Chennault airline. It seemed that he had been flying supplies for the Nationalist Government back and forth between Nanking and Chiang's headquarters as the Communists advanced. He happened to be in Nanking when the Communists took the city, and although he was a civilian, they promptly put him in prison. When he was arrested he spoke very little Chinese, but during two years in prison he applied himself and learned to speak it quite fluently. Then he bribed his way out of jail, went out on a busy street corner, got on a soapbox, and gave a flaming anti-Communist speech to an ever increasing and sympathetic crowd. The meeting was finally broken up by the police and he was put in solitary confinement. Again he bribed his way out and repeated the same performance. After the third effort the Reds gave up. They decided he was too hot to handle and expelled him from the country. Why they didn't shoot him, no one knows. I would neither have believed the story nor reported it here if it had not been certified as true by the manager of the airline.

A British businessman who had specialized in Russian affairs brought up the subject of the Russian budget. He made the startling assertion that Moscow allots an equal amount of money in her budget for propaganda, for fomenting revolution, and for her huge armed forces. Although I still do not believe that such staggering sums could be appropriated for propaganda and revolution, others in a position to know a good deal about it agreed with this estimate. I have never seen it reported, and of course no one outside the Kremlin can be sure, but it does fit the facts. Five full-scale, Communist-directed revolutions are now in progress in the Pacific alone: in Korea, the Philippines, Indo-China, Malaya, and Indonesia. The cost of the successful Communist operations in the turbulent Near East—in Iran, Egypt, Tunisia, and elsewhere—must also be tremendous. In Italy and in France the Communists seem to have unlimited money and their "cultural tours" to most of the countries of Europe, Asia, and Africa must cost astronomical sums. Meanwhile, they quietly win elections in Africa, in South America, and wherever free government is not strongly rooted among a stable population.

Estimates vary as to the number of "Russian advisers" in Mao Tse-tung's Red China. On Formosa estimates ran as high as 500,000; in Hong Kong they thought perhaps 100,000. It reminded me of Mexico City during World War II, where the Russian Embassy maintained three hundred men of fighting age at a time when there was not enough business to justify ten. They were the cream of young Soviet leadership, preparing for their future work of subversion in Latin America.

Sometimes on this trip it seemed to me that we were losing the cold war to the Communists by default; we are being overwhelmed by the skill and sheer volume of Communist propaganda. We are spending $40,000,000,000 on arms and not so much as $1,000,000,000 on all propaganda and counter-revolutionary activity put together. We must spend more on propaganda and make it infinitely better. Americans know how to sell every article of commerce under the sun; I am sure we can learn, if we really try, to sell our purposes and our articles of faith. So far as counter-revolutionary activity is concerned, we of the free world have just been sitting, doing nothing, for too long. Our present modest efforts must be enormously accelerated to give the Communists some troubles of their own. We cannot afford to leave the offensive to the enemy forever.

Naturally one of the first topics to come up in almost every discussion in Hong Kong was the British recognition of Red China. Here the American view is worlds apart from that of the British. Our own Vice Admiral Oscar C. Badger, out of his long experience in the Pacific, summed it up well when he said: "I am opposed to the recognition of the present Communist government of China. I believe that the unanimous stamp of approval by Western nations of a government so unpopular, so tyrannical, and so at odds with all acceptable principles of civilization would result in loss of Western prestige and would result in the encouragement of similar movements by minorities in other world areas and the further spread of Communist tyranny and slavery among people who basically seek peace, independence, and the opportunity to establish for themselves a better way of life."

It is ironic that Australia and New Zealand, the two British Dominions in the far Pacific, have refused to abandon Chiang Kai-shek and recognize Red China, while their mother country has taken the opposite course.

Both British and many Chinese leaders sharply challenged the almost universal American belief that Britain recognized Red China to save Hong Kong and its trade. Actually, they point out, eighty per cent of the trade of Hong Kong is with the free world. "London decided to recognize Red China on the long view," said one. "It was on the gamble that there would be no World War III. The Far Eastern Division of the British Foreign Office felt very strongly that, since Mao Tse-tung had conquered all the Chinese mainland, recognition, however distasteful, was necessary. No other government could represent the 450,000,000 people in China.

"On the long view, they were sure that China would become more Chinese than Communist. She would want to trade, she would have to trade; and China has more than twice as many people as Russia. No Chinese ruler would for long be willing to be a puppet of Moscow."

The argument was superficially persuasive but to me the idea of promptly recognizing a bloody conquest was repulsive, even disregarding the fact that our wartime ally Chiang Kai-shek was still the head of a government on Chinese soil. From painful experience the world once learned that "you can't do business with Hitler." It should have learned long since that you can't deal with Stalin except through strength. Even the Tiger Balm King had learned that. On Formosa I wondered about huge billboards of tigers advertising "Tiger Balm." "That's the most famous patent medicine in China," was the answer, "an ointment which is supposed to cure almost everything. The company also makes other remedies including a pain killer and Chinkowhite Wind Mixture for gas on the stomach. The owner is one of the richest men in the world. He has homes in Hong Kong, Singapore, and other capitals." The Tiger Balm King tried to play both sides of the fence. He kept his Hong Kong newspaper strictly neutral, having a chain of stores on the mainland and hoping that in return, when the Communists came in, they would leave them alone. But he learned his lesson; they promptly seized every one of his stores. Since then he has turned violently anti-Communist.

The Chinese I met in Hong Kong who had recently been behind the Bamboo Curtain felt that the Reds had made a grave blunder in their harsh treatment of the small businessman. I heard this repeatedly in both Manila and Formosa, but I waited until I got to Hong Kong to check the stories carefully.

As one experienced Chinese said: "The policy of the Communists is to tax the small merchants out of existence. This is dictated directly by Moscow. What Moscow doesn't understand about China is that the small merchants in China are also the manufacturers of China. In China there are practically no big factories to nationalize. The individual small businessman and his wife, his children, his nephews, his nieces, and his aunts make up Chinese industry. They make their goods in the back of their store and they sell them in the front. The backbone of China's industrial capacity is the little merchant who both manufactures and sells."

It is equally definite that the Communists committed another bad economic blunder when they forced the small businessmen to put most of their savings into war bonds to support their Korean adventure. The Nationalist Government had done its best to get the merchants to give up their hidden gold and silver to provide stability for the inflated currency. The Communists had a new technique. One businessman who had been through it in Shanghai told me: "The Reds had all the employees of my shop come and sit with me to demand that I raise money to buy war bonds. They stayed all morning insisting; I in turn insisted that I had no money. Then they stayed all evening and all night and all the next day. They wouldn't let me leave the room and finally I had to give in. I sent and got my last savings and gave them for Communist war bonds. The result was that I had no capital left for my business; I couldn't buy raw materials; I couldn't pay the men their wages—so I had to close up my shop. Then I knew that I might be arrested and shot because I wasn't running my business any more; so here I am in Hong Kong."

This story was typical of what has gone on all over China since the Chinese entered the Korean war. The Communist policies almost wrecked production. They finally discovered their error and are again trying to encourage small business and home manufacture, but there is great doubt whether they can rebuild the structure they almost destroyed.

The Peiping radio has been officially reporting mass executions of "landlords, imperialists, and enemies of the people" since early 1951. There was no question about the fact; what I wanted to know was the extent of the executions and the effect upon the people. Again I had heard many reports in Formosa and Manila but I wanted to get firsthand accounts if I could. It was not difficult; Hong Kong is tragically full of people with personal experience of Communist savagery. Their estimates of the number already executed by July 1951 ranged from 1,000,000 up to 2,000,000. Most people thought the latter was the more probable total.

"In the cities," one recently arrived Chinese refugee told me, "many of those the Communists execute are actually professional criminals. No more than half are political executions. Of course the much-advertised mass trials are not trials at all. The fate of the prisoner is settled in advance, sometimes at a secret hearing. Then the people are gathered together and a group of prisoners is 'placed on trial.' The people are exhorted to denounce them and, as mass hysteria grows, one after another is condemned. Then they are taken out and shot for the benefit of the mob in an orgy of blood lust. Nothing so terrible has ever happened in the whole history of China."

In the country it is different. One Chinese who had lived all his life in a small village told me about it and many others confirmed it. "In the rural areas," he said, "they have an exact formula. Five hundred out of every ten thousand must be killed. Usually they are supposed to be 'landlords' and often they are brought from as much as fifty miles away, which in China is a great distance, so the people of the village won't know who they are. When the trial is held, the people are all gathered together and called upon to denounce the victims. After they are condemned, the peasants are made to beat them to death, continuing even after they are dead so all will have blood on their hands."

Even what seems to be a stupid violation of the most sacred aspect of Chinese life—the family unit—is a sharply calculated move. The Communist-published newspapers of China provide evidence in abundance. The official Communist News Agency reported on April 19, 1951, for example, the case of a man whose son asked his brother to bring the father to Canton for a visit. When he arrived the first son, who was an inspector of the Kwangtung Provincial Board of Public Security, accused his own father of being a high-interest moneylender and of hoarding gold. The aging father was put on public trial before his own son as judge and sentenced to death. The son executed the sentence.

On April 11, 1951, the Communist News Agency reported: "A girl student named Chen Kuo-ching rushed from her school to the scene of a public trial to accuse her mother as a secret agent against the Communists. 'Secret agents are all against human nature,' the daughter said, 'and I, therefore, do not want to recognize my mother as she is a spy who should be executed by the authorities.' She was dealt with by the trial and executed."

On May 2, 1951, the New China News Agency reported that Miss Tom Tan, a student at Shiao Ching Normal School in Kwangtung Province, accused her father as a "man of enormity." She charged that he was an enemy of the state and urged that he be executed. He was promptly brought to trial and killed.

The same news agency reported that another student, Lee Chi, publicly denounced his father, saying, "If a man like my father is not to be executed, how are we going to face the people?"

These are only a few of thousands of similar cases reported by the official Communist government news agency. The most terrible aspect is that the Free Chinese admit that the program is succeeding in breaking the family unit.

The purge of intellectuals has been similarly effective and savage.

The proud boast of the Communists that they have abolished corruption in China was also confirmed in part; their revolutionary forces are not corrupt in the sense of taking bribes, though as they stay longer in power old habits come back. Just as we have heard many reports of corruption in Russia today, there were also increasing reports that the Chinese tradition of the "squeeze" was returning, but as of the summer of 1951 taxes were still being collected with honesty and rigidity. This was a terrible shock to the Chinese people, who had never paid taxes at the rates that were levied. Normally, if the peasant had a bad crop or his wife was sick, he could always persuade the collector to leave him his seed rice for the next year or to remit part of his taxes to take care of his wife. Sometimes a bribe was necessary; sometimes not. The system worked over centuries and everybody understood it and got along. The Communist habit of collecting the full tax was demoralizing both the peasant and the businessman.

On top of all their other troubles, the Chinese people as a whole know they have taken the most frightful losses in Korea. From many eyewitnesses I was able to confirm that trainloads of wounded have been moving into Manchuria and North China. Transport is so bad that no one expected that any of them would ever get to South China but again firsthand accounts reported trainload after trainload of wounded coming as far south as Canton. "Our people may not all be able to read and write," one Chinese put it, "but they are wise enough to know that those trainloads of wounded coming all the way down to Canton mean that they have suffered terrible losses." At last I was fully convinced that my checkup in Korea on Army statistics concerning Chinese casualties was correct. The United States Army has not exaggerated: the Chinese have taken a frightful beating.

Even these terrible losses, however, are not decisive in Chinese opinion. The people are told that, whatever losses they have suffered, the Americans have suffered far worse, that the Americans have been badly beaten and are suing for peace. The government circulated throughout China photographs of American Army officers riding with white flags to Kaesong for the truce talks. As a result, we took a bad licking in the propaganda war for the minds of the people.

The Chinese are a proud people. In the half century since the Boxer Rebellion they had become convinced that they could not successfully fight the white man as every outbreak was sternly put down. Now for the first time in fifty years the Chinese are being told that they have won a war against the white man and many believe it. "Even though they hate the government," a Chinese scholar said, "their sense of personal and national pride has been aroused by the Communist claims of victory in Korea. Fifty years of humiliation at the hands of the white man is being wiped out."

There is no question that a vast number of Chinese did resent the white man's colonization; but now they are beginning to learn about the Russians too. Whether the number of Russian "advisers" in China is 100,000 or 500,000, there are too many as far as the Chinese are concerned. For quite a while these advisers were discreet; they stayed in their own compounds and rarely went out except at night. As time passed they have become careless and bolder; a great many, too, are young men who want to show off, get drunk, and have a good time. Despite all restraints, they are increasingly in evidence. There are also increasingly frequent reports that they have raped many wives of the officers and men of the Chinese Red Army; just recently the Communist news agency has been reporting the murder of a number of Russians in Chinese cities.

Does all this mean that Chiang Kai-shek could win a free election in China today? I put that question to almost everyone. The answers were as numerous and as different as the number of people I asked, but the sum total of opinion of those who had been in China within the preceding few months was that, despite Chiang's low estate when the Communists won the mainland, most of them believed he would today have the support of the majority of the Chinese people. "The good old days" always look better the further you get away from them and China is no exception. Chiang personally always had the respect of the Chinese people and, whatever the defects of his government, had a strong spiritual hold upon them. But this will not be enough to liberate China. Millions will not rise just in response to a landing. One eminent Chinese scholar said to me at the Consulate Residence: "A new set of principles should be worked out for the Free China movement. The people will not accept the old slogans today; if a real program is advanced I believe they would rally to it provided it was accompanied by military strength and a chance to win."

In Hong Kong the Chinese were gravely concerned about the Soviet cease-fire proposals for Korea and their consequences. "If a cease-fire should go through," said one of their leaders, "the political discussions which follow will present a grave crisis to the cause of Free China. Just last week a prominent Communist came to Hong Kong, announcing that in those political negotiations Mao Tse-tung would win a great victory. He claimed that Red China would have to be admitted to the discussions in the United Nations; that alone would be victory enough. When this happened, he boasted, the British and the Americans would split wide open over the issue of formal admission of Red China into the United Nations and on the delivery of Formosa to Mao Tse-tung.

"The Communist leader was right," my friend continued. "We believe here that this ultimate political offensive by the Communists to split Britain and the United States on these critical issues will be more effective than any military offensive. We also believe it will be followed by a Soviet peace offensive all over the world, and when it is at its height, the Reds will then launch their great invasion of Indo-China. That will be a black day."

"Are you convinced that Red China will move next against Indo-China?" I asked. My Chinese friend smiled and shrugged his shoulders. Then he reminded me that only the day before the Chinese Red radio had triumphantly announced the completion of a 115-mile railway spur terminating at the Indo-China border. He also handed me a United Press report which read: "The Reds are now able to transport supplies to Indo-China via rail all the way from Peiping which is in turn connected with the Trans-Siberian Railway.

"Chinese reports during the past week said the flow of supplies from China to Indo-China via Hainan Island has greatly increased. The completion of the railroad followed the arrival in Peiping earlier this week of an Indo-Chinese Communist delegation, evidently to seek more aid. The group was headed by one of Ho Chi Minh's principal guerrilla leaders, Hong Quoc Viet."

We both agreed the building of the spur was an ominous sign and returned to the question of British and American relations: "Do the intellectuals in China believe that Britain and America would split over the issue of delivering Formosa to the Reds?"

"Yes, they do, and we in Hong Kong believe that it is an imminent danger. The possibility undermines the morale of all of us who want to be Free Chinese even though many of us are not enthusiastic about Chiang Kai-shek. You mustn't forget that Chinese merchants do most of the business in this part of the world and they are important in all the Pacific countries. If Formosa and Chiang Kai-shek should finally fall, then there would be only one Chinese government. Inevitably the overseas Chinese would go over to the Communists. We think that would spell the end of freedom in Asia," he concluded.

Unhappily this was a common opinion. A slightly different point of view was expressed by a Chinese businessman whom I got to know very well. He represented an American firm and had a very broad point of view. Alone at breakfast one morning, I asked him for his opinion of the attitude of the overseas Chinese. "My people are peaceful, you know," he said. "We are a cheerful people, too. If the average Chinese has a bowl of rice and is left alone he will work hard, live happily with his family, be a good neighbor and a good citizen.

"As a businessman I was completely disgusted with the Chiang regime. I will confess to you that I had hopes that Mao Tse-tung was a real patriot and would bring about a strong, united China. I really favored his recognition by the British Government."

"When did you change your views?"

"I first began to have some serious doubts," he replied, "when I heard of the heavy taxes they were putting on the peasants. Then when Mao Tse-tung entered the Korean war it began to look as though he was a Moscow puppet after all. When he started the mass trials and executions I was horrified, and every day that passes makes it clearer to me that the Communists are the worst enemies China ever had."

"How do you feel about the attitude of the overseas Chinese in other countries?"

"I think most of them have gone through pretty much the same soul-searching experience that I have. First we were hopeful; then we were doubtful, and now most of us have absolutely no use for Mao Tse-tung. Somehow he must be defeated or he will destroy China and all Southeast Asia."

Among the large volume of letters that came to me at Hong Kong the most moving was one signed by fifty-one leading Chinese scholars in exile who announced that they spoke for two hundred more who had authorized the use of their names. Printed in Chinese and accompanied by a translation, it was signed by such men as Dr. Neynen Huang, Harvard University, M.A., president of Canton University; Dr. Sih-fung Tang, Columbia University, M.A., dean of the Chu-Hai College, Hong Kong; Dr. J. L. Chin, University of Chicago, Ph.D., professor of Yen King and Peking universities, Peiping. These were brave men living in a city teeming with spies and conspirators, having been driven out of China when the Communists purged the universities of all except those who blindly followed the party line. Never knowing when the Reds might move to take Hong Kong, they nevertheless boldly sent me the testimony to their faith and then released it to the newspapers with their names attached. In part their letter read:

"Like hundreds of thousands of other free Chinese, we have fled from the Red Terror in the hope of seeing better days to come. Taking pride in the liberal traditions of Chinese civilization, we are irreconcilably opposed to the Communists for their attempt to eradicate the most valuable part of our cultural heritage. We are confident that the beacon of freedom that is shining in Formosa will one day light every nook and corner of the Chinese continent once again.

"It grieves us to recall that we have allowed the forces of evil to get the upper hand in the last few years and that we have not fought bravely enough in the battle between freedom and slavery. But we are taking the bitter lessons to heart and are determined to make amends. We dedicate ourselves anew to the cause of freedom and will co-operate wholeheartedly with all who are similarly inspired, whether they be in Asia, Europe, or America.

"The Chinese mainland has fallen into the clutches of the Soviet Union through the instrumentality of the Chinese Communist Party. The latter, though dominant for the time being, is grossly ignorant of China and the Chinese people; they do not know that Communism does not fit the objective conditions of the country. Those intellectuals who have received a Western education, as well as the common run of men imbued with Chinese cultural traditions, never believe that Communism can be a progressive influence and promote popular welfare. The Chinese Communist Party has negated every traditional institution, but has not made any positive contribution to satisfy the needs of the masses. It has substituted dogma and dictatorship for freedom. Though the people are cowed into submission for the moment, the time will come when they will throw off the Communist yoke and assert their rights as free individuals.

"However complex the international situation may be, the human craving for freedom and democracy and the desire to make the best possible use of atomic energy for human welfare seems to be universal. The central theme of all contemporary problems appears to be the promotion of a better and fuller life by means of science, democracy, and the application of atomic energy to peaceful pursuits. All that would of course be impossible without liberty.

"After having conquered the Chinese mainland, Stalin and his henchmen are turning the 450,000,000 Chinese into cannon fodder in their program for world conquest. As the United States is the main prop of the free world, she has become the butt of Communist propaganda. That is why Mao Tse-tung's so-called 'volunteers' are fighting in Korea under the banner of 'resisting the U.S.A.' The American boys must have learned by now how savagely and ruthlessly the Communists have fought. Stalin's puppets are whipping up a frantic anti-American movement, which we Free Chinese deplore and which Americans must take as a serious warning.

"We Free Chinese are determined to fight Communism to the bitter end. We shall fight until the whole Chinese continent is free from the Communist menace. We are sure that your recent visit to Formosa must have impressed Your Excellency with the resoluteness of the common people and that of the National Government in their struggle against the dark forces of international Communism. Though we may differ among ourselves on questions of internal policies, we are united in our opposition to the Puppet Regime in Peking. President Chiang Kai-shek is now, in the eyes of the 450,000,-000 Chinese, the symbol of anti-Communism, just as he was the symbol of anti-Japanese aggression in 1937–45.

"We do not necessarily belong to any one school of thought, but we are all agreed in our fundamental antagonism to the theory and practice of Communism. We stand for the historical and cultural continuity of our beloved country, and Free China is the embodiment of our highest ideal.

"We care nothing for party, factional, or group interests.

We are united as freedom-loving and democratic individuals. Fully conscious of the immense difficulties confronting us, we are confident of the eventual triumph of Good over Evil and of Truth over Falsehood."

It seems to me that as long as scholars such as these are willing to risk their lives in the cause of truth, freedom will live on.

The Chinese in Hong Kong have not lost their sense of wry humor despite the difficult conditions of life. One who for obvious reasons must be nameless told me that it had fallen to his lot to be the host to an important American Midwestern publisher who visited Shanghai after the war. Naturally the host did everything he could to make his guest comfortable and, as he tells it, "When I took my guest to the airport he told me how much he appreciated the hospitality he had received. Then he said the only way he could really express his gratitude and affection was to give me his watch. With a handsome gesture he took the watch off his wrist and presented it to me and I, of course, accepted it with thanks. The watch that my guest gave me was silver," he said with a twinkle. "I had observed at luncheon that the watch he was wearing was gold. I wondered how many silver watches he was carrying in his suitcase."

A note of tragedy was in the voice of a young Chinese I had known in America as he told me about his six-year-old daughter, who is still in his native city in China. "My little girl loved playing with rubber bands," he told me. "Every time I wrote her I used to send a few. But she returned to me the last batch I sent, saying sternly in her best six-year-old Chinese that they had been made in America and therefore she could not take them because they were evil."

In Hong Kong I first learned of the Communist Chinese practice of wholesale extortion. One Chinese publisher, I was told, had been waited upon by a Communist representative from the mainland who advised him that his brother was a prisoner and that unless his paper turned Communist the brother would be tortured and killed. It was a dreadful dilemma and he fought it out through many sleepless nights. Finally he gave the Reds his answer: "If I turn my paper Communist, you may release my brother. But then you will seize another relative and demand more of me. In the end you will ruin me and I will never know whether you spared my family or not. I cannot accept your proposal." I was to hear much more of this in other capitals. In the months since I have been home reports have reached the American press in increasing numbers of extortionate demands on American Chinese families. In addition to the honor of being the first Communist ruler of China, Mao Tse-tung has chosen for himself the role of boss of the biggest blackmail racket in history.

I gained my first real understanding of "squeeze" in Hong Kong. In America we call it graft but in China it is part of everybody's pay, from houseboys to government officials. Nobody is paid a living wage; everybody is expected to make something on the side. An American who had lived in Hong Kong for many years put it this way: "I tell my houseboy to go out and buy me a hat. The houseboy, though he is completely honest and trustworthy, will make five per cent on the hat. It's the rule. The trouble begins only if my boy takes twenty per cent, thirty or forty per cent. That's bad. He's broken the rules; he is corrupt and must be dismissed. Five per cent is proper; more is stealing."

Sometimes in our own self-righteousness I think we are too easily shocked by Asian customs which are different from ours but have their own common-sense background. I recall an anecdote about the Burma Road after the British had re-opened Free China's life line after Pearl Harbor. On one stretch of the road a local bandit levied toll on all truckloads headed for Chungking. An American who knew the East was sent down to put a stop to this extortion. He soon reported back that it made more sense to leave the bandit alone. Every time a Japanese plane bombed the road the bandit ordered out the villagers to repair the damage. His "squeeze" on the traffic cost much less than we would have spent to maintain American crews and equipment to repair the highway.

In America we pay living salaries, and graft in either public or private life is a crime. In Asia, since few are paid enough to live on, they are expected to make up the rest of their living. This practice went on for thousands of years before Columbus discovered America. I suspect it will go on, whoever runs China. We cannot make Asia over into our image. If we try it we will just make enemies of the Asians and fools of ourselves.

Our stay in Hong Kong was unexpectedly and delightfully extended by two days. In planning the trip I had been repeatedly urged to meet Malcolm MacDonald, British Commissioner General in Southeast Asia; he was the leading British official of the Pacific; he was the "wise man of Asia." To my dismay I now learned in Hong Kong that his schedule, planned long before mine, would put him in Hong Kong when my schedule called for me to be in Singapore. I was not going to travel forty-one thousand miles in the Pacific and not meet Malcolm MacDonald. So I changed my schedule, postponed my departure by two days, and we met for the first time in Government House at Hong Kong. He is short, vigorous, and, with an everlurking smile, is one of the most attractive personalities I ever met. He, Alexander Grantham, and I had tea together and I was glad to learn that he would be back in Singapore by the time I arrived there on my new schedule and would

be there during my whole visit. The change of schedule was a
fortunate one and my contacts with Malcolm MacDonald in
Singapore and Malaya were among the high points of the trip.

The delay made it possible for me to visit the New Territories, across the bay. Crossing in the Governor's launch, we
were met by General G. C. Evans, commander of the British
ground forces of the colony. Driving first through the con-
gested streets of Kowloon, we soon came into some of the
most beautiful rice and vegetable fields I have ever seen. It is
said that this tiny area of land in the New Territories grows
the finest rice in all China; for centuries it was traditional to
take rice grown there to the Emperor. So far as the New Territories are concerned, the rice is valuable but not important:
Hong Kong could live only about three weeks on its total annual production.

We drove along beautiful paved highways almost to the Red
Chinese border. Then we transferred to a jeep. With General
Evans at the wheel, we scaled the sides of a mountain on a
narrow, one-car road which clung perilously to the side of the
mountain with a precipitous drop beside it. At the end of the
road we got out and climbed to the top of the highest hill,
which gave a commanding view of the harbor, the New Territories, and the Communist territory across the line on two
sides of us.

The British have dug in and are determined about defending the New Territories. With 20,000 troops on the job, they
have recently exchanged one regiment for another which had
fought a tough year in Korea. The men are well trained and
well disciplined; their morale is high and the British stoutly
assert that, with the aid of the fleet and aircraft carriers, they
will hold Hong Kong come what may. I had been all over that
subject in a long discussion at Government House. I still
doubt whether that narrow peninsula which tapers into Hong

Kong Harbor could be held against Chinese hordes by anything less than atomic artillery.

From a police observation post, high on a hill, we had a
glimpse of the contraband trade with Communist China. Just
below us was the high wire fence the British have built along
the river, which borders much of their seventeen-mile front
across the peninsula. Through the post's telescope it was easy
to see a group of Red soldiers busily unloading rubber tires
from a junk that had come up the river that night.

This firsthand look at the contraband trade with Red China
gave renewed meaning to the many talks I had had in Hong
Kong on the subject. While we were there the *South China
Morning Post* of Hong Kong carried a two-column story on
Wednesday, July 25, headlined "Boat and Cargo Seized."
Then the subheads: "$120,000 Involved in Court Order for
Confiscation." It seemed that goods worth about $70,000
Hong Kong (a Hong Kong dollar was at that time worth about
sixteen American cents) and a boat worth about $50,000 Hong
Kong had been captured in the harbor, without a license,
headed up the Pearl River. Hidden on the boat were military
field telephones, shock absorbers, shock absorber rings for military jeeps, piston rings, boxes of photograph printing paper,
and rolls of film. Boat and cargo were confiscated after trial
and the master of the boat and its chief engineer were fined
$1000 each or six months in prison. Local business leaders and
officials were sensitive about the subject and insisted sharply
that, while some smuggling does exist, the colonial authorities
have put their backs into the job of stopping it.

The best opinion was that about $3,000,000 a week of con-
traband was smuggled up the river by one means or another.
That is a drop in the bucket to China, and if it is all she is
getting through Hong Kong and the Portuguese island of
Macao, it will do her little good.

Our refusal to ship American cotton to Hong Kong, lest it be smuggled into Red China, is particularly resented by the local textile industry, with its 125,000 employees. Mr. H. C. Yung, chairman of the Spinners Club of Hong Kong, an organization of thirteen local cotton mills with 192,006 spindles, wrote me a letter outlining the problem as they see it:

"The export of raw cotton from Hong Kong is definitely and completely prohibited.

"None of the end-products of any of the Hong Kong mills are sold or shipped to China. The bulk of the yarns and/or cloths produced, after satisfying the demand by local weavers and knitters, are exported to the United Kingdom, Pakistan, Indonesia, French Indo-China, the Philippines, the Malay States, Burma, Australia, East and West and South Africa.

"Large quantities of cloth are being manufactured in Hong Kong for use of the British Army land forces in the Far East, which includes Hong Kong, Singapore, and Korea. In addition, potential supplies of army clothing for the Commonwealth of Australia, Department of Supply, are now under negotiation.

"The embargo by the United States of America on the export of raw cotton to Hong Kong allows the sellers of other growths of cotton to fully exploit the mills in the matter of prices. Cutthroat rates have had to be paid for cotton required for civilian needs and one of the consequences was that the British Army in the Far East, with units fighting in Korea, have had to pay a much higher price for uniforms than would have otherwise been necessary.

"There is no doubt that, in many quarters of the world, there has been a complete lack of understanding of the real position in Hong Kong. While Hong Kong's unique trading position is being gradually realized and now that the restrictive measures against the export of materials of strategical value has been considerably tightened, it is to be hoped that the appropriate American authorities might see their way to granting a suitable allocation of raw cotton to Hong Kong during the coming season.

"This is all the more urgent when one considers that there are approximately 1,000,000 people, as refugees, who have come here, believing that the democratic way of life has more to offer than Communism.

"If the colony is deprived of the necessary raw materials to keep the wheels of industry turning, these people will be deprived of their livelihood and will have no alternative but to turn to Communism for what relief it promises."

Since the embargo was imposed, there has been only a minimum of official trade between Red China and Hong Kong. All of it is non-contraband and most of it travels by rail. When they recognized China, the British tried sending a train up from Kowloon to Canton. That was all right with the Reds and the train went all the way up to Canton. The only trouble was that it never came back. The British sent a second train and then a third. None of them ever came back. Now they just send the train up to the border, about eighteen miles above Kowloon; passenger cars and engines stop there; only the freight cars go on, pulled by a new engine and operated by a new crew. Passengers must transfer to new cars, whichever way the train is going.

While Hong Kong is perhaps one of the most international spots on earth, I found much of the same tragic political short-sightedness that distressed me so much almost every place I went in the Pacific. Almost everybody in the city was thinking primarily about his own immediate problems. Just as the Japanese were thinking only about Japan and the Filipinos were thinking primarily about the Philippines, so were the people of Hong Kong thinking primarily about Hong Kong. This is a natural, human trait the world over, but it is dangerous in these times.

Everyone in Hong Kong agreed, however, that Southeast Asia was the Rice Bowl; that it had to be held; that the French must do it and that nobody knew how they could if the Chinese invaded.

Strangely enough, only the Chinese had thought it through. Maybe you have to lose your country before you can fully recognize danger. The almost unanimous Chinese opinion was best expressed by one scholar who said: "Unless the Americans and the British get a plan and a policy, all Asia and the whole Pacific will fall. If you unite with the French and the British to guarantee the nations of Southeast Asia from Communist aggression, they will stand. Nothing else will save them—or you, in the long run." This was familiar language. I had suspected it was the truth before I left home. The opinion had been confirmed in Tokyo and frankly stated by the best leaders on Formosa, the Philippines, and Hong Kong. It was increasingly clear to me that only strong action for a defense treaty for the whole area can preserve a free Pacific.

7

Indo-China

To-day you have to choose between freedom and slavery. . . .
For even if you should be so fortunate as to escape bonds or
death, servitude will be your lot, a servitude more cruel than
hitherto; and what is more, you will be an impediment to the
liberation of others. . . . Do not lose heart; think of all that
is at stake.

Speech of Brasidas reported by
Thucydides c. 422 B.C.

LENIN once proclaimed that "food is politics." No sooner
had the Communists consolidated their dictatorship on the
Chinese mainland than they acted on Lenin's cynical principle. Southeast Asia produced two thirds of the world's exportable rice and it was at Southeast Asia they struck.

Pouring down from the mountain passes on the south
border of China, Red guerrilla troops launched their grand
offensive at the heart of Southeast Asia. With the conquest
of China complete, the offensive was designed to drive the
French from Indo-China. Burma and Thailand were expected to fall without effort. Malaya and Indonesia would
then be gone spiritually, the Philippines largely surrounded,
Australia and New Zealand isolated, and India outflanked.
Japan would lose her source of rice, her raw materials, and her
trade area; her people and her huge industrial capacity were to

fall into Stalin's waiting arms. Three hundred million people —more than twice the whole population of the United States— with all the riches of the Indies, were thus to be conquered. Or so the Communists dreamed.

Overwhelming the French outposts in the mountains, guerrilla forces of Ho Chi Minh, leader of the Communist Viet Minh movement in Indo-China, moved into the rich Tonkin Delta. Indo-China tottered and the fate of all the free Pacific hung in the balance.

At that moment in December 1950 the unstable French Cabinet gathered itself together in Paris and in an inspired decision called on General Jean Marie de Lattre de Tassigny to take command as High Commissioner and Commander in Chief of the French forces in Indo-China. Flying halfway around the world from Paris to Saigon, De Lattre went immediately to the fighting front. He found the first airport where he landed poorly defended, the troops slovenly and dispirited.

"Who is in command here?" he blazed. A colonel admitted that he was. "You return to France tomorrow, in disgrace!" said De Lattre.

From one end of the front to the other he flew, rode in jeeps, and walked. Storming, raging, removing commanders, promoting new ones on the spot, exhorting, encouraging, he thrilled men with leadership, with fighting courage and grim determination. In a dramatic appeal to the traditional French courage under fire, he restored morale, reorganized his wavering forces, and the rout was stopped.

General de Lattre returned briefly to Saigon in the south for consultations with his home government and with Brigadier General Francis G. Brink, head of the American Military Aid Advisory Group, concerning essential supplies. Then he flew back to Hanoi, the capital of the Tonkin Delta, twenty-five miles from the fighting front. His first act was to revoke the order of his predecessor for the evacuation of women and children. Against the rumble of guns in the distance, De Lattre announced to the French, the Reds, and the world: "I am bringing my wife from Paris to Hanoi! We are here to stay."

Fighting in villages from house to house, in rice paddies and in jungles against appalling odds, the French held. But ammunition and supplies were running desperately low.

Fortunately a few Americans understood the crisis. Washington had given Indo-China a top priority on American aid and several cargoes of guns and ammunition arrived at the last desperate moment. Overnight, under enormous pressure, the precious supplies were unloaded; by truck, by cart, and on the backs of men, they were rushed to the front lines. The Reds were stopped. For once our aid was neither too little nor too late. It was enough and just on time.

Many Americans have asked whether our aid to our allies is really useful. In this case a few million dollars' worth of American ammunition turned the tide of war, saved Indo-China, the Rice Bowl of the Orient, and the whole free Pacific.

Six months later, at a dinner given by General de Lattre upon my arrival in Saigon, in the presence of his staff and of Emperor Bao Dai, the great French general threw his arms around General Brink and said: "He was my salvation."

Here we were in Indo-China where the sages had said tensions were so great that I should not come, where the tiniest incident could cause a diplomatic or military crisis. Instead, the French, as well as the local leaders were happily dining together at the Palais du Haut Commissariat. Here was De Lattre as a most gracious host, the Emperor enjoying himself so much that he did not go home until twelve-fifteen in the morning, the head of our military mission being hailed by General de Lattre as his salvation, all amid an atmosphere of trust, confidence, and mutual respect.

I had suspected that much of what I had heard and read about Indo-China at home, in Tokyo, Formosa, and Hong Kong was either biased or inaccurate. It did not take long to become sure of it. The only entirely accurate statement I had heard about Indo-China was that things were still very grim.

The government of France was as ill prepared to wage a war here as America was in Korea and waged it over the bitter opposition of the Communists and Socialists in France. More than one sixth of the whole budget of the French Government is even now being poured into the war for the Rice Bowl, where they support 114,000 of their own metropolitan and colonial troops. This is in addition to their nearly two thousand French soldiers who have fought with valor in Korea and distinguished themselves on Heartbreak Ridge.

There are two schools of thought about history. One is that events make men. The other is that men make events. In the dramatic struggle for Indo-China I have no doubt that one single man, General de Lattre, before his tragic death in January 1952, made some of the most important history of our century. He was a French hero in World War II, later imprisoned by the Vichy Government for his continued resistance to the Germans. With the aid of his wife and his young son he escaped a special guard of fifty German soldiers and made his way to England in disguise. He was commander of the French First Army in the liberation of southern France and in the march north in the defeat of Germany. Beyond retirement age, General de Lattre had still another great career: he saved Indo-China. At least it has a future today, however clouded it may be.

He talked about Indo-China with explosive and infectious enthusiasm. Just above middle height, hawk-nosed, with deep-set eyes, De Lattre was one of the most exciting personalities I ever met. Unabashed by language difficulties, he spoke a broken English with much more power and effectiveness than most people who know the language well. Admittedly, he was temperamental and sometimes acted with abruptness. Few men with such staggering responsibilities could be without temperament or impatience of detail. General de Lattre was one of the greatest fighting men of this world and his successes in Indo-China proved it.

He knew the meaning of sacrifice. The son who helped him escape from prison during the war grew up to be an officer in the French Army. On May 30, 1951, at the age of twenty-three, Lieutenant Bernard de Lattre, the only son of his commanding general, was killed in Indo-China.

General de Lattre fought on. He was a consecrated man who believed the soul of France was being revived by her noble struggle against Communism in Indo-China. Recalling the recent death of his own son and speaking with the deepest emotion, he said to me:

"The American mother weeps for her boy in Korea. The French mother weeps in the same way for her boy in Indo-China.

"The Americans want nothing from Korea but to halt aggression and leave that poor country in peace. We French have pledged ourselves to withdraw from Indo-China when there is peace.

"We are both fighting this same menace—this Communism. We are joined together in this crusade."

Indo-China today consists of three independent kingdoms within the French Union: Viet Nam, the largest, Cambodia, and Laos. Saigon in Viet Nam is probably the sole completely beleaguered capital in the world. The only way I could plan to reach the city was by air. As we circled Tan Son Nhut airport coming in for the landing, I counted twenty-three great earthen bunkers guarding the field, protecting anti-aircraft guns and planes, while the whole airport was surrounded by barbed wire. A wave of wet heat struck us in the face as we stepped out of the plane. It was the midsummer rainy season and in ten minutes we were soaked through with sweat.

Donald Heath, American Minister to Viet Nam, met us at the Saigon airport and as we drove through the city he pointed out the way the jungle had been cut back a good fifty yards on each side of the road. "That is to prevent the Reds from finding cover near the road to snipe at cars and land convoys," he said. "Of course, we can never drive out of the city until after mine-detection crews have cleared the land mines that are laid in the highways each night by the guerrillas. The crews go out early, though, at about six in the morning; fortunately the job isn't very difficult because the mines are usually handmade and so crude that they are easily detected."

After a shower at the Ministry Residence, I decided to rest for a few minutes before getting dressed for my courtesy calls on the Emperor and General de Lattre. It was then that I met my Saigon lizard. He was brown, about five inches long, and was busily running around the ceiling above my head. Having seen a few in Bermuda, I was not disturbed but just the same I never thought any form of reptile was very attractive. "I am sharing my bedroom with a little guest in the form of a lizard," I told Mrs. Heath when I went downstairs.

"Oh yes," she replied, "I think you will find two lizards in there. We cherish them, you know. They won't hurt you and so long as they are around they eat up all the flies that get in. The only trouble is," she added sadly, "that they are cannibals and once in a while one of them eats the other. Then we have to get another lizard."

Downstairs I noticed that the whole house was open to the outdoors; even the front door had no glass and was just iron grillwork. "The mosquitoes won't bother you," Mrs. Heath assured me. "We simply don't have any."

Donald Heath has been a career man in the State Department for many years. He is short and slight of stature, with a thin face, not the robust type one would expect to find in this explosive and dangerous assignment, but I soon learned why he was there. He speaks excellent French and his long training in treading lightly where political land mines were plentiful has stood him in good stead in his delicate task. He heads a staff which has mushroomed from a small consulate before the war to a mission of more than two hundred Americans today, the majority of them in the MAAG group.

The Heaths came to Saigon in the late spring of 1950. They did not hesitate when they were asked to take a post in a city from which came daily reports of bloodshed and violence. Since they had been evacuated from three countries just ahead of invading troops and shot at in two, Saigon would be nothing new.

Like all State Department career people, the Heaths traveled from one post to the next with most of their earthly possessions in their trunks. They found the city in a state of siege: most of the shops were closed and bare of goods; hand grenades exploded every night in the streets within a few blocks of their home. Looking out of their wide unshuttered windows, they could see tracer bullets from machine guns firing in the streets. Illiterate coolies were paid a few piasters by the Reds to throw hand grenades into restaurants where French soldiers were eating. Often the coolies did not know how to handle grenades and they were killed or had their arms blown off as their reward. There was widespread violence as the Communist Viet Minh waged a savage, cruel war of assassination and murder.

Two days before I arrived in Saigon a hand grenade had been

thrown in the outskirts of the city and two French warrant officers were killed; but the improvement in just twelve months was amazing. The basic police job had been assigned to the developing native government; an honest, stern, and highly competent police chief was appointed; within a year his force developed real skill. Its sources of information are good and apprehension of criminals is becoming swift, with punishment certain and severe.

As I walked down the main street of Saigon looking at stores and talking with people, I saw one of the reasons for this progress. A French warrant officer, followed in single file by three soldiers, marched down the middle of the sidewalk with that slow heavy gait known as the riot march—a deliberate, solid, relentless pace. The officer looked straight ahead as he walked, with a drawn revolver in his hand. Each of the men behind him looked fixedly to the left or to the right, carrying a tommy gun on his arm with his finger on the trigger.

They were in stern contrast to the peaceful surroundings. It is for good reason that Saigon is called the "Paris of the Orient." The prevailing type of architecture in the city is French, so far as public buildings, hotels, and stores are concerned—predominantly pink stucco that recalls the Riviera. The city has a stately cathedral and one of the most beautiful boulevards in the world, with four lanes of traffic and two wide malls with great tamarind trees down the center of each. At one end is the Opera House, almost as beautiful as ever, although the damage of war inside makes it still unusable. The city also has an attractive zoo, set in the midst of a lovely park and botanical garden, but today the cages are empty and the entire animal population consists of one sad-looking elephant. Perhaps, when human beings fall out, honest animals keep their freedom.

In the main shopping section the streets are wide and every shop is open and filled with goods. Many of the stores are branches of well-known Paris establishments, and for a while as I walked from one to another, hearing nothing but French and seeing only French goods, it seemed to me that I might just as well be on a boulevard in Paris. Then all of a sudden we came to a shop owned by a Hindu and, a little farther along, one run by a Cambodian; every so often there was a shop run by Chinese and in addition there is an entire Chinese suburb of the city.

The Saigon streets today are filled with people, with American and French automobiles, with carts drawn by men and beasts, and, most of all, with rickshas. In Hong Kong and most of China, anyone who has the money to pay for transport hires a coolie who pulls him along in a little ricksha. The French have abolished by law the man-drawn ricksha and the traffic in Saigon is dominated by the little two-wheel rickshas with a bicycle or a motorcycle attached to the rear. In the briefing notes attached to the schedule our American mission had prepared for my party, there was a delightful postscript: "In the event you find yourself on your own, 'cyclo' or 'pedi-cab' is a serviceable means of transportation. The price is anywhere between two and five piasters for the man-powered (bicycle) type and between four and six piasters for the motorized variety. Three piasters is a fair price for a ride of about ten blocks in the former type and five piasters in the latter.

"Taxis are available but not recommended; prices will vary according to what the driver thinks he can get away with. You will find it almost impossible to make yourself understood, even in French, when directing the cyclo and taxi drivers."

There was no doubt about the last point. At every crossing we had to stop, look, and jump. From every direction the little motorcycle-pushed rickshas came tearing along at twenty miles an hour. All of a sudden the passenger would stick out his arm in the direction in which he wanted to turn and yell at the driver, who would swerve violently, with the wheels screaming, and off they would go in the new direction. "The funny thing," Mrs. Heath commented, "is that, with all the confusion, there seem to be very few accidents."

The costumes here were different from those we had seen before. We were getting close to the equator and it was increasingly important to be cool. Most of the native men on the streets wore a sort of loose white shirt that hung down outside a pair of thin trousers. The women's costumes, many of them strikingly beautiful, included a pair of slacks that looked like a thin pair of pajamas, covered by a long overall garment buttoned at the neck and flowing almost to the feet, with a slit on each side running up to just below the waist. The costumes were red, blue, green, and some white and black, making the streets of Saigon one of the most colorful sights I had ever seen.

When we got out of the central shopping section the scars of war were everywhere. Saigon is a great seaport sixty miles upstream from the ocean on the Saigon River, or rather it was before ten years of war and rebellion sharply cut down its commerce. A French heavy cruiser was tied up alongside one dock. It looked almost as big as a battleship and it seemed impossible that it could have gotten that far up the river. Behind it was a troop transport and tied up at the navy dock were five mine sweepers. The mine sweepers are the busiest ships on the river. Each morning they clear the river of mines released the night before by the Reds. In addition they accompany each ship that comes up or goes down the river, to be sure no new mines have been sown. Gun crews assigned to ships for the sixty-mile trip stand on the alert to reply to shelling or machine-gun fire, which often comes from the jungles bordering the narrow portions of the estuary. The naval depot was a huge and busy place, well guarded with anti-aircraft and machine-gun emplacements and a high wire fence surrounding mountains of war material.

The most tragic and moving sign of war was the sight of thousands upon thousands of homeless refugees uprooted by civil strife and driven into the city. As far as we could see in both directions, the banks of the river were lined with sampans; in many areas there were two or three layers of sampans extending out into the river, tied side to side and stern to bow, each holding one or two families. Birth and death went on in this compressed, unsanitary living space. Yet there was obvious tender regard and affection between the members of the family, mothers doing the family laundry in the river, others nursing their children, fathers often holding or bathing their children in the stagnant waters.

Conditions were actually much better than they seemed at first. As one of our own ECA men said: "We've had a tremendous influx of refugees, most of them coming from the country areas where the Red terrorists drove them out. But there is no actual starvation and little serious hunger. These people are willing to work and usually they can find employment. Our doctors report there is little malnutrition. Generally the atmosphere is quiet as the people wait for peace to allow them to return home."

The water front was an amazing sight at night. In the narrow space between the street and the river, the sampan dwellers set up what seemed to be thousands of little tables. Often six or eight people would be sitting around them, taking their leisure while the women cooked the evening rice and a bit of fish or vegetables over little braziers on the ground. In between were tables set up by enterprising merchants selling fried fish or

bowls of rice. Often there would be two or three French soldiers sitting at one of the tables enjoying a citronade which
was an excellent variation of American lemonade and as common in Saigon as tea in China.

Ho Chi Minh has been a Communist agent all his life, yet
many naïve Americans and others have hailed him as an honest
patriot fighting for the freedom of his countrymen.

As far back as 1916 he was active in Communist circles in
Paris and in 1923 the Communist Party of France sent him as
a delegate to the Krestintern (Red Peasant) Congress in Moscow where he served two years as a colonial delegate on the
Permanent Committee of the Congress. In 1925 he became
adviser to Borodin at the Soviet Consulate in Canton and in
later years traveled throughout Southeast Asia organizing Communist fronts. In 1931 he founded the Communist Party of
Indo-China while serving as the head of the Far Eastern
Bureau of the Comintern in Hong Kong. In 1941 he founded
the Viet Minh Communist front in South China and has
remained the head of the Communist movement in Indo-
China ever since.

The French have occupied Indo-China for most of the past
century. Originally they moved into Saigon during a war between neighboring kings, gradually extending their rule
through Cochin China in the south, Annam in the central
area, up the coast to the Tonkin Delta, and finally into the
adjoining kingdoms of Cambodia and Laos. Despite the many
contributions France has made to the area, the nationalist
movement was never completely suppressed and revolts were
put down with great severity. As a result of this repressive
colonial regime, even before World War II Communist influence was increasing, though the number of Communists was
always small.

The quick defeat of France in World War II and five years of Japanese occupation of Indo-China did great damage to French prestige among the natives, and five years of Japan's anti-Western propaganda made a lasting impression. Ho Chi Minh had been out of the country during most of the Japanese occupation, until he returned secretly some months before the Japanese surrendered to work underground on a coalition of popular front parties known as the Viet Minh. After the Japanese surrendered in the north, the Viet Minh gained control of a huge area; they also received a large supply of arms which supplemented the weapons the Americans had dropped to the anti-Japanese guerrillas during the war. In the south the French resumed control and the country was divided, much the same as Korea—and with results that were equally catastrophic.

Reversing their ancient colonial policy, the French recognized Ho Chi Minh's popularity as a so-called nationalist leader and acknowledged him as the head of a newly constituted Viet Nam government, by an agreement signed on March 6, 1946. The new nation was to include Annam in the central section and its neighbor Tonkin in the north.

Ho Chi Minh continued to consolidate his political following, paying little attention to the grave social and economic problems of reconstruction in Viet Nam. By this time the traditional Emperor, Bao Dai, had abdicated, taking the private name of Nguyen Vinh Thuy; Ho Chi Minh appointed him "Supreme Political Counselor" and for a time used him extensively to buttress his own position. Ho often traveled with Bao Dai to convince the people that he was no longer a revolutionary but the actual head of a new government.

In June of 1946 Ho Chi Minh went to France to press his claim for the inclusion of Cochin China in Viet Nam and for more extensive autonomy for his new government. There he betrayed his Communist training and it became more and more apparent that he was interested only in building a Red dictatorship as he raised his demands each day like a typical Communist negotiator, deliberately making peaceful settlement with the French impossible. The negotiations ran on from June to September, when he finally succeeded in making them intolerable, broke them off, and returned to Hanoi in Viet Nam where he secretly prepared one of the most savage massacres of modern history.

His preparations took three months to complete. Just six days before Christmas, 1946, the grounds around the homes of European residents in Hanoi were infiltrated by native assassins. At a signal throughout the city, the invaders pulled out their knives and attacked whole families, slaughtering thousands of innocent men, women, and children. Other risings, fortunately less well prepared, occurred elsewhere in the country. The best estimate is that some eight thousand were killed and several hundred more were kidnaped and carried off as Ho Chi Minh escaped to the hills. The surprise of the attack and its impact were so great that the French were almost driven from the northern part of the country. Heavy reinforcements were rushed from France to Viet Nam and the French finally established control of the principal cities, gradually extending their power throughout the country. Today the French forces are defending the principal cities and ports, which contain most of the population and the rice-producing areas; but in addition to guerrilla activity in the south, the Communists are still in control of much of the coast of the China Sea, and parts of the Tonkin Delta in the north at the Chinese border.

They say, "The countryside is Viet Nam by day and Viet Minh at night," meaning that the government maintains peace in the daytime while at night the Viet Minh guerrillas take over. The terror extends even to the areas near Saigon and had recently become more ominous because it was far more intelligent. Not long before my arrival the Reds blew up a large oil storage depot about a mile out of the city. When police and firemen set out to fight the fire, they were stopped by road blocks and ambushed with withering machine-gun fire. Since I left, a transport has been blown up in the river by a mine, killing two soldiers and wounding twenty others. With the end of the rainy season in December 1951 major fighting resumed in the north.

Rubber plantations are guarded by small private armies and must be patrolled day and night to prevent raids by guerrillas who slash and destroy the rubber trees. To prevent the guerrillas from extorting food from the peasants, more and more of the latter have moved into the villages. They come into compounds in the nearest villages for their evening meal and to sleep. After breakfast they return to farm their own land, often protected by armed guards. As soon as the rice is harvested it is brought immediately to the villages, where it is raked, pounded, and ground. Increasingly the Viet Minh guerrillas find only a new kind of scorched earth when they come by night to rob the peasants of their harvested grain.

Nevertheless, Ho Chi Minh still has a wide following throughout the country and his guerrillas are wily and effective. A few months before I came to Saigon three Europeans who operated a rice plantation about a mile out of the city were on their way into town one morning when they were stopped by what appeared to be a police car. Men in police uniforms approached the car and without warning produced machine guns, killing all three. The guerrillas often dress as women or as Buddhist priests, carrying their rifles and machine guns under long flowing garments. Violence, cruelty, and apparently senseless attacks are still the rule as the Com-

munists largely succeed in their first main objective: to cut
down the food and rubber production of the country, making
the government financially unstable and many of the people
hungry and miserable.

Off the south coast of China and close to the coastal areas
controlled by the Viet Minh is the great Chinese island of
Hainan. It is just close enough to Indo-China so that junks
carrying supplies to Ho Chi Minh's Communists can leave at
dusk and reach the mainland at dawn, which makes inter-
ception difficult. The Russians are reported to be building a
new submarine base on Hainan. No one I met in the whole
Pacific had accurate information about its progress but naval
experts are agreed that this is the base from which the Russians
plan to send forth their submarines to harry the South Pacific.

With forces now estimated at more than 150,000, Ho Chi
Minh has succeeded in terrorizing the whole of the rich and
fruitful Tonkin Delta. The guerrilla terror spreads throughout
Viet Nam with its 23,000,000 people and less effectively in the
other two nations of Indo-China: Cambodia with its 3,500,000
people and Laos with about 1,500,000.

Long before the massacre in 1946 Emperor Bao Dai had
reached his own conclusions about Ho Chi Minh. The Emperor realized that he was being used as a figurehead and that
Ho Chi Minh was bent on setting up a Communist dictatorship. So long as the French recognized Ho Chi Minh there
was no chance for Bao Dai to stop the trend; refusing to be
used as a Red puppet, he seized upon the pretext of an official
visit to China to take his family into exile in Hong Kong,
later moving to France.

While the myth still lingers on in the Orient and even in
some of the press of the world that Ho Chi Minh is a patriot, the
massacres of December 1946 made it clear for even the most

gullible that he was a ruthless Communist traitor. The French, of course, could no longer recognize him as the head of a government and after months of soul-searching, they finally turned to Bao Dai, asking him to return home as Chief of State. But Bao Dai had ideas of his own. He, too, wanted freedom for his countrymen and he did not propose to exchange the role of a Red puppet for that of a French puppet. The bargaining was long and hard. Before agreements were reached, Bao Dai had demanded and received concessions broader and wider than Ho Chi Minh had ever attempted: Cochin China would be included within Viet Nam; the new government was to be sovereign, with internal autonomy; it would have its own army under its own command except in time of war, its own diplomatic service and the independent right to contract treaties and agreements. The French agreed to sponsor Viet Nam for membership in the United Nations.

In exchange, the Emperor agreed to guarantees of French property, as well as certain cultural interests and military bases; Viet Nam and French foreign policy were to be co-ordinated; a customs union was to include Laos and Cambodia, since taxes collected on exports and imports at the seaports of Viet Nam involve goods and revenues of both Laos and Cambodia. All three nations were to have a uniform currency.

Today Viet Nam, Cambodia, and Laos are almost as independent within the French Union as are Canada, Australia, and New Zealand in the British Commonwealth. Bao Dai has won the freedom and independence that all the bloodshed and violence of Ho Chi Minh failed to bring about and his government is recognized by thirty-three nations.

As one experienced American in Saigon put it: "In five years the French and Viet Namese have taken action without precedent in history: the initiation of independence and the transfer of sovereignty from one government to another while both are at war against the common enemy. Of course, such a transfer cannot be completed by a single act or at a single point of time. The British Commonwealth of Nations grew over a long period of time as will the French Union, of which Viet Nam, Laos, and Cambodia are members. Some of us think the French have transferred too many powers too quickly; others think they should grant still more powers; but every one who has honestly studied the problem agrees that amazing progress has been made and that with peace a sound evolution will be accomplished, suitable to the temperament and background of all the nations involved."

On my courtesy call on Bao Dai at the palace, Donald Heath and I were greeted by one of the most striking sights of the entire trip—the palace Honor Guard. In spotless white uniforms, with their pants bagged in at the top of high white paratrooper boots, they were colorful and impressive. As we reached the top step of the palace terrace the Viet Namese Royal Band struck up "The Star-Spangled Banner." I felt a lump in my throat as these Viet Namese gave an excellent, if somewhat slow, rendition of our national anthem; next they played their own national anthem, which was considerably livelier.

There could not have been a greater contrast between this visit and that to the Emperor of Japan. Here we were met by the head of the Imperial Household and before we had walked twenty feet into the palace we saw the Emperor standing alone waiting for us in a room off the hall. Bao Dai is thirty-nine years old, somewhat chunky in build, and he looked trim in a white sharkskin suit. We were immediately joined by Prime Minister Tran Van Huu, the President of the Republic. Mr. Heath acted as both American Minister and interpreter, the conversation being in French, since neither the Emperor nor the President spoke English. They both speak beautiful French, although some time later I decided that the Emperor also understood most of the English that was used.

It was not long before it became clear to me that Bao Dai is a very much brighter man than he is generally considered. He has real charm and a directness of speech quite unusual among Asians. He is also a man of real courage. He did not have to come back to Viet Nam with all the risks and burdens involved; he and his family could have stayed comfortably in France for the rest of their lives, but he preferred to win freedom for his people.

The Emperor loves tiger hunting and fishing and is criticized for it mainly by people outside Viet Nam. I suspect, however, that if he did not indulge in these sports, to which royalty generally is addicted—as are most human beings when they can get a chance—his people would have thought there was something wrong with him. During dinner that evening the subject of fishing came up and Bao Dai told me of his regret that there were no bass in the mountain areas where he loved to fish. That was a challenge. I told him: "Naturally I think we have the finest bass in the world in New York State. I'll be glad to send you some if they can be shipped."

That got me in trouble. The Emperor was so overjoyed that he offered to send me an elephant in return. It was a little difficult to explain that we didn't have enough room on the Mansion grounds at Albany to keep an elephant. I recalled Al Smith's experience and said: "A great governor of New York some thirty years ago was given so many animals that he finally had to set up a private zoo in the back yard of the Executive Mansion. They got so noisy that the neighbors complained and he had to send all the animals to a public zoo. It is a great honor you propose, but I should never like to send your elephant to a zoo."

I did not add that what the average American needs least

of all—and can least afford to feed—is a pet elephant. As a Republican, I was delighted at the idea of having an elephant; as a practical matter, it was appalling.

I was disappointed when I got home to find that we could not send the bass immediately. The Conservation Department said that the fingerlings were at such a state of growth that they would undoubtedly die on the trip. But in the spring we shall send him some of our best bass fingerlings and hope they and their progeny will become good citizens of Viet Nam in the years to come.

At a later conference where we went thoroughly into the political conditions of the country, it became clear that Bao Dai has an acute mind and is a first-class statesman. He answered every question I asked him and volunteered much more. He finds his position with the people quite secure as Emperor and the traditional Asian reverence for the crown is very real in his country.

"I have maintained all the ancient customs and rights," he told me. "For instance, any person has a traditional right to stop the Emperor on the road and petition him to redress a wrong. Wherever I travel, people stop me to make requests and I always try to see that they receive whatever help they need.

"What so few people seem to understand is that my country has a democratic tradition which is very old. The Emperor is one of the people and there are sharp limitations on his powers.

"There is an old saying among my people," he said with a smile, "that the power of the Emperor stops at the village line." He then explained that each community is a law unto itself. The Communists promise a piece of land to every peasant, which they ultimately take away from him, putting it into a government-operated co-operative. On the contrary, while all land in Viet Nam is actually owned by the community it is farmed by individual families for their own benefit. The village elders redivide the land every three years, allotting a plot of ground to each family in accordance with its needs and abilities. This practice has gone on for centuries and has never been interfered with except in the areas controlled by the Communists.

I did gather that the village elders are not elected by what we would call a secret ballot. The whole idea of elections is as strange to Asian countries as the rest of our Western ways. Their elders and leaders are selected by their own processes developed through the centuries. One of the tragedies of our American approach to the Far East is that we have expected them to make themselves over into our image. The masses of the people are accustomed to their traditional type of government and the insistence by some of our American writers and political figures upon our kind of elections has been one of the major blunders of our American effort to grow up to our world responsibilities.

When I arrived in Indo-China I was haunted by the assertion I had heard so often in other parts of the Pacific that Ho Chi Minh would win a free election by twenty to one. It was confirmed by most observers that Ho Chi Minh still has a large public following as a presumed patriot. The people still think of him as the knight in shining armor who fought for national freedom when they were ruled as a French colony; they think of him as an ideal, not as a man and least of all as a frail, aged man who is merely a figurehead in the hands of the young Communists who surround him. In one conversation I asked: "What would happen if Ho Chi Minh were assassinated or should die?" There was a mixed response but one man said quite forcibly: "I wouldn't be surprised if the Communists assassinated him in order to have him as a permanent dead hero and martyr. He is more useful to them now dead than alive."

Some of the best-informed Americans sharply dispute the claims that Ho Chi Minh still has a wide public following. They are most insistent when they say that Ho Chi Minh cannot be thought of as against Bao Dai. The two men occupy different spheres—Bao Dai is the Emperor; he is sacrosanct; he is a symbol. Ho Chi Minh is a political agitator who for many years represented what the people thought they wanted. In any event, today Bao Dai is in fact the man who procured from the French what amounts to an independent dominion status for his country, and as the people become familiar with his achievement, it is asserted, he will get much more credit.

Meanwhile, during all the friction that exists between the French and the native leaders, the American diplomats contribute much toward smoothing out the differences. They say, however, that in the final analysis it is Bao Dai who works out the problems. He is not always available and sometimes they wish he would do less fishing and hunting and more work; but when the chips are down, they assert, Bao Dai is the real statesman of Viet Nam today.

The working government is headed by Tran Van Huu, President of the Council of Ministers. Of course that is a contradiction in terms. How can a nation have a President and an Emperor too? Historically and by definition, it cannot. But whatever history and the dictionaries say, the official name of Viet Nam is "The State of Viet Nam"; it has an Emperor, Bao Dai, who carries the title "Chief of State"; it also has a President. It is neither a republic nor a monarchy as yet; that decision is to be made by vote of the people when an election can be held. Born of peasant stock, Huu's early life was spent in rice-paddy farming. By his own efforts and those of his family he acquired a good education and became a successful businessman. He is a strong Republican, having been raised in the Saigon area where the French education was strictly anti-royalist; nevertheless, he works well with Bao Dai; he even shares the Palais Gia-Long with the Emperor when they are both in Saigon.

Huu is a short, quiet man with a good sense of humor, realistic and able. He sees with great clarity that so far as Viet Nam is concerned nationalism has won its victory. His people are now free. Ho Chi Minh's war is no longer a nationalist movement; it is nothing but a struggle for power, waged on behalf of an imperialistic foreign nation—the Soviet Empire.

The government Bao Dai has assembled includes able financial and agricultural experts. Unfortunately its political base is still not broad enough to bring in all loyal elements in the country; when that is done it is expected that Ho Chi Minh's strength will be further weakened. One of the Cabinet members explained some of the difficulties: "We are harassed by the extremists of the left and the right. The left wing are nothing but Moscow puppets and we have learned that if you take Communists into a government they will wreck it. The anti-Communist extremists of the right are almost as troublesome. They are so nationalistic that they demand that the French get out of the country immediately, body and soul, which is ridiculous. What they will not face up to is that if the French troops left this country the Communists would take it over the next morning and all the liberties we have won would be gone."

"What about the feelings of the people?" I asked. "One man I have talked with told me that though they know the Viet Minh are Communists they are so weary of ten years of strife that they would give up their freedom in order to get peace."

"I am sure there are some who feel that way," he answered,

"but there are many more who don't. The most important development of recent months has been the increasing number of people who have escaped from Communist territory to join us in the free areas. Most important of all, a large number of them are intellectuals and recently many of them have been doctors. A great many of them had been passionately in favor of Ho Chi Minh. Now they are completely disillusioned and new ones are arriving every day."

"What do you do with the people who escape and join you?" I asked. "Are you sure you can trust them?"

"Most of them," he replied. "Just lately the man who has been Ho Chi Minh's secretary for many years deserted him and we have already placed him in the government. We knew him before the war as a patriot and we're satisfied he's had a bellyful of Communism."

With the Communists strangling the country's economic production, President Huu has his financial troubles also. For a nation of 23,000,000 people he has a budget of about $100,-000,000 a year. This compares with a budget of $1,000,000,000 for the State of New York with its 15,000,000 people. But Huu is optimistic. "When we get our food production up to normal we will again be exporting great quantities of rice," he explained. "Our rubber production will increase from about the present 50,000 tons a year to at least the 75,000 tons we produced before the war. Our production of minerals will be gradually increased and we can do much for the welfare of the people."

Before the war Indo-China exported 1,500,000 tons of rice. Today it has been cut four fifths by the Communist activities. In addition to tungsten and copra, Indo-China has a high grade of anthracite coal. The coal is still in Viet Namese hands but very little of the tungsten. As a result of the work of the

Viet Minh, most of the tungsten and much rubber go across the border to Red China.

Of course nobody has the answer to the $64 question: once peace is restored and the French withdraw their military forces, how can this country with its $100,000,000 budget take over burdens which cost the French $900,000,000 in 1951? Late in December the French National Assembly voted $1,102,500,000 as the 1952 military budget for Indo-China. The Viet Namese admitted that they could not possibly bear this cost but insisted that they will be able to maintain internal order with their growing army once the Viet Minh has been liquidated. Of this I was not so sure.

Huu has a good answer to all questions about the future. He is not as optimistic as some about cleaning out the Communists within a year but he says: "Look what we have done in just the past year! From chaos and terror in the cities, order has been restored; our police have taken over and learned the job. Look at our government: from no civil service, we have in a short time already developed a very good body of civil servants in many departments. Look at the Army: from no troops at all, we already have 35,000 good soldiers, many of whom are now fighting in defense of our country, thanks to the wonderful training of General de Lattre.

"Look at all we have done and you will think well of the future."

The figure of 35,000 Viet Namese troops was generally used during July, when I was in Saigon. In his annual 1951 report to the French National Assembly on December 28, Jean Letourneau, French Minister for the Indo-China States, reported that nearly 59,000 Viet Namese were now in the army, serving with the French. In addition, he said that 71,000 French metropolitan troops and 43,000 French colonial troops were serving in Indo-China, bringing the total armed forces to 173,000 men. The war for the Rice Bowl is big as well as tough.

An impressive group of Viet Namese and French were present at the state dinner given by President Huu.

I had looked forward to the occasion particularly because Mr. Huu had told me that his two-year-old pet elephant was always present at dinner and the guests greatly enjoyed him. Never having dined with the political symbol of my party before, I thought it would be an interesting experience. It was in a number of ways.

Sure enough, the elephant arrived with the dinner course. Some eighty people were seated at a long table, the men in black tie, the American and European women in evening clothes, the Viet Namese ladies in beautiful native costumes of brocades, silks, and satins. To most of them the elephant was a familiar figure and after he bowed and received a banana he was a very polite youngster. After dinner he retired to his own special corner in the drawing room. Most of the guests paid their respects to him before the evening was out, feeding him from a bunch of bananas hanging near by. If he did not have a stomach-ache by next day it is because young elephants can eat an unlimited quantity of bananas. He behaved perfectly all evening but at the very end as he was being led out by the mahout he expressed emphatic disapproval of the proceedings all over the marble floor.

Saigon is a hard and isolated assignment for Americans. The MAAG group is the largest of our total staff of two hundred, but the ECA, U. S. Information Service, and regular diplomatic representation have also substantially increased. Penned in a city where French and Viet Namese are the only languages spoken, surrounded by Communist enemies on all sides, they live in constant danger; also it must get insufferably boring to see the same faces every time they go out to dinner or have any kind of social event; then there is the ever present tropical heat, the long rainy season from June to November, and the utter impossibility of "getting away from it all." Nevertheless, I was struck by the fact that not one of them made a single complaint, even in private conversations.

They are a dedicated group; I saw no pulling and hauling among them. There was plenty of opportunity, yet nobody caught my ear in private to put in a gripe against another individual or another service. Under Donald Heath's leadership they are doing a fine job to the best of their ability and they know—whether the rest of the world knows it or not—that in this crisis spot of the Pacific they may be saving the peace of the world.

Our military men get along well with the French. Of course there are differences and of course the French feel that the American Government has not kept all of its commitments for military support; but they are profoundly grateful for the help they have received. They know our officers are not armchair generals or filing-cabinet colonels. In the great Communist offensive which brought General de Lattre to the scene, American officers were up in front observing the fighting, taking their chances as if it were their own war, often wading in water up to their shoulders for hours at a time.

Our ECA group struck me as one of the best I had ever seen. Ironically enough, they had had the least money, something like $4,000,000 up to the time of my arrival. They have no delusions of grandeur or desire to throw their weight around. They are hardheaded, practical men who know the problems of Viet Nam will not be solved overnight and that they are there to be a stabilizing and helpful influence. They have used their money skillfully to provide work for tens of thousands of refugees who might otherwise starve or, in desperation, become Communists. Their projects have been useful work: repairing war damage, restoring highways and communications. They have applied for additional funds; whatever they get, I believe, will be money well spent.

They recognize, too, the very delicate problem of relations with the French, who, as a matter of pride, do not like to admit that the Americans are doing so much necessary work. The job is to save Southeast Asia and to keep our friends.

All the members of the American mission suffer from the foreign exchange. The piaster is officially fixed at twenty to the dollar, which means it is worth five cents. In the black market it sells openly at forty to the dollar, which means it is actually worth two and a half cents. But our staff people must spend only money bought at the official rate; they cannot go into the black market, so everything they buy costs them twice what it costs anybody else.

The American mission is bedeviled, too, by VIP missions from Washington. Of all the places in the world that suffer from little understanding, I would venture that Saigon suffers the most. Mission after mission has come out from Washington to Saigon "to study the Indo-China problem." Of course no mission can ever return home without a solution. So one group solemnly announces that there should be United Nations mediation among the Communists, the French, and the Viet Nam government; another mission flatly asserts that the French should immediately declare Viet Nam to be free and withdraw; still another insists that we must find an entirely new "third force" to substitute for the French—the only force in Indo-China that can successfully resist the Communists.

Obviously all of these conclusions are nonsense; there is no happy-thought solution. The tough, hard war against treason and insurrection must be won while political and social changes are made. The situation is infinitely complex and is illustrated, perhaps, by the baffling medical problems. Without Dr. Hilleboe I learned less about them than elsewhere and I missed him; but the problems are much the same throughout Asia.

Tuberculosis, the greatest killer of all, is widespread. Malaria is endemic everywhere, particularly in the mountains. Venereal disease is prevalent. Glaucoma affects an estimated eighty per cent of all the people. The Emperor himself suffers from glaucoma and also from a liver ailment. He told me with a twinkle in his eye that his mother, the Dowager Empress, had come down to the palace not long before and mixed him a special poultice of sea-swallow nest. "It did me a great deal of good," he said solemnly, "but I think the most good has been done by aureomycin."

President Huu suffers from rheumatism and the Dowager Empress prepared another kind of swallow's-nest poultice for him. "Actually," he commented, "my rheumatism has improved greatly and this was the only treatment that has done me any good." After a number of such conversations I began to share Dr. Hilleboe's suspicion that in these ancient and primitive remedies, which represent the accumulated wisdom of many centuries, there may be secrets which modern medicine should ferret out. One medical group is already studying these traditional medical cures and I am looking forward with interest to its findings.

There is no single, simple solution to any of the problems of this ancient civilization. Of course there must be social reforms, though as the Emperor so vigorously pointed out there is more genuine democracy in the traditions and the system of land tenure of his country than in most of the free nations of the world. Social reforms, medical progress, greater improvement in agricultural practices, and the development of a trained civil service and a strong native military force are all necessary. The gradual development of the capacity and interest of the people in government is essential. The government itself must broaden its base and strengthen its leadership. "But," one American observed, "everything hinges on whether Red China moves in. If we take a strong position we may well keep them out. If we don't, and the Chinese move in, the whole Pacific goes up in smoke."

On my visit to the American Legation Building, I met six Chinese, including the consul general of Free China and the president of the Chamber of Commerce. They presented me with flags bearing generous Chinese inscriptions and thanked me in flowery speeches for my interest in and support of the cause of Free China. Whatever is said against Chiang Kai-shek, he has stout friends and supporters.

American officers who have spent years of their lives in the Pacific, some of them assigned to Chiang's armies in the field, also have strong views. One such general, for example, gets furious at the continued harping on the stories of corruption in the Chiang regime. He says they are all false or exaggerated. I do not use his name because I am afraid that since Washington policy has been hostile to Chiang it might interfere with his service career; but when I asked him about the stories of Nationalist corruption he blazed: "There have been more lies spread about the Chinese Nationalist Government than about any government in the world. I know these Chinese officials and there are as fine people in Chiang's government as I have ever known.

"Let me give you one example. I lived in the same city with one Chinese general whom I have heard criticized a great deal. I knew him intimately and I know that he lived in one small room; he had a single suit of clothes to his name and was often hungry. That man was in command of the services of supply in an area where he could have stolen millions if he had been so disposed."

"What about the famous story of Chiang's son calling in all the gold in Shanghai?" I asked. "Two or three times I have been told that the pretense used was to get all the gold in to stabilize the Chinese dollar but then it was stolen."

"I know that story," he replied. "I was in other cities when they did the same thing. It was a well-conceived plan, approved by American advisers, to bring an end to the horrible postwar inflation which was ruining China, the same thing that happened in a lot of other countries. Chiang's son did call in all the gold and made an honest effort to stabilize the currency; but it was too late. Their military losses in the next few months were so grave that confidence in the government deteriorated and the final inflationary spiral started. When the government left the mainland for Formosa the gold was still intact and I know that it supported Chiang's government for a year and a half."

I was repeatedly impressed by the fierce loyalty Chiang Kai-shek has inspired in so many people, both Chinese and Americans. He is sixty-five now and it is to be hoped that as he passes the burden of leadership on to younger men they will be able to attract the same loyalty.

The future of Chiang Kai-shek and Free China are vital to Indo-China. Even without a Korean armistice it is always possible that the Red Chinese armies may drive south in an invasion of the Rice Bowl. One route could be by the Burma Road and everybody agrees that Burma is soft. Politically it is split into bitter factions. The Nationalist and Socialist dreamers who are now learning to govern the country have been taught some bitter lessons and conditions have improved somewhat. For the time being, at least, they have halted many of their abortive programs for socializing production. Order has been largely restored in the north and military strength has been increased; but Burma "is still as soft as butter" in the opinion of most of the people with whom I talked. There is even a "Russian Farmers' Party" in Burma that has considerable support.

The other main invasion route of Southeast Asia is through the Tonkin Delta in northern Indo-China. The Chinese have just finished building a railroad line to the border of Indo-China. It was quite well known in Saigon that the Red Chinese had been giving rigid training to Ho Chi Minh's Communist guerrillas, preparing them for field warfare. It was estimated that at least 50,000 had gone through three-month training courses and returned to Indo-China with arms and equipment supplied by the Chinese Communists. In July the French were feverishly building their defenses in preparation for the end of the rainy season; in December major hostilities were resumed.

General de Lattre hooted when I told him the stories I had heard in Tokyo and Manila that the Communist offensive failed the preceding winter because they tried guerrilla tactics. He confirmed again my suspicion that most of the information which had been printed and peddled was untrue. "They are guerrillas by nature," he exclaimed. "It was when they tried to act in the open as organized troops that we were able to defeat them. But this winter it will be more difficult and we are getting ready."

With only qualified support from his government, he carried both an enormous political and military burden. In addition, he worked so well with the Viet Namese that the 59,000 troops he trained are regarded as excellent and have joined the French Army in the field. Discussing the fighting qualities of the enemy, General de Lattre referred to a quotation from Mao Tse-tung. In substance, Mao said: "When we face the enemy, never attack until we have two, three, four, five times as many men as he has in the field. We must not attack him just in the front. We must surround him, going whatever distances are necessary to get on both flanks. We must go to his rear and then we must cut him to pieces so we will not have to face him again. Then we can send our troops to the next area of combat. Thus we will have victory."

Generals de Lattre and Brink both pointed out that the Communists have refined an ancient basic Asian approach to service of supply. They simply live off the land they conquer. The Communists have developed four stages of attack: first is the propaganda and supervision group, composed mainly of native traitors, which infiltrates ahead of the armies; the operation may take months or years but it is an integral part of the military operation; the second group corrupts public officials and persuades them to desert to the enemy at the psychological moment; the third goes in with money, munitions, and other supplies for native Communist guerrillas and for later use by their own troops. The fourth is the army of invasion itself.

I was curious to know what really kept the French fighting in Indo-China. They have conceded self-government to Viet Nam, Cambodia, and Laos. While this is a fine trading area and rich in natural resources, it cannot be valuable enough in money to repay the French for the blood and billions they are spending for its freedom. Since the outburst of hostilities in Indo-China 28,000 French soldiers and 1014 officers have been killed or were missing in action by the end of 1951. The Viet Minh hold 5000 prisoners of war, of which 900 are French. The flower of French military leadership is being sacrificed in Indo-China. The damage of this war, cumulating with that of World Wars I and II, is incalculable. Why are the French risking their own security at home by such frightful sacrifices?

One answer is that they are defending Indo-China as a matter of national pride, despite the large costs and the political divisions it has brought about within their government.

General de Lattre gave another answer. "This is the critical fight of the world," he said. "If Indo-China should fall, then all Southeast Asia would fall too. The Reds would knife through to Rangoon and with submarine bases there they would command the Indian Ocean. India would be cut off. Japan would starve for lack of food and raw materials.

"But if Indo-China is held, Southeast Asia can stay free. We will not see India fall. The whole Pacific can remain free and probably we will not see World War III.

"The Russians lost 30,000,000 people in the last war. Eighteen million of those dead were their youth. They need time to develop a new generation of soldiers. Then they will go ahead with their plan to conquer the world. Meantime they have launched through their satellites a deliberate drive to get the manpower to extend their empire without using Russian troops. Already they have had staggering successes in central Europe and in all China; but they can't feel secure in China; they don't know whether in ten or twenty years Mao Tse-tung or his successors might turn out to be new Titos.

"The only way they can be really positive of their successes is to take the rest of Southeast Asia and surround China with loyal Soviet satellites. They don't want any more Titos, so they must get Indo-China, Burma, Thailand, Malaya, and Indonesia. Then they are sure they will eventually have Japan, the Philippines, and Formosa, and all the wonderful resources and manpower of the Asian countries.

"Look at these young Viet Namese we are training here," he exclaimed. "Where else in the whole world can you take young men and in six weeks make them into fine soldiers?

That is what we have been able to do with the young men of Viet Nam. They are part of the manpower Russia wants.

"We are winning in Indo-China against Ho Chi Minh," General de Lattre concluded. "But if China sends in her Red troops—then it is a different story. Then it is for the world."

These words had a ring of prophecy as they came from the great man who was, even then, giving his life's energy to the cause. Now he is dead. But his words and his deeds live on. This struggle in Indo-China is indeed "for the world"—the free world. Must we wait until the Chinese attack in Indo-China to put in motion the cumbersome and probably futile machinery of collective defense by the free nations? If we do, it may be one of the greatest tragedies in history. I cannot understand why this gripping struggle for such titanic stakes is so little known or appreciated in the Western world today. I suppose it is because Indo-China seems so far away, so vague, so small. Perhaps it is because people think of it as just another French colony in which nobody has any interest except the French. Perhaps so far as we in America are concerned, it is because we have so little direct trade with that part of the world.

Another possible reason is that this apparently small peninsula falling down from the southeast corner of Asia looks so insignificant on the map; and the islands below, the former Dutch East Indies, seem even more insignificant; but their value to the free world is colossal. Indo-China and its bordering neighbors, Thailand and Burma, occupy the whole peninsula and extend the length of the southern border of China from the China Sea to the Indian Ocean. In these three countries alone there are 62,000,000 people; in addition to rubber, tin, tungsten, and copra, they normally produce two thirds of the exportable rice of the entire world. As a source of food and raw materials to be exchanged for manufactured goods they are essential to the continued existence of a self-supporting Japan. If they should fall, it seems impossible that the free world could long count on Malaya or the former Dutch East Indies, now the great Republic of Indonesia with 79,000,000 people and immense natural resources. It is true that many of these nations are new in the business of self-government, but they should be encouraged to join the brotherhood of free nations of the world, for without them the whole structure of the free world in the Pacific would collapse. They form the cornerstone of the Pacific defenses of America. And Indo-China is the cornerstone of the cornerstone.

I am convinced that our government must move now with decision, in advance of crisis. We must draw a line and give warning that it must not be crossed; that if the Chinese Communists invade Southeast Asia we will retaliate with all the force and with every weapon at our command. With such a guarantee and freedom from fear of conquest, I am convinced Indo-China can restore order and win through to peace.

It would be a catastrophe if Southeast Asia should fall; it would be intolerable if neglect in making our position clear in advance should bring about another Korea. Both can be avoided by stern decisions now. Action through strength is the only action Communists understand. If we give leadership to the free nations by acting now, instead of waiting for crisis to engulf them, Southeast Asia and the free Pacific can be saved. If there is no action, they will be lost. It is as plain as that.

8

Angkor

I met a traveller from an antique land
Who said: Two vast and trunkless legs of stone
Stand in the desert. Near them, on the sand,
Half sunk, a shatter'd visage lies, whose frown
And wrinkled lip, and sneer of cold command,
Tell that its sculptor well those passions read
Which yet survive, (stamp'd on these lifeless things,)
The hand that mocked them and the heart that fed:
And on the pedestal these words appear:
"My name is Ozymandias, king of kings:
Look on my works, ye Mighty, and despair!"

Ozymandias by Percy Bysshe
Shelley

IT SEEMED to me that I was entitled to take one day out of sixty for pure vacationing and sight-seeing. Only two hundred and twenty miles northwest in the kingdom of Cambodia stand the fabulous ruins of Angkor. I had always wanted to see the remains of the capital city of the once great Khmer kingdom, which had been lost to civilization since the fifteenth century and reclaimed from the jungle only in the last hundred years.

This would also give me a chance to visit the Cambodian capital of Pnom Penh to pay my respects to the King and his Cabinet. This was made most attractive by the assurance that the King had already invited us to dinner and would be happy to command a dance by one of the few troupes of palace dancing girls left in a disordered and materialistic world.

No one could be certain whether a plane could land at the airport at Angkor; the last plane that had gone up there got stuck in the mud and it took a week to get it out. There was no telegraph and no telephone communication at that time with Angkor because Viet Minh guerrillas were operating in the intervening territory. It was less than two hours by air, so we could fly up and take a look; if the pilots thought they could set the plane down on the air strip they would; if not, we would have to call it bad luck and return to Saigon.

After flying for two hours over almost unbroken jungle we sighted a vast lake as we approached Angkor. In the rainy season the lake, which bears the euphonious name "Tonle Sap," overflows its natural banks and is more than fifty miles long and sometimes nearly as wide. Mr. Heath assured me in all seriousness that it was the finest fishing lake in the world with a seemingly endless supply which kept the natives in the neighborhood well fed with fish with a minimum of work. In the dry season the lake becomes much shallower and smaller. It is recorded in the writings of responsible travelers and in government reports that during the dry season the fish congest the waters so badly that they interfere with the oars of boatmen rowing on the lake. This I did not see. I can only report it as the best fish story of the trip.

Before long the incredible towers of Angkor Vat appeared above the jungle. Almost surrounded by impenetrable forests, the massive rectangle of the temple with its many towers, buildings and outer galleries caused a gasp of astonishment from all of us who had never seen it before. As the plane circled above it we could see why this jungle monument to a dead civilization was one of the wonders of the world.

When we approached the airport the prospects for landing did not seem bright. The air strip seemed to be all right and a little to one side there was some dry ground on which were a number of cars with people clustered around them; but surrounding all the rest of the strip was water. On one side there were some twenty water buffalo wallowing half submerged for their daily soaking; on the other side, where the water was shallow, sixteen or eighteen cows were nibbling at bits of green thrust up through the surface of the water; on each side of the strip were half a dozen naked children.

We came down for a pass at the full length of the strip to see whether it seemed dry enough to land. With no radio communication from the field, the pilot had to rely on his own estimate of the strip's condition. He decided it was dry enough, so we circled again and came down, touching the strip at the extreme end; by applying the brakes gently but quickly, the pilot stopped the plane before it went into the muddy water at the other end of the strip.

As the door opened we were again hit by the blast of damp July heat which hangs over the jungle area day and night. We were met, too, by His Majesty's representative, the provincial governor, and the French cultural attaché, who bundled the party into a miscellany of cars and jeeps, and we bounced off down the road. The governor speaks excellent French and two native dialects but no English, so with Mr. Heath again acting as interpreter, he explained that he had been sent out from the capital of Pnom Penh by the King not long before to take over the province. It was the largest province in area and the smallest in population in the kingdom but culturally important because it included the city of Angkor. "It's quite safe around here," he assured us. "Our local bandit leader has recently deserted Ho Chi Minh and proclaimed his loyalty to the King;

he has announced that he personally guarantees the safety of all tourists who visit the city."

We were riding in an old Packard limousine which the King had handed down to the governor after using it for several years. This ancient and honorable vehicle seemed to fall apart each time we hit a bump but the driver plowed steadily ahead, ignoring all mechanical difficulties.

As we neared the city there were more and more straw-thatched huts, most of them raised up on high stilts to keep out of the floods of the rainy season, when there are often as much as five inches of rain in one day. The good luck we had generally enjoyed on the trip stayed with us and we saw Angkor Vat under a blazing, cloudless sky.

It is a majestic and breath-taking sight. A causeway thirty feet wide and a quarter of a mile long leads to the central terrace through an artificial lake which surrounds the entire temple. The causeway is paved with huge stone blocks and flanked by balustrades, now largely in ruins, representing the body of a gigantic snake—the seven-headed sacred Naga. At the end of the causeway, up a flight of stone steps, is the first level of the temple, which is completely surrounded by an open-windowed gallery. Inside, rising high above the gallery, are the second and third levels of the temple crowned by a massive central tower.

The architecture of the temple is primitive. The Cambodians of a thousand years ago did not know how to make an arch, though the Romans had understood the principle a thousand years before that; as a result, each doorway and the ceilings of the gallery and the towers themselves are constructed of huge blocks of stone in rising layers which draw closer together until they join at the top in an inverted V. It is amazing that the galleries, roofed over only by stones which were rubbed together until smooth and then joined at the top, still show few leaks after seven centuries. To cover up the crudity of the stonework above, false ceilings of beautifully carved wood were hung below; these, however, had long since decayed and fallen away.

Approaching the first gallery, we climbed the stone steps, each of them deeply worn by millions of bare feet over many centuries. It is believed that devotees, pilgrims, and the general public were admitted to this level, while the higher levels were reserved for the exclusive use of the royal family, the priests, and the ministers of state. Even so, the steps must have been climbed by countless millions over the years because as we mounted from one level to the next the steep, narrow stone slabs were worn to a dangerous slant. We had to cling to an iron railing to arrive at the top, with its towering view of hundreds of square miles of jungle and the spires of other temples occasionally obtruding above the trees in the distance.

As we finally reached the dizzy heights of the highest tower, we were faced with a new problem. Our guides told us that the steps by which we had come up were quite unsuitable for descent. Other steps, which seemed steeper and even more worn, but with a firmer handrail, were the proper way to go down. So, gently putting down one foot at a time and hanging onto the handrail like grim death, we slowly descended a seemingly endless and almost perpendicular flight of steps. The French cultural attaché went first. Though he had made the trip many times, he stepped very gingerly indeed. Ed Galvin followed, even more gingerly, and then I, still more so. After at least a year I got down. Breathing a great sigh of relief, I turned around to look up. I shall never forget the sight of Paul Lockwood, six feet four, weighing two hundred and twenty pounds, feeling his way down those steps. It was physically painful to watch him try out each step to see whether his foot would slip, put his weight on it, and then bring the other foot down while his large leather camera case banged against his side.

The only time I felt completely humiliated on the whole trip was when I saw the Cambodian governor follow us down the steps. Barely touching the handrail and walking straight down from step to step, it was as though he were coming down the wide flat front steps of the State Capitol in Albany. I guess you have to be a Cambodian to know how to go down those temple stairs.

Inside the terraces, at every corner or turning place of the towers and the rising tiers, are carved figures ranging in size from a few inches to fifteen feet, most of them dancing girls. The French cultural attaché, a fine young scholar with an eye for details, said that no two of the carved figures in all the labyrinth of the temple had ever been found to be alike.

The gallery which runs around the first level of the temple is two and a half miles long. The outer side is a continuous row of windows separated only by pillars; on the inner side are two and a half miles of stone carvings and bas-reliefs which once were painted and gilded. As we walked along, the French cultural attaché explained that there is, of course, controversy among scholars as to the meaning of some. Many were perfectly simple, depicting military expeditions of the Emperor, his triumphs and the warlords and kings he had conquered. The more important the vanquished kings were, the more umbrellas over their heads. Thousands of soldiers and dancing girls are presented in bas-relief and some of the panels still bear traces of the original gold and red paint. Others are highly polished from the millions of hands that have passed over them during the centuries.

Ancient epics of India which are represented make it clear to the scholars that this area of the world had been settled by conquering Indians many centuries before the temple was built. One bas-relief shows in detail what is believed to be the history of the ceaseless warfare between the Brahman priests

of India and outside invaders a thousand years before the birth
of Christ. One presents the death of the mythological Hindu
monkey king, surrounded by his weeping monkey subjects.
There are also representations of the judgment of mankind
after death, with thirty-two phases of torture and punishment
in full detail in a sculptured Inferno.

None of the endless carvings in all their beauty and skill
seems to answer the argument among the scholars as to
whether Brahman or Buddhist influence dominated and at
what period. It is agreed, however, that in the early thirteenth
century some thirteen thousand people lived in the temple;
eighteen high priests, twenty-seven hundred serving priests, six
hundred dancing girls, two thousand acolyte priests, and the
balance guards and servants. We met the successors of those
priests while we were there—some of the 60,000 Buddhist
bonzes who serve the 3,500,000 Cambodians. The bonzes in
their brilliant saffron robes carry on the religious tradition
which is basically Buddhist but shows Brahman influence.

Legend insists that the last Khmer monarch who ruled over
Angkor perished in the central tower. The four entrances to
the highest tower were walled up at the King's command, the
legend goes, so he might die alone with his gods, rather than
fall into the hands of the conquering hordes of Siamese who
were storming the city. The southern entrance to the tower
was opened in 1908 but no bones were discovered.

While much of its history is lost in the mists of the past, the
best estimate appears to be that Angkor Vat was built in the
late twelfth and early thirteenth centuries at almost the same
time the nobles were wresting Magna Charta from King John
of England. It is estimated that King Jayavarman VII of the
Khmer kingdom required the services of thirty thousand slaves
for forty years to complete the temple. Ten thousand additional slaves were required to carry water for them; how many

tens of thousands of slaves died in the course of construction and had to be replaced by new ones no one is willing to guess. Many of the slabs of stone are six feet long and three to four feet square, all having been quarried miles away and hauled by the sweat of men onto barges which were then towed to the site of the temple.

During the building of Angkor Vat the Khmer Empire included most of Southeast Asia and the kings of Khmer—as Cambodia was then known—commanded armies of 15,000,000 troops. While those troops probably were unhappy fishermen and peasants forced into warfare, the riches of the kingdom behind them must have required the support of most of conquered Southeast Asia.

It was hard to believe that this sleepy jungle village was once a city of 1,000,060 people, during the reign of the Khmer kings from the ninth to the fourteenth centuries. In the fourteenth century the Siamese rebelled in sufficient strength to defeat the Emperor of Khmer and ravage Angkor and its temples. After that, the legend is, that Chinese, fleeing from the pressure of the Mongol conquests, drove the Siamese out. With no monarch left to preserve and guard the fabled city, the jungle gradually swallowed up the temples.

So far as I was concerned, the whole trip would have been worth while just to see Angkor Vat. It is called the eighth wonder of the world but I am doubtful what wonder would rank ahead of it. Perhaps it is only the eighth wonder because it was the most recently discovered. For five hundred years this whole civilization, with its fantastic architectural monuments, was lost to the world. Not until the middle of the last century did a wandering French missionary rediscover it, and only in 1902 did the French scholar Pelliot translate the only known manuscript written about Angkor at the height of its power and glory. The manuscript was written by Chew Ta Kwan, who was sent in 1295 by the Chinese Emperor Cheng Song as envoy to the kingdom of Khmer.

The French archaeologist in charge of the Angkor Vat ruin has labored for fifty years at the task of clearing the jungle and restoring the temple. We saw the aged scholar, now in his seventies, perched on the roof of one of the stone buildings directing the restoration work of native laborers. As long ago as the eighth century smaller temples and shrines around the sacred city reached the staggering total of six hundred. Excavation work goes ahead slowly, impeded by successive world wars and now by Communist guerrilla activity. Hundreds upon hundreds of Buddhas have been excavated from the accumulated centuries of rotted jungle and flood-borne silt which have torn at the temples and worn down and all but buried them. The great Takeo was wholly lost to view in the dense vegetation until 1920.

We sat down at a lunch stand across the road from the entrance to the causeway, exhausted and half starved. None of us cared to risk the water or the food at the lunch stand, and the longer we watched the columns of flies lighting on everything edible or drinkable, the less hungry we got; but it was the only place to eat. Fortunately Mrs. Heath, who knew the problems of Angkor, had put up lunch for us, enough for the whole party, including the governor, the French cultural attaché, and the drivers.

As we ate, the inhabitants of half a dozen nearby huts were busily cultivating their fields, driving their pigs, or talking with the handful of underfed guides who stood around under the tree across the road, hoping against hope for an unattached tourist. There were no lavatory facilities, of course, but the jungle serves all purposes.

After lunch we set out along the road through the jungle to visit Angkor Thom, the walled royal city of the Khmers. In the short trip to the royal city we saw two huge temples in varying stages of decay. We also passed a gigantic gilded Buddha seated on a raised platform under a high thatched roof. The French cultural attaché said it was quite modern, reckoning that it had been erected within the last sixty years.

Angkor Thom is nearly two miles square and, though it is not nearly as well preserved as Angkor Vat, it is the favorite of many archaeologists. The royal palaces have all but disintegrated and the Temple of Bayon (the Tower of Gold) and the Temple of Baphen (the Tower of Brass) are in ruins. But the former glory of the city is apparent. Huge terraced areas where gladiatorial contests and elephant fights were staged are still to be seen. Despite its walls, the jungle once completely claimed the city, before restoration began. Great trees are now growing all over the ruins, and roots, themselves the size of tree trunks, run along the masonry and over the walls. Some of the enclosed portions are so hidden by jungle growth that little light penetrates them. They are inhabited by thousands of bats, while troops of monkeys play in the trees above as man's halting restoration wages an indecisive battle against nature's invasion.

Our weather luck held out. The only rain on the entire trip to Cambodia was during the flight from Angkor to the capital city of Pnom Penh. For half an hour we flew through a cloudburst; then the air cleared and we arrived in perfect weather. The word certainly must have gone out from Formosa to every place on my itinerary because here again were a dozen loyal leaders of the Chinese community presenting their compliments and urging the cause of a Free China. Here, too, was Don V. Catlett, the American consul and chargé d'affaires, who starred with a straight face through the comedy of the elephant the King of Cambodia shipped to Mr. Truman. In spite of almost unsurmountable difficulties Catlett ultimately solved all problems, except the ability of an elephant to survive the trip.

We arrived almost on time for our courtesy call on His Majesty Norodom Sihanouk Varman, King of Cambodia. "This is Friday," said Don Catlett, "so the King and all his Cabinet will be dressed in their blue sampots."

"What's a sampot and why blue?" I asked.

"The sampot is the Cambodian national costume. It is fastened around the waist and then tucked up between the legs. It looks like a bulky pair of shorts that end at the knee. At the palace they have a different color for each day and Friday is the blue day." And so it was.

Arriving at the palace gates, we were met by the gaily dressed palace band and Honor Guard and ushered into the glittering throne room. The King was seated on a golden chair fifteen feet in front of the throne. On either side of him, facing each other, were two rows of Cabinet ministers—all dressed in the blue sampots and colorful jackets. The twenty-nine-year-old King came forward to greet each of us and introduce us to the members of his Cabinet. He seated me beside him and we had a pleasant conversation, through an interpreter, of course, since he speaks in French, though he also understands a great deal of English.

Our next visit was to the French commissioner, Jean de Raymond. It is still hard to believe that the pleasant, rather tired French career officer who welcomed me so cordially is now dead. We had tea with him and talked about Cambodia and France and Communism; that evening he dined with us at the palace. Two months later he was stabbed to death by a house boy planted on his staff by the Communists.

Dinner at the palace was in the King's private quarters. Their simplicity was as impressive as the throne room was magnificent. The King was faultlessly dressed in a white sharkskin suit and black tie. The thirty people at the dinner party included our party, members of the Cabinet and their wives, and the entire diplomatic corps, which meant the French High Commissioner, Don Catlett, the Free Chinese consul, and their wives. I was surprised to learn at dinner that the King writes modern jazz and has had one piece published in America. I was even more surprised to find in this jungle capital that the King had a private printing plant in the palace. The menu had been elegantly printed that day and it recorded a beautifully cooked French dinner.

After dinner we adjourned to the drawing room, where we were given a program, also printed that day, describing the three dances which would be presented by the King's dancing girls. The King explained to me that he had emancipated the dancing girls from the palace, so they no longer came to the palace at the age of six or seven to learn the traditional dances, living there until they reached the ripe old age of twenty or twenty-one, when they were too old to be dancers and could go out and marry. The dancers now live in the city and commute to the palace when they are needed. The description of one dance, "The Legend of Preah Saing," read as follows:

"Preah Saing is a Prince charmer, but when he is traveling he disguises himself as an ogre and provides himself with a magic wand.

"Princess Rechana, the daughter of King Preah Bat Samal, on being introduced to that ogre, falls in love with him for, by God's favor, she sees him in his real appearance, with a golden complexion. She hands him flowers as a token of her love.

"On receiving those flowers, the ogre is very pleased and comes near her, but the Princess, losing her first vision of him and beholding him as an ogre, gets frightened, is much disappointed and weeps so much that she falls unconscious.

"Lest the Princess die, the ogre drops his disguise to comfort her.

"When the Princess recovers from her fainting fit she sees Preah Saing as he really is and feels a great joy.

"The Prince and the Princess marry."

The headdresses and many of the costumes of the dancing girls were identical with those of the carved figures I had seen earlier in the day on the walls of the temple of Angkor Vat. Clothed from neck to heels, the girls moved slowly around the room accompanied by a hidden orchestra playing on stringed instruments music which to my Western ears bore not even a purely coincidental resemblance to either tune or rhythm. The principal feature of the Cambodian dancing art appeared to me to be the ability to turn on one foot, holding the other leg bent at right angles while feet, toes, and fingers tell the story.

The King is well educated and a charming host. It was greatly to his own surprise that he succeeded to the crown because at the death of his predecessor his uncle was regarded by many as the logical successor. But in Cambodia the crown is not hereditary, passing to whichever male is named by the royal family conference. The uncle was passed over and the present King was selected. This absolute monarch over 3,500,000 people is a modern-minded young man who insists that his kingdom be a constitutional monarchy, having ordered the first election in the history of Cambodia in 1947. From all reports the campaign was unique. The natives in the Cambodian jungle had never heard of elections but when the King called for one they were obedient and agreed to vote. Many of the candidates raised their campaign funds by traveling through the jungle selling ballots to the illiterate natives who wished to obey the royal command to vote.

The results were disastrous and the King finally had to dissolve the new Parliament. The young monarch is not only pleasant, however, but persistent: he ordered a new election in 1951. While I was there he was engaged in active electioneering. Since this was an entirely new wrinkle to me to see a King campaigning in an election, I asked him what he was saying in his speeches to the people. "I tell them that Communism has nothing to offer that we do not have in our country," His Majesty replied. "I tell them that we have more land than any man can farm. I point out that any man can mark out his own land up to twenty acres, clear it of jungle, and have the finest land in the world."

"How does he pay for the land?" I asked.

"He doesn't have to pay for the land. He simply has to register the land with the tax assessor and pay a small tax. Then he can use it as long as he pays his taxes. Twenty acres is more than any man can farm alone but if he clears that much it will be enough to support him and several other families."

The King's confidence was justified. When the Cambodian Minister to the United States called upon me in this country some weeks later he told me that the Parliament was a very good one. I shudder to think, however, what may happen when the Communists organize to win an election in Cambodia. They are now principally engaged in guerrilla activity, trying with some success to starve out the government by reducing production, making highway transport unsafe, and cutting some areas off entirely from tax collections.

As a result the little kingdom is having its troubles. It used to be a heavy exporter of rice, pepper, dried fish, and fish brine. Today its exports are sharply reduced as a result of guerrilla sabotage. Eighty per cent of the arable land of Cambodia is still in jungle. This fertile and relatively undeveloped region on the southern rim of crowded China is a natural target for the land-hungry millions to the north. Cambodians wonder how long the Chinese Reds will resist the temptation to move in. They are also afraid that if the French should withdraw their troops after peace is restored the more numerous Viet Namese might decide to swallow up Cambodia and Laos. If this should happen the fate of Angkor Vat might be re-enacted in our own times; so the French remain quite welcome at Pnom Penh.

The vital need of this little jungle kingdom is, of course, better political leadership, but that is not unique; it is true of the whole world. For humanity's sake, I hope that there will always be room in this dreadfully serious world for the sort of place where the members of the Cabinet change the color of their sampots every day of the week.

9

Malaya

To meet the challenge of Communism, Democracy must learn to improve its own way of life along its own lines by its own choice. . . . There must be equal freedom and opportunity for all of whatever race, class or creed and the Government must take root in the life of the people. The best fortress for the Government is to be found in the love of the people, whose confidence and willing cooperation must be won.

From an address by Dato Tan Cheng Lock, president of the Malayan Chinese Association, October 1949

ON AUGUST 3, 1948, Malcolm MacDonald made his dramatic broadcast from his official residence in the palace at Bukit Serene. Only a few months earlier the Communist bandits had officially set up their Politburo in the jungles of Malaya, announcing to the world that on August 3 they would occupy Bukit Serene in the State of Johore, Malaya, across the Straits from Singapore. In a broadcast to Malaya and all Southeast Asia, MacDonald hurled his defiance and taunted the Reds on the failure of their timetable. As Commissioner General for the United Kingdom in Southeast Asia he announced to his millions of listeners that he was broadcasting from his palace because the Russian commissar who had been scheduled to make the broadcast was absent by reason of circumstances entirely beyond the commissar's control.

While Bukit Serene has yet to be occupied, the Red challenge continues in Malaya and has settled down to a savage war of attrition by a handful of guerrillas who have thus far succeeded in defying the whole British Empire.

The guerrillas—or bandits as they are always called in Malaya —are members of the Communist Malayan Races Liberation Army. The best estimate is that the bandits deliberately keep their fighting strength at about 4000, divided into ten regiments of 400 men apiece. They are supported by the Min Yuen, the underground Communist party in Malaya. If a thousand bandits are killed, there seem always to be a thousand more to take their places. Operating under rigid Communist discipline in small bands in the jungle, their numbers appear to be limited only by the amount of guns and ammunition available. Striking out from their mobile camps in the jungle and then quickly disappearing, these 4000 bandits have harried and baffled a force of nearly 150,000 British troops, police, and local guards. In August 1951 casualties at the end of three years of what the government calls "The Emergency" had already totaled more than 8000 in killed and wounded, about evenly divided on both sides.

The Communists have thus far failed in their customary first objective of wrecking the economy of the country. Malaya's production in 1951 was the highest in its history, with exports considerably exceeding imports. In that year this tiny area produced the largest volume of dollar-earning exports in the whole British Empire. This long narrow tongue of land hangs down from Thailand at the bottom of Southeast Asia, ending in the British Crown Colony island of Singapore. Five million people live in the nine Federated States of Malaya, which has a total area of fifty thousand square miles, about the size of the State of New York. Snuggled along the shore at the end of the peninsula is the island fortress of Singapore, barely twenty-seven miles long and fourteen miles wide.

If America is a melting pot, Malaya and Singapore are crucibles. Here is a mixture not only of national origins but of racial, ethnological, and religious groups which presents one of the most baffling complexes in the world today. While each of the nine sultans who have nominal rule over the Federated States of the Malay Peninsula is a Malayan Moslem, only forty-five per cent of the population are Malays, an almost equal number are Chinese, and the remainder is made up of a scattering of Indians, Europeans, and Americans. Singapore itself has very few Malays; out of a population of 1,000,000, more than 800,000 are Chinese with the remaining 200,000 from Malaya, India, Europe, America, and Indonesia.

The Acting American Consul General, John Goodyear, had arranged a reception for us on the afternoon of our postponed arrival. Out of the 250 people who were invited, four were in London and 246 were present. The reception was about to start by the time our plane from Saigon fought the last of the head winds and landed at the Singapore airport, so I hurried off to change at Government House, where Paul Lockwood and I were to be the guests of the Governor General, Sir Franklin and Lady Gimson.

The reception turned out to be unusually pleasant despite the temperature, which was about a hundred degrees in the shade. Every race, color, and creed was represented: Malay, Chinese, Indian, American officials and businessmen, my host and hostess, Malcolm MacDonald and his wife, as well as British businessmen, representatives of a number of Asian Governments, and the French consul general. I had a chance to visit with nearly everyone and found a number of people who knew many of my friends at home.

The subject of rubber and tin prices came up almost immediately and that hottest of controversial issues in Singapore was underfoot during the entire visit. At a press conference the next morning, the reporters asked a great many questions about conditions in Japan, Korea, Formosa, and Indo-China which I answered quite fully for at least three quarters of an hour; however, the only report of the press conference in the local papers the following day was the front-page news that I had said I would be glad to meet with the rubber and tin producers. Nothing else seemed as important as the American Government's fight to lower rubber and tin prices, which was bitterly resented in Singapore.

I was happy to get back to Government House after the reception, wringing wet and exhausted from a day that had started in Pnom Penh at six in the morning. My Singapore home was situated on top of a hill in the walled and guarded government compound, built in the days when a structure of imposing size symbolized to the world the might of the British Empire. In size and architecture it resembles the Metropolitan Museum of Art on Fifth Avenue in New York and seems quite as spacious inside. One entire wing is devoted to guest rooms; mine was perhaps twenty by fifty feet with ceilings that seemed to be at least eighteen feet high. One corner was glass-enclosed and contained a bed and an excellent air-conditioning machine, so excellent that the stream of cold air it gave off was too much for my tropic-thinned blood. After letting the machine run for a couple of hours that night, I turned it off and opened the door. That raised another problem because for the rest of the night I was the happy hunting ground for what seemed to be all the mosquitoes in Singapore.

The white people who live in that part of the world have an amazing nonchalance about mosquitoes. British and American alike, they will look you straight in the eye and give solemn assurances that there are no mosquitoes whatsoever. Because of the continuous heat in this area, which sits almost on the equator, the houses are almost completely open. Birds and mosquitoes fly in and out, becoming quite disconcerting at dinner sometimes; everybody admits that the birds are there but never the mosquitoes. I had the same experience on Formosa, and at the state dinners in Saigon I had the impression I was being eaten alive. After mentioning it once or twice during the trip I decided that the subject was not worth discussing. Nobody understood what I was talking about. Apparently a nice fresh corn-fed American is fair game for the mosquitoes, but after he has been there for a while they no longer take any interest in him. Until then, a good insect repellent is a necessity.

After church on Sunday I spent the rest of the day with Malcolm MacDonald at Bukit Serene. This oriental palace is situated about twenty miles away from Government House across the causeway which joins Singapore with the mainland. Atop a hill overlooking the harbor, its front terrace commands one of the most beautiful views I have ever seen. By this time I had concluded that all harbors are beautiful and had given up trying to decide which was the loveliest.

The palace itself is about a block long. The ground floor includes spacious entrance halls housing Malcolm MacDonald's priceless collection of Asian paintings and objets d'art. A tower at one end looks down on the whole scene on the landward side, including a swimming pool seventy-five feet in length, with tiled terraces and an attractive recreation house. The palace was built by the Sultan of Johore for his Scottish wife. Betraying an attitude entirely inconsistent with traditional Scottish thrift, she divorced him before she could ever occupy the palace. As a result, the Sultan has rented it to the British Government for the use of the Commissioner General of the United Kingdom for Southeast Asia, who happens also to be a Scot.

Here lived the man I had changed my original route to meet and then postponed my schedule in Hong Kong in order not to miss. At the age of fifty, Malcolm MacDonald had spent most of his life in public service. A member of Parliament from 1929 to 1945, he had served as parliamentary Undersecretary of the Dominions, Secretary of State for Dominion Affairs, Secretary of State for Colonies and Minister of Health in Winston Churchill's wartime coalition Cabinet until he went to Canada as British High Commissioner from 1941 to 1946. In Canada he met and married a beautiful Canadian girl whose first husband had been killed in action. As Commissioner General, Malcolm MacDonald holds a rank equivalent to that of Cabinet minister. Although he has no administrative duties, he has broad policy-making and advisory functions in the British territories of Malaya, Singapore, North Borneo, Sarawak, and Brunei. He also advises the British Government on policy for the whole area stretching through Burma, Thailand, and Indo-China up to Hong Kong and down to Indonesia. He is called by many "the wise man of Asia." As is most unusual in such cases, he lives up to his reputation. He is the son of Ramsay MacDonald, the late Labor Prime Minister of Great Britain.

Malcolm MacDonald is completely informal and friendly in manner. With an easy, spontaneous grin and a nature which makes him like people for their own sakes, it is not hard to understand why he came up the British public service ladder so far and so fast.

This Sunday a swimming party and luncheon had been arranged long before I changed my schedule, so I was just an extra guest at Bukit Serene. The other eighteen or twenty guests were Chinese friends of the Commissioner General whom he had invited for a social afternoon. They were a group of close friends, husbands and wives, some of them with their children along. All spoke perfect English and it was a great treat to me to have a chance to relax, get a swim, sunbathe, and have luncheon on a purely social basis without any talk of wars and politics or even the price of tin. After lunch everyone had a siesta but I forwent a nap to enjoy the rare privilege of reading a New York newspaper for the second time in the month since I had left home. Never have I felt so cut off from news of the world and I realized once again how provincial we all get in our newspaper-reading habits. It is so hard to get the news out of newspapers to which one is not accustomed, particularly in foreign countries.

After the guests had left Malcolm MacDonald and I sat on the terrace and talked for a couple of hours in the calm of a late summer afternoon as we watched the glory of the setting sun in a cloudless sky over the bay. Mrs. MacDonald and Paul Lockwood joined us for dinner, after which the Commissioner General and I continued talking far into the evening. He is a wise man with a fine sense of balance, recognizing that certainty is unattainable in politics—that there are no blacks or whites in the incredible complexities of Asia; as in the best Chinese paintings, there are only various shades of gray, with only a fleck of red or gold.

If the British should suddenly give dominion status to Singapore and Malaya and withdraw their troops, both would unquestionably fall to the Reds; but the status quo is equally intolerable. If the free world continues on the defensive, it cannot survive. The law of life is change and motion. Our problem, as leaders of the free world, is to take command of the change and make it good; make it creative and evolutionary. Change can also come too fast; Burma is an example. There nationalism was so intense that, with no preparation for self-government at all, they insisted on breaking all ties with the British Crown and achieving immediate independence. They have since paid a terrible price in economic dislocation, hunger, warfare, destruction, and chaos.

I was pleased to find that everyone in Singapore shared my great admiration for General de Lattre and his miraculous skill in rebuilding the French defenses of Indo-China at a time when they were in a state of collapse. It was interesting that the fiery and determined De Lattre and the calm, philosophical MacDonald shared a mutual high respect and warm personal regard for each other.

It was during this evening that Malcolm MacDonald proposed that we fly up to see the conditions of jungle warfare in Malaya the next day. A telephone call arranged for the RAF plane and early next morning we took off from Singapore for Kuala Lumpur, the capital of Malaya. The British brigadier in charge of operations against the bandits in the south rode in the seat opposite mine and told me of his problems on the flight up. He is fighting an invisible enemy who strikes in the dark and disappears into the jungle. It is like the forest warfare with the Indians in colonial days in America. The Red bandits are battle-hardened and jungle-trained, elusive and wily. As in the Philippines and Indo-China, they started as a guerrilla force to fight the occupying Japanese in World War II with arms and supplies dropped to them by the British and Americans; they developed their hit-and-run guerrilla tactics in the hard school of jungle warfare, where they had to be faster and quicker than the Japanese troops to stay alive.

The Japanese occupation also drove an estimated 500,000 Chinese from Singapore and the other cities of Malaya to the fringes of the jungle. There, with their families, they sought refuge from the Japanese and scratched out an existence as squatters on the land. Far from the cities or villages where the police guard could protect them, they were easy prey for the Communist guerrillas after the war. By a combination of propaganda and force, the guerrillas extorted from the squatters the food, money, and other supplies needed to continue their warfare against the government.

When it became plain that the usual military and police operations were futile in exterminating the bandits, the British sent in a distinguished soldier as director of operations in Malaya, Lieutenant General Sir Harold Briggs. A veteran of many years' service in India and of three years in the Burma campaign, General Briggs evolved what is now known as the Briggs Plan, designed to tackle both the social and the military problems. First the military was organized in camps scattered at strategic points, from which they could engage in reconnaissance and pursue the bandits whenever they appeared. Second, the police posts were more widely scattered throughout the state to work in complete co-operation with the military out of a central headquarters. Third, the bandits were to be gradually starved out and their political support withdrawn by removing the Chinese squatters and the scattered jungle communities into central compounds. This was a gigantic operation. It involved the wholesale transplanting of a half million people scattered throughout all Malaya. The program was in full force while I was there, with new schools, new facilities, and a sense of security which they had never enjoyed before.

Small communities were enlarged by building thousands of homes at government expense; then the village was surrounded by barbed wire to keep out the bandits and their agents. Once the village was completed, the government forces visited the squatters in the area and "invited" them to move into their new homes in the village. In the beginning some were not too happy, but once they found themselves in better homes, protected from the nightly fear of Communist visitations, the atmosphere improved greatly. In addition to the 4000 armed bandits, there are estimated to be at least 10,000 members of the Communist Party in Malaya who are active and successful propagandists. It is supposed that there are some Reds in every village, but as the squatters find security and protection in the villages at night, going back and forth to farm their fields under armed convoys in the daytime, their confidence has increased and the effectiveness of Communist propaganda has diminished. Still, there were many who were willing to carry food out of the villages to the bandits. While I was there the British were launching a new system of controls over the food supply in the villages, limiting the number of stores where food could be handled, and making inspections to prevent the smuggling of supplies to the guerrillas.

The Briggs Plan was working. Three hundred thousand out of 500,000 Chinese squatters had already been removed into protected villages when I was there and it was expected that the balance of this vast human transplantation would be finished within a few months. The plan was hurting the Reds. The best evidence of this was that the Communists shifted their efforts to get food and supplies from the squatters and went after the rubber plantation workers. As a result the rubber plantations were also compelled to bring their employees into compounds, in addition to maintaining armed guards for the protection of their employees and their rubber trees.

There was one other facet to the Briggs Plan: a substantial reward was offered for the capture of any bandit, dead or alive. While we were in Singapore there was considerable grim amusement about a Chinese wife who had just turned in her own husband, an important guerrilla leader. Without inquiring as to the domestic difficulties which motivated the lady's action, the British paid the reward and prepared to bring the bandit leader to trial. Even in the midst of this desperate struggle the British have maintained civil liberties and no one is condemned except upon evidence establishing his guilt beyond a reasonable doubt.

As we flew from Singapore to Kuala Lumpur we could see the dense and impenetrable tropical jungle covering the mountains which run down the center of Malaya. The mountains are flanked by cleared land along each coast, rich areas which yield rice, coconuts, tapioca, sugar, copra, palm oil, pineapples, tea, yams, and bananas. The rubber plantations, with row upon row of trees on the many thousands of acres, make Malaya unique in the world. For here in this small area is grown almost exactly one half of the rubber supply of the entire world; of the 1,500,000 tons of rubber produced in the calendar year 1950, Malaya produced 700,000. From seeds brought to this fertile peninsula by the British only a few decades ago, British, Chinese, and Malayan planters have developed the most concentrated and scientifically productive rubber area in existence. Rubber is king in Malaya.

As we approached Kuala Lumpur for a landing, huge mud-colored blotches on the landscape advertised rubber's only rival, the tin mines. The tin lies but a few feet below the surface and is dredged out by strip-mining methods, producing one third of the tin of the whole world. Kuala Lumpur is the world's tin capital. The annual exports of this rich little peninsula are one seventh as great as those of the entire United States.

Though we were met at the airport by an armored-car escort, it was hard to believe that Kuala Lumpur was the center of some of the most desperate struggles between Communism and the free world. As we drove through the city to command headquarters, it seemed pleasant and quiet, with well-stocked shops, palm-lined streets, and sedate public buildings, the whole scene looking dull and well ordered as its mixed population went about its leisurely way under the broiling equatorial sun. Once we reached headquarters, all was changed. The command room for Malaya was strictly a war room. On a huge map in the secret operations room was laid out the whole disposition of the armed forces, the police, and the resettlement authorities. Every place where the bandits were believed encamped was marked. Defense operations then under way were also charted. In this room all branches of the government, both British and native, work together around the clock, directing operations from one end of the peninsula to the other. As one after another of the heads of the various services stepped forward to give his briefing statement it was an impressive display of a mighty joint effort.

When we left the city to go out into the field, our escort was increased. Armored cars preceded and followed us, the turrets of each constantly swinging back and forth to be ready for instant action in the event of attack.

Most of the time the jungle was some distance from the road and Malcolm MacDonald explained: "Usually the bandits don't leave the jungle except when it is necessary to conduct a raid. They don't ordinarily ambush traveling parties except where the jungle comes close to the road. It wasn't far from here, however, that I passed along the road a few weeks ago and forty minutes later a police car was ambushed. The police gave the bandits a good battle, killing two of them, but two of our own chaps were killed in the fight and the bandits got their guns before they ran into the jungle."

I told the Commissioner General a story that I had heard from a man who had twice seen, off the Malayan coast, a submarine which submerged when his plane went down to get a close look. "We've heard similar reports," he replied, "but up to this minute we've found no proof that the bandits are receiving supplies from the outside. They still have the guns and ammunition which were given them when they were resisting the Japanese and they keep on getting guns and ammunition whenever they raid a police outpost.

"We're strengthening these outposts, however, and the raids are diminishing. While there's some evidence that the high command of the bandits has Russian advisers and they may well be brought in by submarines, we've been unable to prove it so far."

At Selangor, our first stop in the field, the combined operations room was a smaller replica of the command headquarters, but confined to its own province. At Kajang, our second stop, we got down to the military grass roots. Here the combined operations room dealt with one section of one state and the details of each operation then in process. I was particularly impressed with the top secret intelligence room where the bits and pieces of information that filtered in were all fitted together into the mosaics on which successful action was based. On one wall photographs of the leaders of all the bandit groups represented a typical Communist organization from the Politburo down through the lower ranks. There were a number of blanks on the chart but in the majority of places were pictures of bandit leaders, some alive and some dead. Captured bandits were brought here to be shown how much was known about them and their leaders. Whenever any important bandit leader surrenders, the government launches him on a lecture tour from compound to compound and village to village, to tell the people the evils of Communism and describe the guerrillas' mistakes and failures. One of the most recently surrendered leaders had announced to the press that he was now against the bandits and would co-operate with the government in suppressing them. Paradoxically, he added that he was still a good Communist but that he could no longer support the bandits' methods or the injury they were doing to the people of Malaya.

Every picture on the wall was of a Chinese and I was astonished to learn that the Communist rebellion in Malaya involves practically no Malays, ninety-five per cent of all the bandits being Chinese. The loyal Chinese greatly outnumber the Reds, however, and three of the four men in charge of this top secret intelligence office were Chinese.

The headquarters of the 1st Suffolk Regiment camp at Kajang was one of the finest military installations I ever saw. The tents were on concrete platforms raised eight to ten inches from the ground and surrounded by concrete drains. The cots were good and solid, each with its own mosquito netting, and all of the facilities of the camp were first class. A company was standing in hollow square for review and the amazing thing was that they were all draftees or, as the British call them, "national service men." As we walked around the square the commanding general called out: "All national service men raise their hands." Every single man put up his hand. So far as I could learn, these English lads had become thoroughly adjusted to jungle warfare and their discipline and morale were excellent.

They were dressed in green uniforms for concealment in the jungle and wore rubber-soled canvas boots. When I asked one of the men whether his boots weren't too flimsy for the jungle, he replied: "Oh, they're excellent, sir. They usually last about two weeks. We tried regular leather boots but they didn't last more than two or three days in the jungle."

In the hollow square there was also a group of native Borneo head-hunters, sometimes called the Hill Dyaks or Ibon trackers. They are all volunteers who have hired out for the job of tracking down the enemy because they love it. A little under five feet and very dark, these aborigines from Borneo have a long hole in the lobe of the ear, which hangs down more than an inch. Their coal-black hair is never cut and they roll it up under their caps. An officer asked one of the trackers to remove his cap and his hair fell down in waves over his shoulders.

Malcolm MacDonald expressed his particular enthusiasm for the Borneo trackers. "They make fine soldiers," he said. "They have superb skill and matchless courage. They can track an enemy through any jungle in Malaya." The Commissioner General has been more honored than any other man in history by the British Borneo tribes. I found out one of the reasons. In addition to his natural gifts for getting along with people, he is a Scot and he always wears his plaid kilts when he goes to Borneo—"to show them, you know, that I am a tribesman too," he explains.

All these soldiers are proud of the job they are doing and the captain of the company of the 1st Suffolk Regiment, which was on review, sent to his tent for a Communist flag. With a good deal of pride he told how his men had captured that flag from a group of bandits they had fought and killed just a few days ago. He was, he said, proud to present it to me as a souvenir to show they were giving the bandits a beating.

The Gurkha Signal Training Wing was something new. For many years the Gurkhas have been superb soldiers with a tradition of service in the British Army. Most of them are unable to write their own language, and they know no English. For this reason, it has been necessary in recent years to put an English platoon or company into a Gurkha regiment to operate communications with the rest of the army—an expensive and cumbersome procedure since the Gurkhas have their own tribal habits and their own religious practices affecting food.

One British officer got the idea that this was a lot of nonsense: the thing to do was to teach the Gurkhas English and then to teach them how to handle and operate radio. Everybody else said this was impossible. He replied that the present setup was impossible and got permission to try. He was right.

The brightest young Gurkhas were selected and they took eagerly to this novel training. First they were taught to write their own language; then they were taught English. We visited one class of twenty Gurkhas where a young English sergeant was giving the English course, standing in front of a man, pointing to his nose, and saying, "Is this my nose?" From the intent little Gurkha came the prompt answer in quite beautiful English with a decidedly British accent: "Yes, that is your nose." Then the sergeant moved to the next man and, pointing to his own shirt, said: "Is this your shirt?" The Gurkha answered: "No, that is not my shirt. That is your shirt." The sergeant told us that in a few weeks he graduates his classes speaking completely workable English.

In another room Gurkhas wearing earphones were sitting tensely in front of radios, adjusting the sets and sending messages back and forth to each other in their new halting but good English, while outside a graduating class was rigging wireless field equipment. The experiment was a success. From now on the Gurkhas will have their own English-speaking units in the field, able to communicate directly with all of their comrades-in-arms. While the government forces could not trust the telephone for secret messages, they still could use the radio because for some reason the bandits thus far appeared to have none.

I had heard a great deal about Sir Henry Gurney, the High Commissioner for the Federated States of Malaya. His reputation as an administrator and his wide experience in the delicate relations with Asian peoples gave him unusual qualifications for his difficult role, which combined the functions of a governor general, liaison man between the sultans of the Malay States, sponsor of the developing self-rule of a mixed and illiterate people, and commander in chief during bitter revolutionary warfare.

I had also, of course, heard a good deal about General Briggs, whose plan was having such a profound effect upon the territory and was being copied in other countries, including Indo-China and to some extent the Philippines. Both men were at luncheon in Kuala Lumpur at King's House, as the residence of the High Commissioner is called. It also turned out to be a welcome-home luncheon for Lady Gurney, who had just returned after a year at home in England. The Minister of Education and his wife, both Ceylonese, were there and I was impressed not only with their charm but with the size of the diamond implanted in the left side of the wife's nose and the red spot in the center of her forehead, indicating her Hindu caste. All of these people, British, Malay, Chinese, Indian, and Ceylonese were living on terms of cordial, easy social relations, working toward a common objective under the terrible tensions of guerrilla warfare. "We have many things to do," Sir Henry said during luncheon, "but the most important is to show the people that we have a better way than the bandits can offer. I believe we are doing it. One example is our new technical school here in Kuala Lumpur. It's the best in Southeast Asia. Already a number of the surrendered bandits have graduated from the school to become successful artisans and fine citizens.

"We're not using our schools for propaganda; we're just giving training and education, letting the opportunities of freedom speak for themselves. Good future leadership for Malaya is coming along and we are encouraging Malayan political leaders to lead. I believe we are making great progress toward self-rule for Malaya within the British Commonwealth."

Two months later the headlines blazoned the assassination of Sir Henry Gurney on a highway outside Kuala Lumpur. He was ambushed by the bandits on the same road we had traveled the day we were together. His driver was killed by the first volley. Mortally wounded, Sir Henry pushed his wife to the floor of the car and staggered down the road, deliberately drawing fire away from her until he fell dead.

In the face of every kind of danger, including the assassination of managers, foremen, and workers in the rubber plantations and the tin mines, the work of the world goes ahead in Malaya, producing the rubber and tin that the world so desperately needs. The private armies required for the defense of the plantation workers are exceedingly costly. One man told me that he had to leave a thousand acres of rubber completely untapped in order to remove his workers to a safe area for their own protection. A Chinese operator of a small plantation told me that the bandits had slashed and thereby destroyed a hundred acres of newly grown, untapped rubber trees. It takes seven years to grow a rubber tree and one slash with a jungle knife destroys it. The cost of Malayan rubber and tin includes the blood of the men who are turning it out.

The rubber and tin producers were outraged by the harsh words hurled at them by a United States Senate Committee and by officials of the Government of the United States. They were accused of withholding rubber and tin from the world market; of being a cartel; of attempting to wring an exorbitant profit from the needs of the world; and of price-fixing. When I saw their representatives, they presented a vigorous defense, pointing out that inflation had multiplied the price of rice to their workers eight times over and that wages today were five to eight times higher than those paid before World War II. They presented statistics to show that many other commodities had gone up from two to five times as much as rubber and tin, yet those commodities were raised in free areas where it was not necessary to maintain private armies to protect the workers or to build new villages to give them safe housing. There is a full, open rubber and tin market at Singapore where the world's buyers and sellers meet; no man or group could fix the prices—only a government. They also pointed out forcibly that none of them had withheld produce from the market or could afford to do so. A new factor had recently intervened. A few Communist agents had infiltrated among Malay and Chinese workers, exhorting them to demand fantastic increases in wages under pain of death. These new tactics by the Communists were successful on many of the small plantations owned by Chinese and Malay operators and it was anticipated that the techniques would be expanded throughout Malaya.

One semiofficial report indicates that in just six months the bandits in one state collected, by extortion and the sale of stolen rubber and tin, three hundred thousand Singapore dollars or about one hundred thousand American dollars.

The producers complain that they are being condemned by people in America who know little about the conditions in Malaya and nothing at all about the production of tin and rubber.

I also met with the Americans who buy the rubber and tin. They took a middle position, that costs had increased heavily and they thought that some place in between the demagogic positions taken by some leaders of our government and the producers of Malaya was the right one. One thing everyone agreed on: the fervid and extreme language used by the American politicians in denouncing the producers in Malaya and Indonesia had done our relations with those countries great damage. I think there must be some more respectable way of solving complex economic problems than by long-distance name-calling.

All factions, including our own American economic experts, agreed on one other conclusion: the Communists have failed in their prime objective of starving out the people of Malaya. They have forced an increase in costs but they have failed in their attempt to wreck production. They are dealing with men who are braver than they are and who will stick to their jobs even though sudden death may be the penalty.

In all the Pacific, genuine nationalism is mildest in Malaya and Singapore. Yet no flat statement, even this one, is wholly true. There is a definite movement for self-government in Malaya but it is restrained by a strange combination of circumstances. One is that the Malays are a minority in Malaya. The Malay is quiet, peace-loving, and not particularly ambitious; he is not politically inclined by nature and he gives his allegiance to the sultan of his state rather than to the abstract concept of a federal government. An ever increasing group of educated and progressive Malays would like to see a government of their own but they are acutely afraid that the equally numerous Chinese, who are more hard-working and prosperous, would control it. The Chinese already run the business of the country. The Malays do not want to see the Chinese also run the politics.

At the end of the war the British took a long step toward self-government for Malaya by setting up a Malayan Union in which they gave the Chinese substantially equal representation. This aroused the political consciousness of the Malays for the first time and they vigorously opposed the new constitution; they were glad to have self-government but not on equal terms with the Chinese. Under the leadership of Dato Onn bin Jaa'afar, Chief Minister of Johore, they succeeded in persuading the British to change the constitution so as to give the Malays a preferred position in their own country. As a result, British schools, civil service, and political policies have tended to favor the native Malay over the Chinese immigrant.

This, in turn, aroused the Chinese. Though they had always regarded themselves as overseas Chinese, with little interest in local politics, now they took a vigorous interest out of resentment at the effort of the British to develop Malay leadership. With the Malays enjoying a preferred position, the Chinese sought equality. Trying to confer self-government is a complex business and the British have a thorny problem on their hands with no group having a majority and each jealous of the other.

Even this picture is not entirely accurate because among the Chinese community I met a number who scorned the idea that they are overseas Chinese; they proudly point out that their families have lived in Malaya or Singapore for four, five, or six generations. Sir Ham Hoe Lim, member of the Executive Council of Singapore, thinks he is just as good a British subject as the Prime Minister of England himself. He has a right to those sentiments. While the British who were interned in the war were treated reasonably well, the Japanese inflicted typical oriental cruelties upon some of their Asian prisoners and the dread torture known as "the water cure" was administered to Sir Ham while he was a prisoner. No information was ever wrung from him and his loyalty remained unshaken; after the war he was knighted by the King for his heroism.

The leader of the Chinese movement for self-government

and equality of treatment is Dato Tan Cheng Lock, an enthusiastic, charming, and vigorous businessman. I saw a good deal
of him and was greatly impressed by his point of view. His
writings, which he presented to me, portray a remarkably
mature and unselfish political outlook. For example, in an address to the Malayan Chinese Association, he frankly said:

"It is high time that the people of Malaya became interested in Malayan politics. However a man may think he is
uninterested in politics, the practice of politics will not be
uninterested in him. We all must pull our weight or we shall
most assuredly be pulled.

"It is the policy of the Association to interest itself actively
in helping to solve the social problems affecting the Chinese
in Malaya including those arising out of the prevailing state
of emergency. All in this country must learn to become Ma-
layans first. Racialism is a myth, and a dangerous myth. It
is a cloak for selfish economic aims which in its uncloaked
nakedness would look ugly enough. The secret of life is balance; the body must be in balance. The mind must be in
balance. The community must be in balance."

Dato Tan has been a leader in the fight against Communism
and has vigorously supported the action of the government in
moving the squatters into protected compounds. He took
sharp issue with an official statement of the American Government which said that the overseas Chinese were "soft" and
a source of weakness in the fight against Communism because
of their strong racial feelings and ties to their homeland.
Indignantly denying this, Dato Tan made a major speech on
May 16, 1951, saying of his fellow Chinese in Malaya: "They
have proved to be on the whole excellent, peace-loving, loyal
and law-abiding citizens, respecting the rights of the other
nationalities wherever they have settled down in the Pacific.
Their economic efficiency and relative prosperity, resulting

solely from their indefatigable industry, thrift and business acumen have generated some feeling of jealousy and resentment amongst other peoples which has shown itself in anti-Chinese sentiment.

"Ten million overseas Chinese outside China in South East Asia should be well treated and not discriminated against. They should be encouraged to throw in their lot with the peoples of the respective territories in which they have settled, so that they may become a living proof to the Chinese in Communist China of the superiority of free enterprise, social order and the western democratic way of life, and a standing object lesson to them demonstrating the evils of tyrannical Communist rule in the countries within the Soviet orbit so destructive of human dignity and liberty. Only in this way can Communism be defeated and Russian Imperialism foiled.

"The Government of Malaya in particular should embark upon a systematic campaign to tell the peoples of Malaya the truth about the inevitability of the coming defeat of Communism both as a social ideal and in other respects."

The result of all this is that the British find themselves with mature, loyal leaders of the two dominant groups, the Malays and the Chinese; but their points of view conflict so sharply that, so long as the British try to advance the Malays to self-government of their own country, they encourage Communist sentiment among the Chinese. All this is further complicated by a third major political group—the Indians. They are the smallest, comprising only about ten per cent of the population, but they are the most active politically. When the British, in advancing self-government for Singapore, ordered its first election, they were astonished to find that, although the population is eighty per cent Chinese, a large proportion of the members elected to the Singapore Parliament were Indian. The simple answer was that the Indians turned out to vote and the Chinese and the Malays did not. As a result, for the appointive places in the Parliament, the Governor General, Sir Franklin Gimson, had to appoint representatives of the two other groups to provide a balance.

Caught among the conflicting racial groups, the British, nevertheless, have a great asset in the fact that over the centuries they have governed Singapore and Malaya exceedingly well. There is general agreement that there is no basic hostility against the British on the part of the native populations; on the contrary, there is a high degree of loyalty to the British Crown. Within that loyalty the problems of self-government are being solved in friendly fashion. At a small luncheon with Malcolm MacDonald, I found that Sir Ham, Dato Onn, Dato Tan, and R. Jumabhey, the Indian leader, could discuss with me freely, without heat and on the friendliest basis, the problems they were struggling to solve.

Meanwhile, guerrilla activity presents a constant danger. All groups agreed that if the power of government were dropped too suddenly into the hands of the people they would collapse under the burden and the Communists would take over. All agreed, too, that whatever form of local government came about must be evolutionary and within the Asian tradition.

At Singapore I had a chance to bring into focus a great many conversations with overseas Chinese about their fundamental feeling toward China. It was true that most of them have no philosophical opposition to Communism and regard it with rather a detached view as being nothing more than another economic system which can scarcely be any worse than others China has experienced. Their indifference was shaken by Mao Tse-tung's armed intervention against America and the United Nations in Korea; the crushing taxes imposed by the Reds upon both businessmen and peasants alike; then by the brutal purges, followed by the campaign of systematic extortion from the overseas Chinese. These developments moved a large majority of the overseas Chinese definitely against the Red regime. While some still insist that there must be "a third force," most agree that Chiang Kai-shek is the only symbol of Free China and that he should be supported.

The real paradox is that the British throughout the Pacific, when they take their hair down and talk frankly, are sympathetic to Chiang Kai-shek, although their government recognizes the Reds; while quite a number of the Americans are hostile to Chiang, though our government has refused to recognize the Reds.

When I went to the American Consulate General for my conference with our Singapore staff I found that every chair in the United States Information Service was occupied; everyone agreed that they could fill a reading room many times as large for twenty-four hours of the day. American magazines, periodicals, and technical books are devoured avidly by people of all ages and of every race of Asia, in their search for information as they come up the ladder of independence.

It was at this meeting that a letter was delivered to me from a local Indian justice of the peace in which he enclosed a two-week-old front page of the Singapore *Straits Times* dated Thursday, July 19, 1951. At the top of the page, occupying the center four columns, was a photograph of helmeted troops holding back a crowd of rioters, in the disgraceful demonstration at Cicero, Illinois. Over the photograph was a four-column streamer reading: "And all this because a Negro rented a flat." It was an Associated Press picture, carrying a caption which read: "Steel-helmeted police and guardsmen were called out recently to deal with a mob of more than 4,000 who demonstrated in the all-white Chicago suburb, where a Negro family rented an apartment. When the Negro family moved in, anti-Negro demonstrations started almost immediately. The family's furniture was thrown out of the windows and trampled upon. Police cars were smashed and five bombs were thrown into the flat." The shameful episode had happened weeks before but the *Straits Times* gave half of the top of their front page to it when the picture arrived in Singapore.

The Indian justice of the peace who sent it asked in scathing terms how America could pretend to stand for freedom and democracy while colored people were treated this way in our country. I could understand his point of view; but the treatment of the story in Singapore made me completely furious. It had received prominent play here in the United States and rightly so. It was an isolated incident, thoroughly disgraceful, and should have been publicized to hold up to shame and public scorn all those involved. But in Singapore, with its mixed population, not one per cent of which was white, that picture, weeks old, was treated by the British-owned newspaper as the biggest news from the entire world on that day.

It gave the deliberate impression to these proud and sensitive yellow and dark-skinned people that all Americans treat all dark-skinned people that way. It seemed to me to be a deliberate propaganda attack against America.

Our consulate staff was equally furious and they advanced the interesting theory that this kind of journalistic horseplay was the result of British policy. They believed that it was not current policy but said that in the old days the British had preferred to keep Singapore free of all non-British influence and it had been a subtle policy to disparage other nations whenever possible. The USIS people said that they had checked and found that our American wire services, the Associated Press and the United Press, had formerly never sent out that kind of news to countries where it would do us such damage; but the competing British Reuters Agency did send the stories and the AP and the UP were finally forced to send them in order to compete. Moreover, our Americans found that the two British newspapers in Singapore had a standing order for the fullest report of any racial disorder in the United States.

That night the members of the fledgling Parliaments of Singapore and Malaya were holding the first joint dinner in their history for me. I had intended discussing world affairs but this Cicero incident so thoroughly outraged me that I proposed to the people in our American Consulate that I speak on this subject in blunt and strong language. They were enthusiastic. I told the story to Sir Franklin, who was also outraged. He was positive no such British policy had ever existed and concluded that it was an aberration of the local English-language newspapers.

When I told the story to Malcolm MacDonald at lunch that day he was equally disturbed, assuring me that in his official capacity he could make the flat statement that there was no such British policy and never had been. He said it was wholly the fault of the local newspapers, which were looking for circulation out of sensational stories, and urged: "Make the speech and make it in the strongest language possible."

The dinner was held at an attractive resort hotel out on the end of Singapore Island. The sides of the dining room were open and the cooling breezes of the evening made it temperate and pleasant. The table was in the shape of a hollow rectangle with everyone facing the center under a curious conical-shaped ceiling. As I moved around before dinner I noticed that I was hearing conversations but could not see the speakers. The manager explained that the acoustics of the ceiling were such that, wherever one sat, even a whisper on one side of the table could be heard clearly at the exact opposite side. I was quite careful of my dinner-table conversation as a result.

In the tradition of the British Parliamentary Association, the dinner was exclusively confined to the members of the two Parliaments and their invited guests: no husbands, no wives, and no press. There were some forty members present, of every race and color, including four women. The Indian lady member was an active political leader here in Singapore and bore the symbols of her own native culture, the diamond in her nose and the caste mark on her forehead; the Chinese lady member of the Parliament was a social worker; the men included doctors, merchants, teachers, a tin miner, and a rubber grower. They represented the two experiments in parliamentary government which were being conducted almost under Communist guns amidst one of the most thoroughly mixed populations in the world. We talked of many things, including the desperately high prevalence of tuberculosis, estimated at nearly eighty per cent in some sections of the city.

After Malcolm MacDonald had given the courtesy toast to the President of the United States, I gave the toast to the King; then the Governor General, Sir Franklin, rose and delivered a short and exceedingly gracious speech of welcome, ending with the customary toast to the guest.

I replied extemporaneously with a number of pleasantries and then delivered my speech. I spoke first of the importance of Southeast Asia in the free world and then of my admiration for the courage with which my hosts were proceeding to produce the goods the world needed so much and for the patience with which they were developing responsible self-government. Then I continued:

"For these reasons it is appalling to find barriers built against a mutual understanding of the social and economic conditions in our respective countries. It is, of course, a fact that trouble makes news and peace and progress make no headlines. Yet this does not seem to me to excuse the fact that so much distortion is laid before the people by media of public opinion.

"For example, I am shocked to find that an incident of racial prejudice, involving a few hundred people out of a nation of 150,000,000 is front-page news in Singapore and elsewhere and is considered worthy of a four-column photograph on the front page of a newspaper.

"There is no excuse for an incident of racial or religious or national abuse by one group of another. But to present the occurrence of such an incident as the major news from the United States on any one day is shocking and grossly misleading. What is wholly ignored is that the incident shocked the public conscience, was abhorrent to all our people and was both vigorously suppressed and prosecuted by the public authorities. This is the true reflection of the American point of view, which I find entirely omitted.

"A major point of Communist propaganda has been this distortion of life in the United States and the claim that the rare incident of ruffianism represents anything basic in our country. It is just as false as would be the claim that a waterfront brawl between two sailors in Singapore was a true picture of life in this delightful and harmonious colony.

"Of course the simple fact is that in the United States every race, every color and every religion have mingled. . . .

"Such ancient prejudices as linger in some sections are dwindling and I venture the prophecy that when the eighty-eight years since the Emancipation Proclamation have stretched to the century mark the ugly concept of discrimination will have been extinguished. . . .

"We in America are not free of our own misconceptions.

It is unfortunate that we hear more of the troubles with Communist brigands in the Philippines, in Viet Nam, in Malaya, and in Indonesia, than we do of the broad constructive social and economic progress which is being made. I hope to do my own share in presenting that fuller, more rounded picture which is essential to the basic unity of free men everywhere.

"We can only escape the tyranny of ignorance and force by a firm resolve to know and understand each other."

I explained that in New York State we had banned by law discrimination in employment, education, or in places of public accommodation on grounds of race, color, creed, or national origin; that the law had achieved wide acceptance among our people and had been copied by many other states. No good American, I pointed out, felt anything but shame over the remaining evidences of discrimination, and despite them, we were waging an ever more successful battle against intolerance of all kinds. Meanwhile, to present America as a basically intolerant country was a denial of the basic truth upon which the nation was founded.

After the dinner we broke up into small groups and talked of the problems of Malaya, Singapore, and the free world far into the night.

Sir Franklin and Lady Gimson were reluctantly looking forward to retirement at the end of December, since Sir Franklin reached sixty in the year 1951. Lady Gimson was already packing for their final return to Britain after their thirty years in colonial service. It was not a cheerful prospect because the pension is not large. However, each of their daughters was married and expecting a baby and they were both anxious to be home to see their grandchildren for the first time.

Singapore will miss Sir Franklin Gimson. A sturdy colonial administrator, he is an equally stout advocate of the development of self-government for native peoples as rapidly as possible. He is blunt and the people understand him. He is one of the British officials who was outspoken in his disapproval of recognition of Red China. I said: "You tell me you have made your opinion clear in the official conferences, do you mind if I quote you?"

"Not at all," he replied. "It is imperative that the Free Chinese forces be strengthened to prevent the Reds from moving into Indo-China, after which they would have Burma and Thailand. We can defend Malaya but the loss of those countries would be very serious to the world."

After what I had seen, I was sure that Malaya would be defended—for a while; but I thought that if the other countries fell Malaya would be dead spiritually. There is a limit to how long people can resist if the world around them falls.

I was sorry to say good-by to Malcolm MacDonald. It seemed to me that we had known each other for years. The quiet of his judgments, combined with his human warmth for everyone from Borneo head-hunters to Chinese philosophers was deeply appealing. When the Conservative Government was elected in the fall, I had a strong temptation to convey privately the hope that his learning and flexible skill would not be withdrawn from this crisis area. But propriety prevailed and I kept my nose out of Britain's affairs. So far, however, he is still Commissioner General in Southeast Asia.

10

Indonesia

The immense tracts of unoccupied or thinly peopled territories in Sumatra, Borneo, and the numerous islands scattered over the archipelago, may be able to receive colonies, arts, and civilization from the metropolis of the Indian seas [Java]. Commercial intercourse, friendly relations, or political institutions may bind these dispersed communities into one great insular commonwealth. Its trade and navigation might connect the center of this great empire with Japan, China, and the southwestern countries of Asia."

From The History of Java,
by Sir Thomas Stamford Raffles,
1817

DJAKARTA, capital of the Republic of Indonesia, was different from any other city we visited. Just as Saigon is an Asian Paris, so Djakarta looks like an Asian Amsterdam. Solid, chunky Dutch architecture dominates the scene, and the wide canals which flow through the streets of the city have strong, slanting banks paved with stone.

Close up, the face of Asia thrusts through the demure Dutch façade. Dutch architecture has been sharply modified by the need for ventilation in this eternally hot tropical climate and the sides of most of the buildings are open to catch the breeze.

Old-fashioned Dutch streetcars with trailers that would fit the needs of Amsterdam seem slightly scandalized as they clang furiously through the swarms of pedicabs, bicycles, automobiles, and trucks. Unlike the trolley conductors in Holland, the government employees who run the streetcars make no serious effort in the rush hours to collect fares from the thronging passengers who fill the cars, stand on the platforms, and hang onto the steps. The trolleys are typical of the whole city, crowded, disorderly, insecure. This already overcrowded city had been inundated by contemporary Asia's endless stream of refugees, some seeking security from the troubled countryside, some looking for work, others for education. There was an acute shortage of water and the power shortage was so serious that every night large areas of the city were entirely cut off from electricity for many hours.

A few years before the war Batavia, now renamed Djakarta, was a trim and orderly city. Today, with no increase in basic services or utilities, it has six times as many people—2,000,000 instead of 300,000—with only twice as many houses. Pouring into the capital from all over the archipelago, tragic refugees from hunger and banditry live three or four families to one small tile and bamboo house, in one-car garages, in jerry-built shacks, in the streets, in the gutters, and in every alley.

The Dutch canals have gone completely native. Half filled with turgid, brown, sluggish water, they serve as bathroom, laundry, and sewage disposal for the vast population. They reminded me of Mark Twain's comment on the healing powers of the sacred river Ganges; the water, he remarked, was so dirty that it killed the germs.

Our 482-mile flight from Singapore across the equator to Djakarta was one of fabulous beauty. Rarely out of sight of land, our course took us over the luxuriant jungles and plantations of the west coast of Sumatra and countless smaller islands. Every shade of blue and green shone beneath us in the ever changing waters of the South China Sea.

I happened to be in the co-pilot's seat fifty miles out of Singapore as we formally checked out of the closely guarded British air screen and made our first contact with the airport at Djakarta. "You will check in with us at exactly one hundred miles out," came the harsh, almost hostile tones of the control tower; "we know your course and we will watch you on radar. Report your progress regularly as you approach." The grim business of twenty-four-hour defense against possible air attack goes on throughout the Pacific on air fields stretching from Japan to Australia.

Curving up from the south around the west coast of Singapore and Malaya, the vast island of Sumatra is over a thousand miles long. With a total area greater than that of California and with about the same population, Sumatra is the largest of the islands which make up the former Dutch East Indies, the spice islands Columbus was seeking when he bumped into America.

East of Sumatra lies the island of Java, six hundred and fifty miles long—as far as from New York City to Indianapolis—with a population of 50,000,000. Almost the exact size of Alabama, it has a population equal to that of France, with an average of one thousand people to each square mile of the island. It is the most densely populated area of the world. Sumatra and Java are only two of the great islands of this amazing amphibious Republic with its 743,000 square miles of territory and 79,000,000 people.

We were met at the Djakarta airport by Merle Cochran, United States Ambassador to Indonesia. He is a short, round billikin of a man, cordial, jovial, and relaxed. As we drove into the city together he described its various sections and buildings in the matter-of-fact way of a native, with a lively sense of humor and a wholly realistic understanding of the problems of this jammed and confused community. The quite imposing Embassy Residence revealed a good deal about our host. It is a stately white two-story house with a wide terrace in front and is surrounded by spacious grounds. No guards were in evidence and there is no fence around it. It faces a public park and diagonally across from it are a Dutch church and a Masonic Temple. Acquired after the war, the house was stripped and in run-down condition; Ambassador Cochran was forced to refurnish it from top to bottom, mostly with furniture he had collected in the course of his many years as a State Department career man.

Usaw, the Number One boy, was on the job to take our luggage to our rooms. He was bright-eyed, about five feet tall, brown-skinned and intelligent; he knew his business, and though he spoke little English, he took very good care of us indeed. Dressed in a clean white cotton shirt and trousers, he was barefoot but I never saw him without his black fez, an Indonesian adaptation without tassel or other ornament. He and the other household help were Moslems, and while they may violate the strict laws of the Prophet by smoking, they are faithful in observing the Koran's injunction against alcohol.

Despite the impressive appearance of the Residence from the outside, there are actually only three bedrooms, and Paul Lockwood and I filled up the house. Between my bedroom and the Ambassador's are his study and the telephone. Since no one in the house but the Ambassador speaks English, he answers his own telephone. Whether it is a drunken sailor on the waterfront, an exchange student wanting to give him a little free advice on an American foreign policy, or a member of the government, he is likely to find his call answered by the Ambassador of the United States.

There were two spacious bathrooms on the second floor and

Paul Lockwood and I shared the use of the one at our end of the hall. The water heater was a little dangerous and nobody ever uses it to make hot water. My first lesson in Indonesia was to follow the Ambassador's advice in taking a Dutch bath. Two small square stone tubs filled with cold water are against one wall. The technique is to stand next to the tub and take a shower by pouring buckets of water over yourself. I found that with two or three buckets of water I was wet enough for soaping; three or four more buckets washed off the soap, the water running down a drain in the middle of the tiled floor. All in all, it was a very satisfactory bath for a tropical climate.

Our host had violated all local traditions by installing screens in the windows of the three bedrooms. Screens are generally believed to interfere with the daytime flow of air through the house and at night it is the custom to close the windows and sleep under a mosquito net. A desire for fresh air in the tropical night, without mosquitoes in the room, is regarded as strictly an American eccentricity.

The ground floors of homes are commonly wide open at all times and the spacious, lovely rooms of the Embassy Residence conformed to the local practice. There were shutters which could be closed for the night or to keep out driving rain, but they were open all the time we were there, with birds occasionally flying through and the neighbors' cat wandering into the house each night in search of a succulent lizard.

Two hundred members of the government, the American business community, and the diplomatic corps had been invited to the Ambassador's welcoming reception and I was thoroughly bewildered by the new set of names I had to learn. Japanese names had seemed a bit hard at first and Korean names a little harder. The Chinese and Philippine names were not particularly difficult but the problem increased as I went through Hong Kong, Viet Nam, Cambodia, and Malaya. Now all of that had been child's play. The names of a few of the invited guests at the reception, indicating by their length something of their family distinction, were as follows:

Dr. Sukiman Wirjosandjojo—Prime Minister
Dr. Achmad Subardjo—Minister for Foreign Affairs
Dr. Iskaq Tjokrohadisurjo—Minister of Interior
Dr. Jusuf Wibisono—Minister of Finance
Dr. Ukar Bratakusumah—Minister of Public Works
Mr. I. Tedjasukmana—Minister of Labor

This was pretty tough, even for a boy born in Owosso, Shiawassee County, Michigan.

The Dutch had ruled these fabulously rich islands for three and a half centuries with a generally benevolent but iron hand. This rule had been interrupted only twice; by a curious stroke of fortune the first interruption may have saved the United States in the War of 1812; the second interruption saved Australia and New Zealand in World War II.

Between 1811 and 1816, during the Napoleonic wars, the British occupied the Dutch East Indies. If the British had not been spread out all over the world fighting France and the Netherlands while she was also fighting the War of 1812 with the fledgling American Republic, we might well have lost. Even so, the War of 1812 was a stalemate but because of the British commitments elsewhere in the world, including the Dutch East Indies, we negotiated a successful settlement, winning most of our objectives through the Treaty of Ghent in 1814.

One hundred twenty-eight years later, in 1942, the Japanese overran the islands. We since have learned that they intended to by-pass the Dutch East Indies and occupy Australia, which they expected to accomplish without difficulty. The Japanese heard, however, that the Dutch had large military forces on the island of Java which they did not dare leave behind them as a threat to their lines of supply. The Dutch did have large forces—but what the Japanese didn't know was that they were mostly untrained civilians in uniform. When I met the director of the Bogor Botanical Gardens, a middle-aged man who had never carried a gun in his life, he told me how he, like every other Dutchman able to walk, had suddenly found himself in the army when the war broke out. The Dutch did it partly in the hope of creating the illusion of a large army to keep the Japanese away, and partly to give their civilians the status of military prisoners of war if the islands should be taken. Alarmed by the apparent size of the Dutch Army, the Japanese changed their plans and attacked Java first, with considerable resulting delay in the Japanese attack on Australia. The delay gave us and the Australians the precious time needed to build up the military and naval forces which saved Australia when the Japanese later attacked.

During the occupation of the East Indies, the Japanese busily sowed their seeds of hatred for the white man, and though the population had no more use for their new conquerors than they had had for the Dutch, the seeds of nationalism took deep and effective root. Leadership for revolt against the Dutch was ready and waiting as soon as the Japanese evacuated the islands at the end of the war. In the 1920s the Dutch had started sending the brightest young Indonesians to Holland for higher education. When they returned home they began preaching to their countrymen the ideas of freedom and self-government they had learned from the Dutch. As they became too troublesome, one after another was sent by the Dutch colonial government into exile on small islands. Later, the exiles became so numerous that the Dutch concentrated them all on one island.

At the end of the war with Japan, this group announced the independence of the Dutch East Indies and proclaimed a republic under the name of the United States of Indonesia. Their chosen leader was Sukarno, who has no known first name, as is not unusual in Indonesia. The movement spread like wildfire among the people and thousands of tough fighting men, who had been trained in army groups by the Japanese or who had served as guerrillas against the Japanese, united in support of the new government. Even as the Dutch reoccupied their old capital, Batavia, and tried to restore their colonial government, the new Republic set up its headquarters at Jogjakarta behind the high mountain range of central Java. The Dutch found it impossible to restore order and the broad popular support of the Nationalist movement was so great that there were simply not enough men and resources in Holland to put down the Indonesian revolution. The inability of the Dutch colonial administration to restore control, followed by the refusal of the Nationalist group to recognize the Dutch authority, came as a great and bitter shock to the people of the Netherlands. A large share of all of their overseas investments was involved in the East Indies. For three and a half centuries the Dutch had built up the productivity of the islands. Now all seemed in danger of being swept away.

The Dutch could not abandon their centuries of investment and effort and withdraw; but neither could they stay. Finally a Good Offices Commission was established in the United Nations under the leadership of Merle Cochran, our present Ambassador. The work of the commission dragged on month after month. Commission members and their technical staffs would spend three weeks in Batavia negotiating with the Dutch, then drive under heavy guard to Jogjakarta in the mountains to negotiate for three weeks with the Nationalists. With points of view so far apart, peaceful solutions seemed further and further away.

Meanwhile, as the Dutch and Indonesian Republicans struggled for supremacy, the armed forces of Communist revolutionaries, with direction and support from Moscow, seized the opportunity to overthrow the Republican movement, converting it into a Communist revolution. Moving with great violence, they launched a campaign of military attack, assassination, and sabotage. This assault strained the Jogjakarta government even more heavily than the attacks of the Dutch, for a time threatening to take control of Jogjakarta and the whole of the Republic. Slowly, after long, bitter fighting, the Republicans finally gained the upper hand and one after another of the Communist leaders was jailed or executed. In this effort the fledgling government almost exhausted itself, to the point where it was existing under conditions of the most extreme privation. Many of its leaders were living in straw huts or out in the open with no shelter at all; many also were wearing untreated animal skins in the cool mountain climate; arms and ammunition were running desperately low and medical supplies were almost exhausted; there were no bandages at all in many areas and wounds were often wrapped in the leaves of banana trees with a resulting tragic death rate from infection.

In the face of apparently hopeless odds, the Nationalist leaders remained utterly indomitable. Most of them had spent the majority of their lives in exile, waiting, working, hoping for freedom for their country; at whatever cost now, they would not settle for less than full independence.

In December 1948, after the negotiations of the Good Offices Commission had dragged on month after month, the Dutch, despairing of a settlement, launched the Second Police

Action, a surprise parachute attack on Jogjakarta by the famous Ambonese colonial troops. The suddenness and vigor of the onset confounded the Nationalist defenders and overwhelmed them; their leaders were killed or captured as hundreds of innocent women and children were also killed despite the best efforts of the Dutch commander to control his wild and violent troops.

With the leaders of the Republic in jail or dead, the Dutch seemed to be back in the driver's seat. The Good Offices Commission was dissolved and Chairman Cochran returned home prepared to take on his waiting assignment as Ambassador to the new government of Ceylon.

But it was not to be. The old days of Western imperialism simply could not be restored to an awakened and determined land. The Dutch made a monumental blunder in releasing the very Communist leaders whom the Nationalist Government had captured and imprisoned. The Dutch also found that with the members of the Nationalist Government in jail they had more trouble on their hands than when they were free. They could not even negotiate with the Republicans, whose following was so great that, in jail, they proudly refused to talk with the Dutch until they were released and their government restored. Finally, as a result of the chaos in the islands and the pressure of world opinion, the Dutch released the leaders of the Republic, and restored Jogjakarta to their control so negotiations could be resumed. Ambassador Cochran was sent by the State Department to The Hague to lend his good offices in the new talks on this thorny problem.

After a protracted series of round-table conferences through most of the year, sovereignty was transferred to the new Republic on December 27, 1949. Dutch investments were guaranteed and both nations were joined in a Netherlands-Indonesian Union under the Dutch Crown with an equal status for both.

One unfortunate legacy from this long struggle is that the members of the Indonesian Government are suspicious and distrustful of all foreigners, especially of the Dutch. Another unhappy legacy has been the continuation of the old Dutch colonial practice of censorship. All incoming and outgoing mail to Djakarta is carefully read by a government agent. Sometimes the censors don't quite know the implications contained in a letter but they take no chances; if the letter seems to be against government policy, it is "lost" and never reaches its destination.

In bloodshed, confusion, and chaos this newest great nation on earth was born—the sixth largest of the world. Indonesia produces forty per cent of the world's natural rubber, a large share of the world's tin, and a great output of rice, coffee, pepper, tobacco, kapok, quinine, copra, and other agricultural wealth. In addition, it produces an increasing share of the world's oil and has large unexplored resources of coal.

The problems of the new government seemed unsurmountable. The population of this rich area are called Indonesian but it is made up of people who differ greatly in language, custom, and cultural development. They range in color from light to dark, from primitive jungle tribes to the highly educated. Ninety per cent are Moslems, with the balance divided among Christians, Buddhists, Brahmans, and pagans. Faced with problems that would stagger any nation, the new Indonesian Government insists on taking on more.

For centuries the Dutch have occupied the western half of the vast island of New Guinea, which lies off the north coast of Australia, which administers the eastern half of the island. The Indonesians demand that the Dutch include West New Guinea, or Irian, as they have renamed it, in the grant of sovereignty, pointing out that for centuries the Dutch have taught their school children that New Guinea was a part of the Indonesian chain. This is vigorously opposed by the Dutch, who now point out that New Guinea is largely unsettled, inhabited by people who have no ethnic, cultural, or other ties with Indonesia. The Dutch argue that it would simply give to the new government imperial control over subject peoples with whom they have no relationship. The Australians object with equal violence. The subject is a heated political issue with the Indonesians and keeps the bitterness against the Dutch stirred up. Many of the local Dutch in Djakarta favor any settlement to get rid of the issue.

While the whole controversy about the Indies was at its height in May of 1949, I was in the Netherlands and ran into the full force of the Dutch bitterness over American failure to support their efforts to re-establish colonial control. Admitting that they had neither the troops nor the money to re-establish their own control, the Dutch felt that their wartime allies, principally the United States, had betrayed them in failing to provide aid so they could keep their greatest asset as a nation. Sovereignty was finally granted, however, and regardless of the merits, it is certainly to be hoped that a settlement of the Irian issue can soon be reached to improve the relations between the Indonesians and the Dutch. Each needs the other in these difficult and dangerous times.

Indonesia's public health problems are staggering. The Dutch had conquered cholera and smallpox and brought plague down to a minimum; but malaria, typhoid, and dysentery are still endemic, while tuberculosis, as always in the East, reigns as the number one health threat.

The canals of Djakarta present in one form a graphic summary of the monumental problem. For the homeless as well as countless other thousands whose houses have no sanitary facilities, there is no recourse but to use the canals for all bathroom purposes. When bathing, the women lift up their garments modestly to keep them just above the surface as they immerse themselves in the coffee-colored water; near by, others do the family laundry, while still others use the same water to brush their teeth, using the forefinger as a toothbrush.

As I looked out the window of a silversmith's shop one day a peddler came along, carrying his wares in baskets hanging from each end of a typical Asian pole across his shoulder. It was noon and he was hungry and tired. Squatting gently, he let the baskets down to the ground and removed the pole from his shoulders. He took off his shirt and walked into the canal, removing his loincloth as he stepped down into the water. First he brushed his teeth with his fingers, then he bathed, using no soap but rubbing his body vigorously. Drying off as he slowly emerged, he replaced his loincloth, walked out of the canal, and approached a typical one-man restaurant. Between the sidewalk and the canal the proprietor had set up a small portable stove with an umbrella over it. He sold a bowl of rice and a cooked banana to the peddler, who sat down on his heels to eat. After he had rested awhile he got up, put his shirt back on, resumed his load, and went his way. The restaurant owner put a string on the dish the peddler had used, let it down into the canal, rinsed it, and brought it out ready to serve food to the next customer.

Of course I was curious to know how such a city could avoid wholesale epidemics. The Minister of Health gave me his best answer: "The reason there are no widespread epidemics is the low toxicity of the germs." One of his fellow Cabinet members interrupted to say: "But you should tell Governor Dewey the rest of the story, the high death rate among infants."

"Too often the mothers don't get an adequate diet," the Minister explained, "and their milk does not give enough nutrition to the infants to give them a good start in life. Soon after birth babies are fed bananas and other food which has usually been improperly cleaned, resulting in a high infant mortality."

If they survive infancy, it seems that the people develop immunities which allow them to live in the face of conditions under which any other people would die of disease overnight. It is nature's way of protecting Asia's masses.

A Dutch doctor tells of a number of cases of jaundice that came to his attention. He prescribed the only known treatment: rest and good diet, under which it usually takes about six weeks to recover if the patient follows the doctor's orders. To the doctor's astonishment, several of his patients came back cured in three or four days. Inquiry revealed that they had gone home and followed the local custom of eating head lice.

Profoundly impressed by this unknown cure for a baffling disease, the doctor had lice gathered from the heads of workers in a nearby compound, put them in capsules, and tried to persuade some of his other patients to try the remedy. The first one willing to try it was an American, who was cured in three days; nobody knows why. Now the doctor has launched a research project to find the secret of the cure. I was not quite sure myself whether I would rather have jaundice or eat the lice. But after all, this cure is no more repulsive than pus from a sick cow which we use to prevent smallpox.

I was anxious to meet the leaders of this government who by sheer courage and tenacity in the face of impossible odds had won freedom for their country and now in the face of still more impossible odds were proceeding to govern it. I knew they were brave; I knew they were young, most of them in their forties. Ambassador Cochran knew them all and the widespread resentment against foreigners apparently was not held against him. He had lived through all their crises with them and was more responsible than any other foreigner for the freedom of the Republic. One of the Ambassador's special qualifications for his position is that, during the time when these Indonesian leaders were treated by many as mere pretenders to power, he came to know them as responsible, accomplished individuals whom he was proud to regard as friends.

My first courtesy call the day I arrived was on Minister for Foreign Affairs Achmad Subardjo and we got off to an excellent start. He is slight of build, scholarly in manner, bearded, attractive and stimulating. Others had told me that he is difficult to talk with and often will say nothing at all; so far as I was concerned, he could not have been more delightful. During the course of our conversation I mentioned in passing that I was sorry we could not get to Bali to see the famous Balinese dancers. When the Minister came to the reception later that day he told the Ambassador that he had made arrangements to put on a special performance of Balinese and Javanese dancing at his home the following Friday evening.

Unfortunately, the Indonesian Cabinet met through the afternoon and early evening on that Friday, debating the burning issue of the Japanese peace treaty. Indonesia was torn between two courses: the neutralism of India, and signing up with the free world. The fledgling nation insists upon maintaining its independence and at the same time living in peace and friendship with its Asian neighbors; it is trying desperately to remain aloof from what many of its people regard as a struggle between the two great powers, Russia and the United States. The decision on the Japanese treaty was perhaps its greatest diplomatic decision to date, risking, as it would, violent criticism of the few but vociferous Communist members of its Parliament and the Red elements of the press. It was a tough one, too, for a new government which recognizes Red China and feels strong ties with nearby India. The subject came up in almost every conversation and I was deeply gratified that Indonesia made the decision at the last moment in San Francisco to sign the treaty.

On Friday evening while Mr. Subardjo was tied up at his Cabinet meeting, we gathered on the lawn in the rear of the Foreign Minister's house, to sit facing the terrace, which had been transformed into a beautifully lighted stage. On one side was a Javanese orchestra, on the other a Balinese orchestra. The most important instrument in each orchestra resembled a large xylophone, one made of wood, the other of metal. There were stringed instruments and timpani made of a series of copper pots hanging from parallel cords. These were extremely beautiful in tone, though the musical scales were not the same as ours. There were also tiny oboes which made a soft, whining sound but again in a musical sequence not familiar to Western ears. The twenty members of each orchestra in turn played complicated musical compositions in the dark, with neither sheet music nor director. The tonal concepts are so entirely strange to my training that it would take a long time before I became accustomed to them. Balinese music seemed to me much closer to our musical forms than the Javanese; but when I mentioned this to one of the Indonesians he said: "It is very primitive. Javanese music is much more interesting and several centuries ahead in development."

Both the Javanese and Balinese troupes were government-sponsored, representing the highest form of Indonesian dancing art. Again it was highly stylized and, since both the men and the women were heavily clothed, it was, like the Cambodian dances, largely the representation of traditional or mythological stories interpreted by the skillful movement of the neck, the toes, the eyes, and the fingers of the dancers. After the dancing began, the Foreign Minister arrived. Sitting beside me, he greatly aided my understanding of the performance by explaining the significance of each dance.

One of the dances represented the basic religious concept which I had found portrayed on the walls of Angkor Vat and in many of the art forms. It was the dramatic dance of a young man about to engage in the process of meditation by which he identified himself ever more closely with his Brahman god. Following his own dance, he retired to contemplation at the back of the scene as two women dancers came out and during a long and charming dance failed to seduce him from his contemplation. Then came a dancer representing a female Devil, who wore an ugly huge grinning mask and long, black, metallic fingernails extending at least eight inches beyond the tips of her own. First she danced to induce the young man to join her; failing in that, they engaged in battle. The Devil uttered loud noises and demands in classic Balinese but was finally slain by the triumphant young man.

Achmad Subardjo has a fine grasp of foreign affairs and, like so many of the government leaders, views them from a strictly Asian point of view, though against the background of a Western education. The actions of his government will often puzzle us, but in the light of the fantastic problems they face, I will always think of them in the setting of this complex country. The split personality represented by this rising new government is illustrated by the clothes its leaders wear: every member of the Cabinet wore regular western suits; every wife of a member of the Cabinet wore Indonesian dress.

Our visit to the Government Rest House in the mountains, as the guests of the Foreign Minister and Mrs. Subardjo, was our only chance to escape the heat during our stay in Indonesia, and by this time I realized why the Dutch and most other foreigners tried to maintain mountain retreats. The route to the Government Rest House lay through territory where the Communist guerrillas were quite active. Only a few days before a Yale professor and an American representative of *Life* magazine had been killed on a side road leading off the main highway, apparently solely because the assassins wanted to steal their jeep. The only witness to the ambush, a native woman, "committed suicide" before her testimony could be taken. Though the road is generally quite safe by day, our hosts arranged a convoy with soldiers in armored cars riding ahead of and behind us. We started early enough to see the world-famous Buitenzorg Botanical Gardens at Bogor. I am not an expert on botany but I believe that these gardens, founded by the Dutch in 1817, are unequaled anywhere. The Dutch brought plants from all over the world to develop the productive capacity of the Malay Archipelago. Gutta-percha, cocoa, quinine, tea, vanilla, and the oil palm were all imported, the varieties increasing by experimentation throughout the course of a century, from about 2000 to more than 8000. In the greenhouses grow an unbelievable collection of more than 4000 varieties of orchids, ranging from delicate miniatures no larger than a thumbnail to huge trailing vines. The first palm oil tree, brought to the islands in 1848, still stands alongside the main garden road and the curator told me that while the Japanese occupied the island they respected the tree so much that all Japanese soldiers either took off their caps or saluted each time they passed this great landmark in the development of oriental agriculture.

The roads through the gardens are transformed into majestic avenues by stately rows of trees on each side, every tree bearing a different species of vine curling up its trunk. While the Indonesians have taken over the direction of the Botanical Gardens, their technical training is not yet up to the job, so the Dutch botanist who has been in charge for many years is retained as "Joint Director."

Driving into the mountains toward the Rest House, it be-

came noticeably cooler as the road curved upward between intensively cultivated areas, first of wet rice paddies and then, as
we rose higher, dry rice paddies. Finally we reached an altitude
where the rice was replaced on each side of the road by
thousands of acres of tea plants, some of them with tea bushes
as much as seventy years old.

The Government Rest House was beautifully located at the
top of a hill, with mountains rising far above. In addition
to our party and half a dozen people from the Embassy, some
twenty-five leading Indonesians and their wives were present.
I looked longingly at the sparkling clean water of the swimming pool on the lawn but the amenities of conversation with
the other guests made a swim diplomatically impossible.

For luncheon we had the famed Indonesian rice table, an
adventure in delicious food which began with a mound of
boiled rice in a plate. On top of the rice were placed vegetables,
meats, fish, and condiments prepared in at least twenty-five
different ways. There was also lamb and chicken on bamboo
skewers, which had been broiled over charcoal and seasoned
with sauce of coconut milk, peanuts, and many spices. There
were large fish which had been cooked in deep fat until the
skin was crisp and brown and the meat flaky, served whole on
a large plate and covered with sauce flecked with vegetables
and fruits. Shrimp, eggs, and chicken dishes, prepared again
with vegetables and spices, completed the main courses. Afterward the strong, sweet Javanese coffee was served with an
assortment of tropical fruits.

A similar but simpler dish I had on other occasions and
quite favored by the Javanese for breakfast was nasi-goreng. I
was a little startled when I first heard the name of this dish;
but nasi-goreng was a standard dish in the Indies long before
the Nazis reared their ugly heads for their brief time on earth.
Heaped on a mound of fried rice is a mixture of raisins,

shrimp, meat, and peanuts, garnished with shreds of crisply fried egg, onion, and other vegetables. Nasi-goreng is almost as appetizing as rice table, the king of Indonesian food for my taste.

At luncheon the question of foreign capital and investments came up. In Indonesia, as in Malaya, Indo-China, and so many other Asian countries, nearly all major production is still in the hands of foreigners. Dutch, British, Chinese, Americans, and a few French and Belgians operate the tea and rubber plantations; the Dutch and Chinese operate the tin mines; the Dutch and Americans operate the oil fields, which are rapidly growing in importance. The Indonesians produce only a minor share of the major exports and they resent foreign operation of the larger enterprises. This leads to a demand for nationalization, and the present government, which had been in office for only a few months, was considerably more Socialist than its predecessor.

As in most of the Pacific nations, capital is badly needed for the development of the country and they want it to be Indonesian capital; but unfortunately there is no Indonesian capital. So they are on the horns of a painful dilemma. If they should nationalize their great industries the Indonesian Government would own them and would presumably pay for them over a period of years. But then they would get no more foreign capital and they might lose much of the foreign management which makes the difference between success and failure of the plantations, the mines, and the oil wells. Naturally Indonesia is watching the controversy over the nationalization of oil in Iran with acute interest. The final outcome of the controversy will have an important effect in Indonesia.

In this capital-scarce country the leaders are, nevertheless, worried over the influx of new Chinese money for investment.

They don't want a larger share of their resources owned by the Chinese because they regard Chinese capital as unstable. They say it moves around from nation to nation in accordance with the convenience or fears of its owners. When it moves into a country it is all right; when it moves out, it is a depressing influence on the nation's economy.

Another difficulty is that the Indonesian Government is short of money to meet many of its most pressing needs. As in most Asian areas, the foreigners pay most of the taxes. For example, the American oil companies now operating in Indonesia pay out two thirds of their total net income in taxes to the Indonesian Government. The soberer heads in the government know that if they should nationalize the oil industry and lose the American management they would not only lose most, if not all, of this revenue, but they would get no further American capital for the immense developments that lie ahead. In the face of heavy taxation, decreasing productivity of workers, and doubts about future government policy, one American oil company, Caltex, is courageously going ahead with a program of development which is expected to total $40,000,000.

The American businessmen in Indonesia are doing a fine job for America as well as for Indonesia. Most of them have lived in the Orient for many years, developing oil, assembling automobiles, growing or purchasing rubber, tea, coffee, and copra, for great American companies. The largest American oil installations in all of Asia are on Sumatra. General Motors has a large assembly plant which brought about an amusing paradox after the war. An American rubber company had a concession from the Dutch in Djakarta to assemble automobiles and contracted with the General Motors Company to set up a branch plant in Djakarta. Then they found that Ford was the only automobile company which could spare parts at the time to send to Indonesia. So the General Motors branch in Djakarta found itself assembling the cars of one of its principal competitors for a whole year after the war.

Unlike the American businessmen who live in the country, outside visitors often make a bad impression. In Indonesia, for example, an officer of a New York bank visited President Sukarno to extend to him the greetings of the chairman of his board. He discussed local conditions and finally, reaching his climax, leaned over and slapped President Sukarno on the knee, saying: "We have confidence in you." The President tartly replied: "We have confidence in ourselves. What about a loan?" The conversation ended soon and the financial four-flusher retired in confusion.

Despite such incidents I had the distinct impression that we are the best-liked foreigners in Indonesia. Certainly our diplomatic mission under Ambassador Cochran's leadership is held in high esteem. So are many of our technicians, including especially the agricultural attachés and the private engineers. For one example, the Indonesian Government set out to hire consulting engineers with the proceeds of a small ECA grant, to advise on the monumental problems of rehabilitating the country following the years of war and revolution. After a study of the engineers of many nations they picked the American J. G. White Engineering Corporation. I heard so much of the outstanding job they were doing that I asked the Ambassador to invite Henry Tarring, Jr., the head of their Djakarta group, in to lunch. Mr. Tarring is a tall, spare engineer, experienced in the Orient, and has rendered invaluable service to the Indonesian Government.

I was fascinated by his report on Formosa. His firm had been retained as industrial advisers to the Nationalist Government of China before it was forced off the mainland; in February 1949 Mr. Tarring and his staff were evacuated to Formosa. There they found that only trifling repairs had been made in the Japanese-built factories, railroads, and electric plants which had been demolished by American bombers during the war. The Tarring group was assigned the tremendous job of directing their restoration. Without a dollar of American aid for the first year and three quarters, the whole Formosa industrial plant was restored by Chinese efforts under Mr. Tarring's guidance. Aluminum, chemical, iron, steel, textile, cement, mining, pulp paper, and shipping industries were turned from government subsidies to profits. The electric power system was increased from a peak load of 150,000 kilowatts to 192,000. Production of fertilizer was increased from 46,000 tons to 120,000 tons in two years. The railroads were brought into efficient operation, transporting freight tonnages far above those ever attained under the Japanese, all without any new equipment. In the spring of 1949 the average loading and unloading time of ships was twenty-five days; two years later the turn-around time had been reduced to two and a half days. Similar miracles were performed in highway construction, cotton spinning, cement production, timber production, aluminum, and oil refining. Mr. Tarring concluded his review by saying: "These accomplishments have been made without recourse to aid funds from the United States and I give much credit to the Chinese for this remarkable achievement. It has become fashionable to criticize the Nationalist Government and its leaders, but too little is said of their achievements and these should be better known."

If this American engineer can do for Indonesia what he did for Formosa it will be a major miracle. Of course the problems in Djakarta are different. Among them is the problem of ECA operations, which made me blush for my country. Indonesia confirmed my growing conviction that small amounts of American aid in the hands of first-class people are infinitely more helpful than large amounts in the hands of mediocre or bad people. The small amounts of ECA money in Indo-China have been skillfully used to create stability and advance the living standards of the people.

The same is true in Formosa. In Indonesia the few thousand dollars of the American grant used to hire the J. G. White engineers has been the most valuable money we have spent there. The ECA staff has been a comedy, or rather a tragedy of errors. The original small staff with a modest grant was useful. But the local ECA director decided that he wanted $30,-000,000. Going over the Ambassador's head, he sent a written recommendation to Washington for this amount directly through the mails, knowing that his letter would be opened and read by the local censors. This letter, of course, put the Ambassador in an impossible position and it gave the Indonesian Government a full picture of a row between the United States Embassy and the ECA director, who had to be recalled as a result. In his place, a young professor of geography from Colgate University, who happened to be in Southeast Asia, was asked to take temporary charge. He was succeeded by another professor who, directly contrary to his orders, went to The Hague, conferred with the Dutch Government officials, and held a press conference, announcing large additions to the ECA staff in Indonesia. This particularly embarrassed the Djakarta government, since it had just turned back a large Red Chinese delegation. Now it was faced with a horde of American ECA officials, and to add insult to injury the announcement came from The Hague.

Several of the ECA people who were moving out with the new director sent along queries asking about transportation for their dogs, motor cars, servants, and relatives. Some of these inquiries got into the press and the Indian UN delegate in Djakarta wryly remarked: "It looks as though America is going to colonize Djakarta with dogs and relatives."

Ambassador Cochran will loyally defend the ECA in Indonesia but its dismal history was told to every member of our party by dozens of responsible residents of Djakarta, including some of the ECA employees themselves. Having commandeered as many of the best houses as they could, even to the exclusion of Indonesian Cabinet officers who could get no homes, the ECA next made a fantastic proposal to the Hotel des Indes. They offered to build an entire modern hotel inside the grounds of the Des Indes; the ECA was to occupy the new hotel rent-free for two years, after which it would belong to the Des Indes free, and the ECA would pay full rent for its own building from then on. Once again Ambassador Cochran had to intervene and, with the help of some American businessmen, found property owned by the government of the United States where the ECA could build and continue to own the hotel instead of giving it away. The local ECA was outraged over this thwarting of their project and filed formal charges against the Ambassador which, of course, were dismissed after they were examined.

About this time still another ECA man came to Djakarta "to study the situation," announcing that he could stay and take charge if he wanted to, but first he was going to look things over. Two weeks later he announced his conclusion: "This job isn't big enough to interest me. I can go to Germany where I will have millions of dollars to spend and be a much more powerful figure."

Meanwhile, the warehouses and the docks were piled high with crates of goods from America. Nobody knew what was in them; the only watchman on the job was sound asleep when our party visited the docks. Signs of deterioration and pilfering were all over the place. The ECA had helped the government acquire twenty-five Japanese boats to develop its fishing industry. Two of them capsized and sank because they were not properly moored. The other twenty-three were still there, but many were dismantled and parts of the Diesel engines had been stolen. The government had also acquired two PT boats from the United States, but the Indonesians, delighted with their new possessions, took them out and raced them; then while racing they put the engines in reverse and, of course, wrecked them both.

I recalled the comment of the Japanese scholar: "When you send technical assistants to Asia, I urge you to send one good man instead of a dozen poor ones." He must have been speaking from bitter experience. My own conclusion was that if the ECA in Indonesia had a few million dollars and five good men they could dispense with the other ninety-five officials they plan on having and we would make friends instead of enemies.

It seemed to me a tragedy that, with fine Americans available like those who were doing superb jobs in Formosa and Indo-China, this great new Republic should be cursed with some of our worst. I was reminded of the Philippines, where everyone had agreed in recommending an outstanding manager of an American bank, who had lived in Manila for many years, to head ECA after it had suffered a series of catastrophes from mismanagement; out of patriotism he had agreed to do the job temporarily, on leave from his bank, taking a cut from his regular salary of $50,000 a year to $12,000. Then the blow fell: Washington ignored the recommendation and announced the appointment as ECA director for the Philippines of the head of a small agricultural college. He rose to the occasion by announcing that it was a dangerous assignment, but he was willing to take it on as a service to his country. When his statement appeared on the front pages in Manila the consternation was complete: they had lost the services of an outstanding man in exchange for one who knew nothing of the country or the job and insulted their country even before he arrived. His impending arrival was being viewed with apprehension in all quarters when I left.

I was delighted to discover that I could make my visit to Indonesian farms without armed escorts and without a crowd of government officials. Two Indonesians came along as interpreters: one who works for the agricultural attaché at the American Embassy and another from the Indonesian Department of Agriculture. Our first stop was the Fruit Growing Experiment Station about twelve miles out of Djakarta. Here the Dutch developed over many years a large and fine variety of fruit trees, including citrus, papaya, and banana. The citrus fruit looks like a green orange and tastes very much like a ripe one; all of the varieties of fruit have been developed and improved to suit the Indonesian climate, which varies from tropical in the valleys to temperate in the mountains. The young Indonesian director at the station was well trained and enthusiastic about his work; the samples of grafted saplings and the care with which they were handled were impressive. "Our saplings are sold to farmers at cost," he said, "so that the station can support all of its experiments including the salaries of the 150 men who work on it." The station even had a small herd of twenty cows, but I was thwarted in my interest in the herd: the cows are kept at the station for the purpose of getting manure for fertilizer for the trees. Night soil is not used in Java since the ground is a rich volcanic ash, created over many centuries by the eruptions of volcanoes. The rains wash the volcanic ash down from the mountains and continuously enrich the soil, so it needs little fertilizer for most crops.

At the station we abandoned our cars and with the director transferred to jeeps. We then traveled for miles along a winding, deeply rutted road about six feet wide, running between cultivated rice lands; the agricultural experts explained the local crop practices as we all hung on for dear life. On most of the islands the farmers are able to harvest three crops of rice a year. Despite wars, revolutions, and bandits, Indonesia is today producing ninety-five per cent of its own rice, the remaining five per cent coming from Burma and Thailand; with order restored Indonesia can easily produce an exportable surplus.

Finally we stopped at a crossroads where there were three houses. Twenty-five or thirty people of all ages were standing, squatting, or working around the crossroads and, as was so often the case, the men just stared while the women smiled at us in a friendly fashion; though the women were generally quite friendly, they were also quite shy. One of the houses served as a crossroad store run by the family of the proprietor, who works his acre of land part of the day. He was home this afternoon, and as I walked up to the store, the women behind the counter slowly edged toward a back room, peering through the door while I stood talking with the storekeeper and his father. Dried fish, rice, a few spices, and a little cloth were arrayed on the ten-foot counter. As usual, the rice was polished white and I asked the owner whether anyone had ever suggested that the unpolished, brown rice made a better, richer food. "Oh yes," he said, "but nobody likes it." He understood quite well that, if the brown husks were left on, it was better food but he also knew that nobody would buy his rice unless it was husked.

The people in the back country dress much the same as in the cities, the women wearing blouses and sarongs, which, unlike the movie version, are ankle-length, wrap-around skirts made of batik in beautifully dyed designs of brown and blue. Most of the men wore short, thin, knee-length pants and sometimes thin cotton shirts. In the cities the few well-to-do wear shoes, but in the country I saw almost no shoes.

At the first farm we visited we were greeted by a middle-aged Moslem who wore his black fez, a good shirt and trousers, but, of course, no shoes. He was the owner of two hectares or about five acres of land, which made him above average but not rich. One hectare was devoted entirely to fruit growing, every square yard of it beautifully cultivated. He accepted the best Experiment Station advice and his new papaya seedlings grow in between the citrus trees because they come to maturity and die at different ages. The other hectare was devoted to rice farming and to a new form of agriculture which was a liberal education to me.

About an acre of it was given over to inland fisheries. At first I thought they were ordinary rice paddies—twenty or thirty yards square; but they turned out to be fishponds divided by earthen banks with the water kept at the right level by opening small sluices between them. Most of the fish are carp, which we in America do not consider our best eating; in the Orient, with its spices and culinary skill, almost any fish is good food. The carp feed on fungi and on the sewage from the people who live near by. A sturdy long scaffold extends out over each pond, with the end enclosed on all four sides by a straw matting. This is the Indonesian variety of a Chic Sale, and all the neighbors are expected to use it to feed the fish.

This farmer owned three cows, but like the herd at the Station, the cows were kept to provide manure for the fruit trees. They are also milked and the few liters they produce bring a good price in the nearest village but the total amount of milk all three of them give would not warrant feeding one cow by American standards. They are cheap to keep, however, because one of the duties of the smallest children of the family is to go along the roadside and cut grass with a small sickle. As we drove along the road we passed two small boys, each of them carrying an amazing amount of grass in a pair of forked sticks over each shoulder.

In addition to the three cows, the owner also had four water buffalo which, by the standards of any other Asian country I had visited, would have made him a rich man. In Indonesia he was middle-class. The good farmers there do well.

Four young girls dressed in typical sarongs were pounding rice in a small open shed near the house. Working in pairs, each lifted a thick, heavy, six-foot pole, pounding the rice in a stone bowl. In steady rhythm while one pounded, the other lifted, up and down, up and down: it seemed a dull task. When I lifted one of the poles I realized it was also heavy labor; I think that if I had been doing the work I would have shifted the pole from one hand to the other even oftener than the girls did. As the girls finished pounding it a middle-aged woman was taking the beaten rice out of the bowls to sift it in a large shallow sieve. The owner introduced the woman as his wife. As usual, it was almost impossible to get the family straight. I did learn that he had four wives, fourteen children, of whom twelve were living, eleven grandchildren, and three hired men. His wives and children, grandchildren and four nieces, as well as the three hired men and their families, all lived together in a long, one-story frame house. The master himself obviously did little work but he certainly had plenty of help.

Later, when I mentioned to President Sukarno that this particular farmer had four wives, he pointed out quite firmly that that was unusual. A total of four wives is permitted by the Moslem law but most of the members of the government have only one, and plural wives are discouraged. A Cabinet member explained to me later that under modern conditions and the emancipation of women, polygamy is dying out. He said: "My father-in-law had thirteen wives, but I have only one."

To be rid of a wife under Moslem law the husband needs only to say, "I divorce you." The Minister pointed out, however, that before the three little words can be uttered, long and complicated negotiations must be conducted between the families of the husband and wife, including arrangements to pay back the dowry and to care for the children. "Usually this is so long and difficult," he laughed, "that it's easier to stay married."

With all their enthusiasm for independence, the Indonesian people are generally placid and agricultural by nature and the hard business of government is new to them. For example, when I was in Djakarta, there was an army, a navy, and an air force; but there was still no law authorizing their existence or any pay for them. They just existed by fiat. The armed forces represent a merger, so far incomplete, of the regular and guerrilla forces who fought for the Republic and the Indonesian troops who fought for the Dutch against the Republic; with troops in the same army who fought against each other, it is not surprising that they were sometimes as much a problem as a comfort to the new government. Also, when their pay was long overdue, they had a habit of turning bandit for the week end and collecting their pay from the people.

When elements of the navy were unpaid or idle, they became smugglers, which was natural since, during the revolution, smuggling to Singapore to support the Republican government was the official task of the navy. So one of the most difficult problems had been to reduce the size of the armed forces. The government tackled the navy first and had finally succeeded in reducing it from 80,000 to a compact force of 8000 men. Many of its officers were former smugglers who became ardent Nationalists and they were then using their small but loyal fleet of corvettes, American LSTs, and patrol boats to police Indonesian waters. No one had any illusion that the navy could defend these three thousand islands in the event of a major hostile attack, but at least it was beginning to tackle the smuggling problem.

Because export-import duties have always been high in the Orient and a principal source of revenue to the governments, piracy and smuggling have become fine arts over many centuries. If not always respectable, smuggling has at least been a well-recognized profession, and the Chinese and Malays are past masters of the art. While it is no longer patriotic in Indonesia, it is something of a habit, and the Chinese Reds are giving it great encouragement. The present high tariffs of Indonesia and its great shortage of goods, combined with the spectacular prices paid by the Communists for rubber and tin, have made smuggling highly profitable. I met no one even willing to venture an estimate of the amount of vital raw materials still being smuggled from Indonesia and Southeast Asia into Red China.

There are two well-known main smuggling routes to Indonesia: one is across the narrow Straits of Malacca from Malaya to Sumatra; the other is from Swatow in China, down between the lower Philippine Islands and Borneo, to Java. Even when the navy catches these free traders very little happens. One Chinese had been nabbed with a lot of contraband shortly before we got there. He was not imprisoned and his official fine was so small that everybody was laughing about it, asking who got the rest on the side. In addition to the basic problem of creating an effective judicial system, no real inroads against the smuggling will be made until radar and flying boats are added to the navy's equipment.

The army presents different problems. For example, one

Indonesian army officer approached a member of the American Consular Service and said: "My salary is too small to live on and I don't always get paid. So I have decided to enter the smuggling business and wonder if you could recommend a good honest smuggler."

The next job obviously is to reduce the size of the Indonesian Army. I inquired of one Cabinet officer why they kept an army of 200,000 which was by no means disciplined, supplied, or adequately paid. I asked: "Wouldn't it be better to cut the army in half and have a force of 100,000 which was well disciplined, well supplied, and regularly paid?"

"Of course it would," he said, "but what will we do with the other 100,000?"

I had no answer. Demobilizing an army is sometimes just as hard as establishing one, particularly when there are plenty of guerrilla forces for the men to join after they are mustered out. Nevertheless, real progress is being made at reconstructing Indonesian defense under the training of a Dutch general and a military mission of about a thousand officers and men. While there was great hostility toward the Dutch officers at first, the friction is diminishing and a new, efficient Indonesian Army is emerging. There is still practically no air force, but our MAAG people say the Indonesians are good fliers: the pilots now in training will do well as soon as they get airplanes to fly.

The more I learned about the problems of this new island government, the more impressed I was with the progress it had made. Several major revolutions had already been put down, including one, curiously enough, that was led by Dutch soldiers. They organized what is known as the Westerling affair, named for their leader, a renegade Dutch officer. Fighting for Queen and country, as they claimed, they set up a new government with Indonesians as front men. Only after vigorous action was the major threat of this group finally put down. Westerling fled to Europe and the remainder, estimated at 15,000, have continued to act as bandits. At the time I was there, it was believed that they were co-operating with an active Moslem revolutionary group.

The hard-fighting Ambonese had also staged a first-class rebellion against the new Republic, setting up their own island Republic of Ambon. The Minister of Health in the new government came from Ambon and he offered to go to them to mediate the rebellion, arguing that he understood his people, who had served as professional soldiers for the Dutch through the centuries. The Ambonese are savage, mercenary fighters who ask no quarter and give none; their loyalty has always been to the Crown. As the Minister of Health approached the island of Ambon, the rebels sent out word that they would sink the ship if he tried to land. Forced to turn back to Java, he next sent a group of sergeants from the Indonesian Army to prepare the way for a mediation conference. Instead of conferring, the Ambonese took them prisoners, cut off their ears, and made them eat them.

Only then did the new government move in with full force and, after a long and destructive conflict, finally killed or captured all of the rebel forces. The government offered the prisoners three choices: jobs in the regular army, release to go to Holland, or return to their native islands under pledge of good behavior. Many chose to go to Holland, so shiploads of savage Ambonese went to the Netherlands with their families. They are still there and nobody can figure out what to do with them. Maybe they will end up in the European Army. They are fighting men.

The Indonesian Government still has a mountain of trouble with revolutionaries: the large, well-organized, well-disciplined, Communist guerrillas; the remainder of the Westerling forces; and the Moslem extremists known as the Darul Islam. The latter are religious fanatics who are even more nationalist that the Nationalists. They refuse to recognize the secular nature of the new government and are fighting to establish a Moslem theocracy under the absolute rule of religious leaders. Of late they have established some co-operation with the Communists, with whom they have nothing in common except their opposition to the government.

The Communist guerrillas are in a particularly powerful position because there are Communist members of Parliament, Communist sympathizers in the Cabinet, and Communists at the head of two thirds of the labor unions. As always, the Red objective is to destroy production, starving the government out of its taxes and the people out of food and employment. The Communists count on the curious quirk in human nature which makes people turn to the left when they are hungry and desperate even though it is the very violence of the Left which has brought about their desperate condition. Forty Dutch planters were killed in the seven months before my visit in August 1951. Communist-led waterfront and oil strikes were periodically paralyzing the islands and a strike in the power plant at one major city left it in darkness during my visit. The evening of the day we left, the Communists launched an attack on Djakarta Harbor in force, carrying submachine guns and identifying themselves with red armbands bearing the hammer and sickle, as well as a strange device described by one Indonesian official as "that prehistoric bird—the dove of peace." Troops and police were rushed to the scene and only after an all-night battle were the Communists driven off, with many wounded and six dead. After this episode the government staged a series of roundups, gathering in some thousands of suspicious characters, including known Communist leaders and some high government officials. By report, the action had a salutary effect.

In such an atmosphere of turmoil and revolution, it is not surprising that labor should be both unproductive and inefficient. For example, it takes three weeks to unload a freighter in the harbor, compared with two and a half days in Formosa today. On one day there were 141 strikes and the general attitude of a large share of the Communist-led workers is: "Now that we've won our freedom why should we have to work any more?"

The long-continued atmosphere of revolution and the vast refugee population have combined to create a condition of unchecked lawlessness. Miss Roberta McKay, Ambassador Cochran's secretary, is the women's golf champion of West Java, and she and others were held up and robbed so often during their week-end games at the Djakarta Golf Club that a policeman had to be assigned to patrol the fairways.

Earlier in the year guerrillas had attacked a week-end cottage in the mountains used by two American couples from Djakarta. There was no telephone, so one of the Americans slipped out of the house and made his way down the mountain to call the police. The other three continued to return the fire of the bandits until they disappeared at daylight when the police arrived. The man who had stayed behind was shot in the abdomen but recovered, only to be stabbed and killed a little later by a Malay employee of the oil company for which he worked.

"These are just the risks of life, like crossing Broadway or riding in an airplane," one American explained, "but conditions are steadily improving."

In the midst of these stresses and strains the serenity and optimism of the American Ambassador were inspiring. In his years as a career man in the State Department, Mr. Cochran has been almost everywhere and seen almost everything, achieving wisdom in the process. He is wise enough not to flaunt American power and prestige before the sensitive and proud Indonesians. As a result, there are no uniformed marines on guard at the American Embassy or Embassy Residence. He does not even have a refuge in the hills as do practically all the members of the diplomatic corps and the business community. He has avoided it in order to minimize the possibility of incidents. In a country where most of the people are poor and housing is desperately short, he has sought no elaborate quarters either for the Embassy, for himself, or for his staff, though it is expected that a new Embassy will replace the present blowzy, two-hundred-year-old relic which dates back to the time when we were represented by a single consul with a stenographer and a clerk.

Ambassador Cochran is utterly without side and seems to be equally popular with the highest officials in the Indonesian Government, the diplomatic corps, the American businessmen, and the ordinary citizens of Djakarta. It would probably give most diplomats a shock to find the American Ambassador answering his own door in bathrobe and slippers; but the Indonesians like the genuineness of his simplicity and confidence. By contrast they are not impressed with the royal splendor of the Red China Embassy Residence where Mao Tse-tung's Ambassador hides behind high walls topped with barbed wire illuminated at night by floodlights and is almost inaccessible even to his own staff.

Before the war only about seven per cent of the population of Indonesia was literate by ordinary standards, and one of the major efforts of the new government has been to expand the school system. On the day I visited farms I saw a roadside school and stopped to look it over. Dozens of small boys, seven or eight years old, were playing outside and I watched a game of marbles which seemed exactly like the kind of marbles I played at the same age. The school itself was a long, narrow, one-story wooden frame building; packed tight in one room, sitting three at a desk, were eighty-four boys about ten years old, each wearing his fez. Two teachers were in the room, each in front of a blackboard, one teaching writing, the other arithmetic.

There was no partition in the room—just about a yard of space between two rows of desks on each side. In talking with the teachers I found that the school is operated in three shifts: from nine to twelve; twelve to three; and three to six. They explained that usually there would be a partition between the classes, but some remodeling was going on. So the boys on one side of the room listened to one teacher and watched his blackboard while the boys on the other side of the room did the same for the other teacher—or at least that was the theory. And we think we have school-crowding problems here at home!

The Communists are making a serious effort to infiltrate the schools but at present they are concentrating on the high schools and such higher education as is available. In the Chinese schools in Indonesia they have had conspicuous success. Large posters of Mao Tse-tung are posted in the classrooms and the students learn that Russia won the war against Japan, while the United States is pictured as an imperialist monster intent on gobbling up the world. In the Chinese areas of Djakarta, bookstores are almost always Communist-run, as in Hong Kong and elsewhere in Asia. Books and treatises which sell for a trifle push the Marxist revolution, giving detailed instruction on how to take over land and governments.

Two million Chinese do the major retail business in Indonesia and have a powerful influence through their factories, landholdings, and extensive moneylending. Many come from families who have lived in Indonesia for centuries, but as a minority with great business and financial influence, they are, naturally, unpopular, and are increasingly aware of their importance as a balance of power. Like most of the overseas Chinese, those in Djakarta were originally neutral in the struggle between Chiang Kai-shek and Mao Tse-tung; I had the impression that more had retained that neutrality than in other areas, where they have moved decisively to the side of Chiang. Of course there is an articulate and vigorous Communist group and the Red Chinese Embassy is a beehive of secret activity. There is no Russian diplomatic corps in Indonesia; the Red Chinese do their work for them.

Indonesia is another surplus land area at which the Chinese Reds look with hungry eyes. There is untilled land in Sumatra, Borneo, and many other islands, on which rice could be grown to feed millions of Chinese. It was not surprising that shortly before we were there the Chinese Reds had tried to add twenty additional employees to their already overstaffed Embassy. Only four of these had been cleared in advance with the Indonesian Government, although all twenty carried visas from the Indonesian consul in Red China. The Indonesians are learning; they promptly shipped home the extra sixteen in the face of violent protest by the Mao Tse-tung government.

In the face of every Communist pressure, many local Chinese publicly denounce Mao Tse-tung, proclaiming their adherence to the free world, and at the American Embassy there are Chinese employees who are most trustworthy. I met one who had retired after thirty years of honorable and loyal service to our country and still continued to live in one of the row of houses behind the Embassy; another has served twenty-three years in the Embassy. Of course, American pay scales in an Indonesian city are very attractive, but these Embassy Chinese, on the testimony of everyone who knew them, have a genuine loyalty to the United States.

A curious streak of pacifism runs through the whole Indonesian Government. Its leaders want no part in the world struggle against Communism; they would like to be friendly with both sides, somewhat in the same way that Nehru has staked out his devious course for India. But also, like Nehru, they are becoming increasingly tough on their own home-grown Communist agitators and guerrillas. They insist that their first duty is to set their own house in order, not to undertake world commitments they cannot fulfill.

The members of the Indonesian Government do not particularly like to discuss the Korean situation; they want to stay out of it. Even the proposal of an embargo on war materials for Red China was bitterly attacked on the ground that the new government would lose its independence of action if it put on the embargo and also on the ground that Ceylon and Malaya would not observe such an agreement anyway. One high official of the Indonesian Government publicly announced: "We will sell to the devil if it is helpful to us." Nevertheless, the government did quietly impose the embargo upon war materials for Red China, reserving the right to decide what were war materials and what were not.

Presiding over this strange and difficult government and the whole complicated Indonesian scene is the President of the Republic, the fifty-year-old Sukarno. I saw him at the palace of the former Dutch Governor General in Batavia. President Sukarno has already stamped his own personality on this enormous and beautiful marble structure by hanging a large collection of paintings, some by Indonesians and some, to my surprise, by Dutch artists. There are lovely pictures of the women of the islands, of sea scenes, and some small and beautiful portraits of heads of men and women. Behind his desk is a great canvas showing conditions in his mountain capital of Jogjakarta in the most desperate days when he and his government were fighting the Dutch. The canvas depicts tattered Republican soldiers carefully cleaning weapons, putting fuses in dynamite, and bandaging their wounds, while a man off in a corner is sadly counting his last three bullets. The President showed me each painting in turn, describing it in flawless English with the enthusiasm of an art connoisseur.

When we sat down to talk it was obvious that he was tired. He had just completed a speaking tour of the islands lasting twelve days, during which he had made seventy-two speeches to crowds often larger than 150,000 people. Many had traveled miles by foot to hear the leader of their country and he had given of himself with all his enormous energy and faith. I asked him what he was saying in his speeches and he replied: "I am telling them to work hard. They now have real independence. The Dutch rule is gone. I repeat that they are working for themselves and that they must live and produce like free men. I warn them that they must not expect miracles or even that all the old evils will be wiped out overnight. They mustn't expect the living standard to rise immediately and they must not swallow the propaganda of agitators who claim they can give them the millennium."

Even in private conversation he argued his country's claim to Irian (Dutch West New Guinea) with great vigor. "I tell them," he said, "that the problems of Irian will be solved, that we will contest with the Dutch until they give it to us; but I warn them we must not tear up the Round Table Agreement because it is the source of our sovereignty."

President Sukarno talked freely of the difficulties of the nation and, like President Huu of Viet Nam, disposed of some problems by exclaiming, "See how much progress we have made already." He is deeply convinced that the infant Republic, like other Indonesian babies, will flourish now that it has survived the risks of infant mortality.

He is a thoughtful man as well as a fiery leader. He knows the danger of the increasing volume of Communist propaganda which the Chinese are bringing into the country and is disturbed by it. He hopes that the free world will somehow develop a forcible, constructive program of propaganda for the free way of life; it is of the greatest importance, he urged, that the free world capture the imagination of the youth. He pointed to the fact that only two Indonesian youths were attending the World Youth Conference in America while fifty were attending Communist conferences in East Berlin. I raised the point both here and with other members of the government later as to where the money was coming from to finance the fifty who went to the Berlin spectacle. No one knew for sure, but all indicated an opinion that the money had been extorted by the Communists from Chinese businessmen.

Standing somewhat aloof from the day-to-day problems of government, President Sukarno is a magnetic, forceful, and commanding leader of men; he has achieved the independence of his country and 79,000,000 Indonesians are now free; he knows full well that he is the leader of the sixth largest nation on earth; he knows the importance of its riches and he wants to build his country in peace and progress. This George Washington of Indonesia has the capacity somehow to lead his people to stability.

He holds his office by the most extraordinary set of circumstances. He and Vice-President Mohammad Hatta proclaimed the Republic on August 17, 1945, three days after V-J Day; just by common consent they became the acknowledged leaders of the struggle for independence. Then they were named as President and Vice-President in the Round Table Agreement establishing the independent United States of Indonesia, which later changed its name to the Republic of Indonesia. The Parliament was not elected, but was appointed to represent the various groups within the island and the Premier and his Cabinet are responsible to it.

How they will ever hold elections I do not know. At this moment they are talking of an election, but there is no law under which one could be held. They do not know even who could vote. There are no records of the ages of people and most Indonesians do not know their own age. It has been suggested that women should be allowed to vote when they become mothers, but in Asia motherhood comes as early as twelve and usually by fourteen. Moreover, Indonesians are not accustomed to voting and there is good reason to believe that, since the Communists are the politically active group, they might easily steal the election, though they have little genuine support among the people.

I asked President Sukarno what language he used when he spoke to the great masses of people and he said: "Indonesian." The best estimate is that about seventy per cent of the people would understand about seventy per cent of what they heard in Indonesian, which is now the single, official language. Actually it is basic Malay with some development and, though it is related to many of the dialects, it is still commonly spoken by few. The Malay tongue is in many ways quite primitive and the vocabulary does not fill all the requirements of modern life. In many instances Dutch is still found to be necessary for exact statement. The language problems in elections would be particularly acute. Even in many households I met husbands and wives who spoke such different dialects that the only language in which they could talk to each other was Dutch.

In its nationalist zeal the government has attempted to wipe every trace of Dutch names from the islands. Not only every island and every city but every street has been renamed. However, this zeal exceeded the people's understanding and anyone who wants to travel in a pedicab or a taxi must often tell the driver the old Dutch name if he wants to arrive at his destination. Even some of the leaders of the government still use the old names of Java, Sumatra, Borneo, Bali, and all the other islands—except New Guinea. Because of the crisis over its ownership, it is universally called by its new name, Irian.

Indonesia's half-castes face a bitter choice. Under the Round Table Agreement, all persons who were part Indonesian and part Dutch were forced to declare by December 31, 1951, whether they wished to be Dutch or Indonesian. Under the colonial regime any half-caste with Dutch blood, or Indo-European, as they are called, was regarded as a Dutchman and suffered no social stigma. Much of the finest talent of Indonesia has come from this group. But now they were forced to make a choice. If they elected to call themselves Indonesians they faced the possibility of future discrimination because of their Dutch blood. On the other hand, if they declared themselves to be Dutch they might well be forced to leave the country and go back to overcrowded little Holland with nothing to do and no place to live.

The native Dutch still in Indonesia suffer from the hostility of the populace, though 6000 of them provide the main body of trained public servants. They are too few to run such a large country and too many to be absorbed. Without them, no one knows what would happen to the government.

Certainly the government must start paying all of its employees a living wage. Cabinet officers get about a hundred dollars a month. They say it is tough but they can exist on that salary. The lower echelons of government employees simply cannot live on their low compensation. Unless government pay is increased, morale will further disintegrate and corruption increase.

The Republic of Indonesia exists today as a race between development of the techniques of government on the one hand and the forces of rebellion and disorder on the other. I am betting on the government. Its problems are staggering beyond belief and neither the solutions nor the governmental forms will be after our pattern or according to our republican ideas of democracy; they could not possibly be. President Sukarno's leadership is intelligent and powerful; the fires of great patriotism and loyalty burn in him and his associates. They are learning the business of government the hard way. Even as I write this chapter the Cabinet is falling, but I believe a new and, perhaps, even stronger Cabinet can be formed.

The leaders of Indonesia are facing up to the need for broader education, development of resources, and higher living standards for all the people. With the infinite riches of their islands and the basic good sense of their people, they can come through. The 79,000,000 people of Indonesia can be one of the most powerful forces for the freedom of man. They do not want to be involved in the world struggle. They have achieved their independence, even as we did, after long and bitter fighting and they are determined to maintain it. We will not always see eye to eye with them on what should be done; but we share the same objective: freedom for them and for us. If we give them half a chance by learning to respect them and like them, and if Southeast Asia is not overrun, I believe Indonesia can become a free and prosperous nation.

Pacific Anchors

SINCE I RETURNED home the Communist attack in the Pacific has been stepped up. Violence has broken out in Japan as ratification of the peace treaty nears. General de Lattre is dead and the long-expected Communist offensive has been launched in the Tonkin Delta of Indo-China. In Indonesia the Cabinet has fallen over the issue of acceptance of American arms aid. Reacting to the march of events, our own national Administration has finally begun to show concern over the preservation of Formosa in our island chain of defense. To succeed the murdered Sir Henry Gurney in Malaya the British have appointed a stern and successful military leader to break the stalemate with the guerrillas.

Australia and New Zealand are the southern anchors of the Pacific defense line, and are to be protected by the pending treaty of mutual defense. Alaska is the northern anchor. Since it is clear that we would immediately go to the defense of either area in the event of attack, I have omitted from this book chapters on my visits there. I do wish, however, to express my warm gratitude to the people of those British Pacific Dominions and of Hawaii and Alaska for their generous hospitality to me and to the members of my party.

The crisis today is in Southeast Asia. If it stands, the whole defense perimeter will doubtless stand—from Alaska down through Japan, Okinawa, Formosa, the Philippines, Southeast Asia and Indonesia, to Australia and New Zealand. We have taken action—strong action—in creating mutual defenses in the Americas through the Rio Treaty, and in Europe through the North Atlantic Treaty Organization. During the great debate of 1951 over the issue of sending American troops to help shore up the defenses of Europe, the opponents predicted darkly that this was a sure way to provoke war with Stalin; they warned, in all seriousness, that an attempt to become strong would provoke attack while we were still weak. Fortunately for America and for the free world, these arguments of defeatism were ignored, and as a result of the labors and the shining leadership of General Eisenhower, Western Europe is stronger today than ever.

The outstanding fact is that, wherever we have undertaken treaties assuring collective action in advance, there is no war. Peace has thus far been preserved by strength. In the Pacific we have done only patchwork jobs and that area is racked by five wars.

It must be clear that for the sake of our own freedom we should take action in the Pacific similar to that which we have taken in the Americas and in Western Europe. There will be many difficulties, of course, but peace was never won by timidity or inertia. If France remains steadfast in Indo-China, Southeast Asia and the free Pacific can win through—always provided the Red Chinese do not launch a new invasion. I am confident the Chinese will not attack if the United States develops, within the structure of the United Nations, a total Pacific treaty of mutual defense.

We do not need to be committed to respond to attack in any particular way or in any particular spot; we can reserve to ourselves complete freedom of the manner of our action. I am profoundly convinced that such a treaty will save the 300,000,000